Police Misconduct

A GLOBAL PERSPECTIVE

Cliff Roberson

CRC Press
Taylor & Francis Group
Boca Raton London New York

CRC Press is an imprint of the
Taylor & Francis Group, an **informa** business

Dedication

This book is dedicated to the men and women serving and those that have served in our criminal justice system. We, as Americans, are truly fortunate to have had fine devoted professionals ever tending that fine blue line. For your anonymous help in our times of need and to perhaps make up some for the thanks that we have failed to express, thank you.

Contents

Preface

In 2015, U.S. police officers killed about 1000 civilians. No other Western country came near that amount. So, as we read this text, we should ask ourselves why so many are killed by U.S. police officers.

The text, *Police Misconduct: A Global Perspective*, is designed to provide students and persons interested in the police and police deviance with an easy-to-read work on the complex issue of police misconduct. This is not designed as an antipolice text. The vast majority of police officers are honest, hardworking, and dedicated to their profession and to serving their citizens. As with any large groups, companies, agencies, or other types of organizations, there are some "bad apples" in the profession. While I have attempted to remove any indication of my political viewpoints or political opinions, some may have crept in, for which I apologize for in advance.

Even though I am listed as the sole author of the text, numerous persons assisted in the preparation of the manuscript, including the editor at Taylor and Francis Group, Carolyn Spence, and both Jennifer Brady and Michelle van Kampen who were instrumental in the production of the book. Thanks to all of you for your assistance and encouragement.

A special round of appreciation to my colleagues, Ken Peck, John Eterno, Eli Silverman, Diana Burns, Matthew O'Deane, Rick Parent, Ryan Getty, and Michael Doyle, who have submitted materials that are included in the text.

Teachers using this book as a text should be aware that a full solutions manual, lecture slides, and instructor materials are available from the publisher.

Comments and suggestions for improvement regarding the contents of the material may be forwarded to me by e-mail at cliff.roberson@washburn.edu

Author

Cliff Roberson is an emeritus professor of criminal justice at Washburn University, Topeka, Kansas, and a retired professor of criminology at California State University, Fresno, California. He has authored or coauthored numerous books and texts on legal, criminal justice, and sociology subjects. His previous academic experiences include associate vice president for academic affairs, Arkansas Tech University; dean of arts and sciences, University of Houston, Victoria; director of programs, National College of District Attorneys; professor of criminology and director of Justice Center, California State University, Fresno; and assistant professor of criminal justice, St. Edwards University. Dr. Roberson's nonacademic experience includes U.S. Marine Corps service as an infantry officer, trial and defense counsel and military judge as a marine judge advocate; and director of the Military Law Branch, U.S. Marine Corps. Other legal employment experiences include trial supervisor, Office of State Counsel for Offenders, Texas Board of Criminal Justice; and judge *pro tem* in the California courts. Dr. Roberson is admitted to practice before the U.S. Supreme Court, the U.S. Court of Military Appeals, the U.S. Tax Court, federal courts in California and Texas, the Supreme Court of Texas, and the Supreme Court of California. His educational background includes: PhD in human behavior, U.S. International University; LLM in criminal law, criminology, and psychiatry, George Washington University; JD, American University; BA in political science, University of Missouri; and one year of postgraduate study at the University of Virginia School of Law.

chapter one

Introduction to the study of police misconduct

Learning objectives

After studying this chapter, the reader should understand the following concepts and issues:

- What constitutes police misconduct
- The issues involved in noble-cause corruption
- Basic forms of police misconduct
- The right of police officers to refuse to testify
- Restrictions on police investigations
- Problems with the Law Enforcement Officers' Bill of Rights
- The purpose of the National Decertification Database (NDD)

Introduction

According to the report of the President's Task Force on 21st Century Policing, decades of research and practice support the premise that people are more likely to obey the law when they believe that those who are enforcing it have the legitimate authority to tell them what to do. However, the public confers legitimacy only on those whom they believe are acting in procedurally just ways.[1] Procedurally just behavior is based on four central principles:

- Treating people with dignity and respect
- Giving individuals a "voice" during encounters
- Being neutral and transparent in decision-making
- Conveying trustworthy motives

The report noted that research demonstrates that these principles lead to relationships in which the community trusts that officers are honest, unbiased, benevolent, and lawful. The community therefore feels obligated to follow the law and the dictates of legal authorities, and is more willing to cooperate with and engage those authorities because it believes that it shares a common set of interests and values with the police. As we discuss police misconduct, it is quickly demonstrated that, in the present day, a lot of citizens no longer believe that the police are honest and trustworthy.

According to Jerome Skolnick and James Fyfe, videos of the Los Angeles officers beating Rodney King in March 1991 destroyed our vision of the goodness of police in the United States that we had formed as the result of the television series *Dragnet* and Sergeant Joe Friday.[2] *Dragnet* was a radio, television, and movie series about dedicated Los Angeles police detective Friday and his partners. Many consider it the most famous and influential police drama series in media history. It started as a radio show and later, in 1951, became a television series. The original series lasted from 1951 until 1959. It was revived in 1967 and continued until 1970. Reruns are still playing on many television stations.

The senseless beating of Rodney King by police officers was shown repeatedly in 1991 and again in 1992 when the officers involved were first acquitted in California state courts. Later, the officers were tried in federal district court for violation of King's constitutional rights and were found guilty.

Skolnick and Fyfe concluded that there were two Americas. One is urban, cosmopolitan, and multicultural. The other America is suburban, relatively safe, relatively prosperous, and unicultural. The first suffers disproportionately from crime, gang violence, poverty, and homelessness. The second is predominantly white and middle class. The Los Angeles police officers committed their crimes in the first America and were tried in a California state court in the second America (Simi Valley) and were found not guilty. After the jury finding was announced in April 1992, the Los Angeles riots occurred in the first America.

The Los Angeles police cars carried the legend on their doors: *Los Angeles—the city of angels.* After the King incident, many commentators suggested that the city change the slogan on the police cars to read: *Los Angeles—where we treat you like a King.*

While the actions of the police officers in the incident were certainly not a lone incident, the presence of a video camera allowed the incident to be replayed in homes nationwide. The King incident introduced police aggression into the media age. Since then, most incidents with the police are captured on video or other forms of media and, if derogatory, are published nationwide on local television news.

As pointed out by Skolnick and Fyfe, the Rodney King incident, which was electronically memorialized by amateur photographer George Holliday precipitated a national investigation by the U.S. Department of Justice and the U.S. Congress on the excessive use of force complaints against police departments. Skolnick and Fyfe state that the police chiefs knew that an unwritten message among the police was that "Brutality is an occupational risk of a profession that rides with danger and is trained and authorized to use force, even deadly force."[3]

Police misconduct is a complex and varied subject. It is often easier to develop a book that focuses on criticizing the thousands of hardworking individuals who risk their lives every day to protect us. That is not the focus of this book. Here, we will explore various types of police misconduct and provide limited guidance on how to prevent misconduct in the future.

There are over 12,000 law enforcement agencies in the United States alone, and close to one million people are involved in law enforcement in one manner or another. According to a 2010 study by the United Nations Office on Drugs and Crime, the United States has about 207 police officers per 100,000 population.[4] The average for countries in Asia is about 435 police officers per 100,000 population. The worldwide number of individuals involved in policing is therefore in the millions. The vast number probably makes law enforcement one of the largest professions in the world. Accordingly, in a profession this large, there will be some individuals who do not meet the expected professional standard that we expect of them.

One question that the reader should keep in mind when reading this text is: Who should police the police? There does not seem to be a uniform correct answer to this question. By police misconduct, the author is referring not only to criminal acts by police officers, such as the over use of force, but also to those acts that are committed that violate the professional standards expected of an officer.

As the author once discussed with a group of Mexican police chiefs, no one joins the police force and endures the rigors of police basic training with the goal of becoming a corrupt police officer. This brings up the question of how or why an officer transitions from the idea of being a public servant to being one that is corrupt.

In this book, the author will examine police misconduct in various countries around the world. However, readers should keep in mind that the vast majority of the world's police officers are honest and decent public servants. So in this text, we will concentrate on the outliers (Figure 1.1) (Boxes 1.1 and 1.2).

Figure 1.1 Police officer taking a bribe during the prohibition era. (Photo courtesy of the Library of Congress Prints and Photographs Division.)

BOX 1.1 DUTY TO REPORT MISCONDUCT POLICY: SAN DIEGO POLICE DEPARTMENT POLICY MANUAL SECTION 9.33 (04/30/14)

Members shall immediately report misconduct by another member. For the purpose of this policy, misconduct means conduct that causes risk to the health and safety of the public or impairs the operation and efficiency of the department or member or brings into disrepute the reputation of the member or the department. The conduct could involve a violation of any law, statute, ordinance, city administrative regulation, department policy or procedure, act of moral turpitude, or ethical violation. In this context, misconduct involves a willful act done with a wrong intention and is more than mere negligence, error of judgment, or innocent mistake. If any member has credible knowledge of another member's misconduct, the member should take immediate, reasonable action to stop the misconduct, and the member shall report the misconduct to a supervisor as soon as possible. Supervisors shall assess the validity of any allegation of misconduct by a member. If there is any evidence of misconduct or the allegation appears credible, then the supervisor shall immediately notify their chain of command or the watch commander's once.

BOX 1.2 COMPLAINANTS AGAINST CHICAGO POLICE OFFICERS

The city of Chicago has an Independent Police Review Authority (IPRA) that is responsible for conducting investigations into complaints against police officers for domestic violence, excessive use of force, coercion, and verbal abuse. Other types of misconduct are investigated by the police department's Internal Affairs Division (IAD).

In 2010, the IPRA and the IAD investigated 3861 complaints against police officers and found only 283 to be valid. There were 156 complaints of verbal abuse and none were considered as valid. The only area in which the majority of complaints were upheld was alcohol abuse by officers. There were 22 allegations of alcohol abuse and 13 were upheld. Of the 580 allegations of unreasonable use of force, only 11 disciplinary charges were filed against police officers.

Overall, only 7.2% of the allegations of police misconduct were sustained. For example, it is hard to believe that out of the 580 incidents where citizens claim that the police used excessive force, only 11 officers in Chicago in 2010 were disciplined. **Strictly from a statically point of view is it believable that about 93% of the allegations of police misconduct were unfounded?**

Source: Data regarding the Chicago Police Department were taken from the Chicago annual police report available at https://portal.chicagopolice.org. Accessed on June 14, 2015. Note that the annual report for 2010 was the latest report available.

For the purposes of this book, police corruption is considered a form of police misconduct in which law enforcement officers seek personal gain, illegally discriminate against individuals, use excessive force, fail to respect the rights of individuals, or commit other criminal offenses.

Although studied and researched, the topic of police corruption largely remains a mystery. Rich Martin, in an FBI Law Enforcement Bulletin, noted that Sir Robert Peel was credited with the concept that the police depend on citizen cooperation when providing services in a democratic society. As such, the detrimental aspects of police misconduct cannot be overstated. In terms of public trust for law enforcement, recent polls show that only 56% of people rated the police as having a high or very high ethical standard, compared with 84% for nurses.[5]

Martin notes that over the past few decades, great strides have been made in the law enforcement profession. To begin with, many police agencies have avoided hiring candidates who have low ethical standards and have identified those onboard employees early in their careers who might compromise the department's integrity. In addition, research has discovered new methods of testing candidates for their psychological propensity to act ethically. However, unethical conduct by the nation's police officers continues to occur in departments, large and small.

Martin notes that research into police corruption offers some understanding of the phenomenon in the hope of rooting out behavior that serves to undermine the overall legitimacy of law enforcement. Theories on the role of society in law enforcement, the negative influence of an officer's department, and a person's own natural tendency to engage in unethical behavior have been offered as explanations of police corruption. Martin poses the question: Is this noble goal to rid our nation's police organizations of unethical behavior possible and plausible?

Martin notes that the profession of policing, among many others, has a subculture unto itself. A morbid sense of humor perhaps illustrates one of the most widely known characteristics. In relation to corruption, however, the police subculture can either prevent its existence or be a vehicle to spread it throughout a department. This subculture may be the most difficult aspect to address.

Martin defines a subculture as a group of individuals who generally share attitudes, perceptions, assumptions, values, beliefs, ways of living, and traditions. Because police work entails so many experiences unique to the field, the subculture can almost become stronger than the officer's family ties. Additionally, work schedules outside of the normal realm can lead to feelings of isolation that further strengthen the bond of the subculture. According to Martin, this subculture may prevent or encourage police corruption (Box 1.3).

Procedural handling of citizen complaints

A 3-month study of citizen complaints indicated that many citizens were unhappy with the procedural aspects of the complaint process.[6] Many felt that the law enforcement departments were not interested in pursuing justice. The study indicated that the treatment of citizens was often more relevant to how their complaint was processed rather than the solving of the complaint. The study noted five points to measure a citizen's satisfaction with the process. The five points were

- Overall approval
- Courtesy and politeness
- Speed of response
- Level of concern
- Helpfulness

The research concluded that it is a requirement for law enforcement agencies to provide citizens with an opportunity to express their dissatisfaction with a police officer's conduct. The report concluded that studies have shown that procedural justice regarding dispute handling crosses several aspects of everyday life, such as interpersonal relationships, commercial interactions, citizen–government contacts, and traditional community–police encounters. Procedural justice applies to the resolution of complaints of police misconduct. This concept aids in designing policies and procedures that result in higher levels of citizen satisfaction (Box 1.4).

Extent of police corruption

According to Professors David Bayley and Robert Perito, police corruption is an international problem. Historically, police misconduct has been a factor in the development of police institutions worldwide, but it is a particular problem in counterinsurgency and peacekeeping operations such as the U.S.-led North Atlantic Treaty Organization police training program in Afghanistan.[7] There, police abuse and corruption appear endemic and have caused some Afghans to seek the assistance of the Taliban against their own government.

Bayley and Perito defined police corruption as abuse of authority for private gain. They noted that it is among the world's oldest practices and a fundamental cause of intrastate conflict, providing a focal point for many social groups' grievances against governments. It can be equally crucial after conflict, when fledgling law enforcement institutions cannot control official abuse. Whenever the international community has tried to build a secure, viable society after a conflict, it has faced the need to reform the institution most responsible for law enforcement—the local police force—to reduce its predatory and often pervasive corruption.

The FBI considers police corruption as part of public corruption. According to the FBI, public corruption is a breach of trust by federal, state, or local officials—often with the help of private sector accomplices. It's also the FBI's top criminal investigative priority.

The FBI explains its priority as follows:

> Because of its impact, corrupt public officials undermine the country's national security, the overall safety, the public trust, and confidence in the U.S. government, wasting billions of dollars along the way. This corruption can tarnish virtually every aspect of society. For example, a border official might take a bribe, knowingly or unknowingly letting in a truck containing weapons of mass destruction. Or corrupt state legislators could cast deciding votes on a bill providing funding or other benefits to a company for the wrong reasons. Or at the local level, a building inspector might be paid to overlook some bad wiring, which could cause a deadly fire down the road.[8]

Agencies that have a reputation for being corrupt

In June 2015, the inspector general of police for Nigeria, in a public statement, stated that the Nigerian police had the least corrupt officers of all the institutions in Nigeria. He also pledged to follow up on any corrupt police cases

---

BOX 1.3   EXCERPTS FROM AN FBI WEBSITE ARTICLE: COLOR-OF-LAW ABUSES

The Federal Bureau of Investigation (FBI) is the lead federal agency for investigating color-of-law abuses, which include acts carried out by government officials operating both within and beyond the limits of their lawful authority. Off-duty conduct may be covered if the perpetrator asserted his or her official status in some way.

During 2012, 42% of the FBI's total civil rights caseload involved color-of-law issues—there were 380 color-of-law cases opened during that year. Most of the cases involved crimes that fell into five broad areas:

- Excessive force
- Sexual assaults
- False arrest and fabrication of evidence
- Deprivation of property
- Failure to keep from harm

Excessive force: In making arrests, maintaining order, and defending life, law enforcement officers are allowed to use whatever force is "reasonably" necessary. The breadth and scope of the use of force is vast—from just the physical presence of the officer to the use of deadly force. Violations of federal law occur when it can be shown that the force used was willfully "unreasonable" or "excessive."

Sexual assaults by officials acting under color of law can happen in jails, during traffic stops, or in other settings where officials might use their position of authority to coerce an individual into sexual compliance. The compliance is generally gained because of a threat of an official action against the person if he or she doesn't comply.

False arrest and fabrication of evidence: The Fourth Amendment of the U.S. Constitution guarantees protection against unreasonable searches or seizures. A law enforcement official using authority provided under the color of law is allowed to stop individuals and, under certain circumstances, to search them and retain their property. It is in the abuse of that discretionary power—such as an unlawful detention or illegal confiscation of property—that a violation of a person's civil rights may occur.

Fabricating evidence against or falsely arresting an individual also violates the color-of-law statute, taking away the person's rights of due process and unreasonable seizure. In the case of deprivation of property, the color-of-law statute would be violated by unlawfully obtaining or maintaining a person's property, which oversteps or misapplies the official's authority.

The Fourteenth Amendment secures the right to due process; the Eighth Amendment prohibits the use of cruel and unusual punishment. During an arrest or detention, these rights can be violated by the use of force amounting to punishment (summary judgment). The person accused of a crime must be allowed the opportunity to have a trial and should not be subjected to punishment without having been afforded the opportunity of the legal process.

Failure to keep from harm: The public counts on its law enforcement officials to protect local communities. If it is shown that an official willfully failed to keep an individual from harm, that official could be in violation of the color-of-law statute.

Source: FBI website https://www.fbi.gov/about-us/investigate/civilrights/color_of_law. Accessed on October 2, 2015.

---

in accordance with the nation's constitutional provisions.[9] According to the inspector general, the Nigerian police have made frantic efforts in tackling corruption among the police officers. Nigeria is one of those countries whose police departments have a reputation of being corrupt.

While there are numerous websites that rank the 10 most corrupt police agencies, the author found it difficult to rank them with any degree of accuracy. Accordingly, the agencies with reputations for being corrupt are listed here without regard to their rank.

- *Pakistan*: The Pakistani police agencies are traditionally considered among the most corrupt institutions. The agencies have a reputation for police brutality, extortion, bribery, and for arresting innocent citizens for crimes that were knowingly committed by police officers.
- *Sudan police*: The country of Sudan has a reputation for being one of the most corrupt countries in the world. The corrupt institutions of Sudan include the police. The Sudan police have a reputation for extortion, bribery, and the use of violence and

BOX 1.4   FORMER ILLINOIS POLICE CHIEF, SHERIFF'S DEPUTY SENTENCED FOR MAIL FRAUD, MONEY LAUNDERING, AND TAX EVASION

On May 29, 2015, in Peoria, Illinois, Timothy J. Swanson of Bourbonnais was sentenced to 27 months in prison, 3 years of supervised release, and ordered to pay $229,128 in restitution to victims as well as $55,140 in back taxes. On January 27, 2015, Swanson pleaded guilty to two counts of mail fraud, one count of money laundering, two counts of tax evasion, and two counts of filing a false tax return. According to court documents, Swanson was employed as the City of Countryside, Illinois Chief of Police in 2005 and 2006. After leaving the police department, Swanson joined the Kankakee County Sheriff's Office in 2009. During 2005 and 2006, Swanson obtained the use of two U.S. Department of Defense helicopters for law enforcement activities. To obtain funds to operate the helicopters, Swanson established the Illinois Regional Air Support Service (IRASS) as a tax-exempt organization. No officer or director was to profit from its operation. From at least 2005 through 2012, Swanson solicited police departments, corporations, and individuals to make contributions to the IRASS. From 2006 to 2010, Swanson used a credit card in the name of the IRASS to make personal purchases and used money donated or awarded to the IRASS to make payments on the credit card. Swanson also used this money to purchase Rotors & Wings, LLC., a business that he operated.

retaliation against citizens who complain about police abuses.

- *Russia*: The Russian police are accused of committing police brutality, extorting bribes, and arresting innocent citizens. Their police force has also been accused of using corruption and bribery to meet monthly quotas.
- *Iraq police*: The Iraqi police have a reputation for having a long history of corruption. The police also appear to be ineffective at preventing violence and protecting citizens.
- *Afghanistan police*: The Afghan police have a reputation of extorting money and inflicting violence on civilians at police checkpoints. They also have a reputation of bribing citizens into paying them to avoid being arrested for crimes the citizens did not commit.

- *Mexico police*: Many consider the Mexican police force as one of the most corrupt police forces in the world. In addition, there are constant rumors of the police working to protect the drug cartels. Other charges of misconduct include that the police often ignore reported crimes and fail to investigate them. One probable reason for the corruption is that police officers' pay in Mexico is very low, and that police officers turn to corruption to supplement their income.
- *Haiti police*: The Haitian national police have been accused of violating various human rights and of being involved in crimes such as kidnapping, drug trafficking, and police brutality. There is some indication that the lawlessness of the police may have lessened after the earthquake in January 2010 (Figure 1.2).

Figure 1.2 Police ransacking effects taken from a bus in Hebron in the 1930s. (Photo courtesy of the Library of Congress Prints and Photographs Division.)

Noble-cause corruption

Frequently, police misconduct is justified by officers as "noble-cause corruption," and that the illegal actions were undertaken to achieve acceptable and laudable ends. For example, an unauthorized search by a police officer designed to take illegal contraband off the market is justified by some as noble-cause misconduct. Bayley and Perito cite the findings of the Judicial Commission of Inquiry into corruption in the Ugandan police force in 2000. The commission investigated murder and other abuses by Uganda police officers and the misappropriation of police property. The commission concluded that, while some of these incidents were undertaken for personal gain, most were motivated by the notion of noble-cause corruption.[10]

Noble-cause corruption is described on the PoliceOne website as a teleological (ends-oriented) approach to an ethical dilemma that states law enforcement professionals will utilize unethical, and sometimes illegal, means to obtain a desired result.[11] Frequently, in incidents involving noble-cause corruption, the police officers involved are good people trying to do the right thing.

Dirty Harry syndrome

The 1971 movie, *Dirty Harry*, is an action film in which Clint Eastwood played the role of "Dirty" Harry Callahan, a San Francisco police detective. During the movie, Dirty Harry provokes a psychotic serial killer to draw a weapon on him. Harry then kills the serial killer. The movie portrays Eastwood as a maverick cop who has little regard for rules but who also always gets results. There were four sequels to the movie. The clear message portrayed by the Dirty Harry movies was that the end justifies the means.

Noble-cause incident that went wrong

In the *Commonwealth v. Luna* case, the defendant Carlos Luna appealed his conviction for perjury and the filing of false police reports.* In February 1988, Luna, a Boston police officer, applied for a warrant to search the apartment of a suspected drug dealer, Albert Lewin. Luna, in the application for the search warrant, indicated that a specific informant had supplied him with information about drug dealing in the Dorchester apartment. During the search executed pursuant to the warrant, Luna's partner, Detective Sherman Griffiths, was killed.

Lewin was arrested and charged with the murder of Griffiths. When a state court ordered Luna to reveal his supposed original informant, Luna made up a name and physical description. When ordered to produce the informant, Luna and others engaged in a spurious

* Commonwealth v. Luna, 418 Mass. 749 (1994).

search, during the course of which Luna filed further false reports.

In due course, the drug indictment against Lewin was dismissed for failure to produce the informant, a potentially exculpatory witness. At the hearing prior to the dismissal, Luna told additional lies consistent with his search warrant affidavit and his subsequent false identification of the informant.

In February 1989, a superior court judge directed Luna to file an affidavit about his search for the so-called informant. On March 12, 1989, Luna filed an affidavit with the court and acknowledged that he had included false statements in the search warrant affidavit and that his testimony regarding the Lewin case was not entirely correct.

Dangers of the noble cause

One of the greatest dangers of noble-cause corruption is that police officers may become accustomed to bending the law, leading them to take actions that are increasing illegal and harmful to society when trying to ensure a conviction.

The PoliceOne website notes that there are a number of techniques that can modify the ethical orientation of officers. The website recommends that officers follow two basic techniques:

- Follow Policies and Procedures (P&P): Every department has a standard set of P&P guidelines. When in doubt, especially if you are a new officer, default to these tested and approved guidelines. At the very least, when Internal Affairs comes knocking at your door, you'll not only be able to articulate how you did what you did but, more importantly, why you did it.
- Always Act Professionally (AAP): This sounds simple enough, but any seasoned professional knows how quickly rationality can be pushed aside by pride, stubborn goals, or adrenaline.

The concept of noble-cause misconduct is a contradiction in terms. It is or is not misconduct, despite the motives of the individuals involved in committing the acts (Figure 1.3) (Box 1.5).

Predicable forms of corruption

Bayley and Perito noted that the reports of 32 police commissions identified 35 different forms of corruption.[12] The professors divided the forms into four categories:

- Sale and organization
- Predatory forms
- Subversion of justice
- Gifts and discounts

Figure 1.3 The original mission of the police is to serve and protect the citizens, as shown in the photo were the officer is assisting a young child. (Photo courtesy of the Library of Congress Prints and Photographs Division.)

BOX 1.5   EXAMPLE OF NOBLE-CAUSE CORRUPTION

A less obvious but perhaps even more threatening type of misconduct in law enforcement is noble-cause corruption. This type of misconduct involves, not necessarily the "rotten apples" in the agency, but sometimes the best officers in the agency or the "golden apples." Noble-cause corruption is a mind-set or subculture that fosters a belief that the end justifies the means. In other words, law enforcement is engaged in a mission to make our streets and communities safe, and if that requires suspending the constitution or violating laws ourselves in order to accomplish our mission, then for the greater good of society, so be it. The officers who adopt this philosophy lose their moral compass.

Source: Adapted from Steve Rothlein's letter distributed to the Public Training Council in 2008. Available at www. patc.com. Assessed on June 9, 2015.

Bayley and Perito noted that the most common forms of corruption were making false reports and committing perjury, protecting illegal gambling, theft of drugs on the street, theft of seized property, receiving discounts on purchases, and selling information about police operations. The researchers noted that, in studies prior to 1970, drug involvement was not mentioned. Drugs, however, became the major driver of corruption after the 1970s. Drugs replaced gambling, prostitution, and alcohol as the major driver of corruption after the 1970s (Box 1.6).

Police misconduct and the media

From the beginning of the development of police units, there has probably been a lot of corruption. In the present-day world, the media portray police corruption as at an all-time high. Each day, the majority of

---

BOX 1.6 FIXING POLICE TRAINING: COUNTERPOINT FROM THE POLICE POINT OF VIEW

In an editorial for *Police Magazine* in March 2015, David Griffith noted that, in the wake of anti-police demonstrations, politicians made a lot of promises to fix policing and to retrain officers to use force sparingly. Griffith claimed that many of the training programs designed to correct these problems appear to be sacrificing real-world common sense about violence in favor of politically correct ideology.[13]

Griffith notes that, in one training program, officers were advised to close their eyes and take a deep breath before responding to irate subjects. He points out that there are some hard truths about stopping "bad guys," whether they are terrorists or just criminals, and that these guys don't want to be stopped so force is often required to stop them. Any politically correct attempt to downplay this fact is therefore dangerous for both the officer and the people the officer serves.

BOX 1.7 MEDIA POWER

In an era when guns, drugs, and gangs occupy city streets, the media may very well prove to be law enforcement's most formidable foe. This is because the media are a source of political and social power. As providers of news and information, their messages influence the attitudes, opinions, beliefs, and voting patterns of the public. For this reason, government officials and special interest groups attempt to influence the content of media for the purpose of shaping public opinion. "Media power" represents the extent to which interested groups command control of media messages relevant to their particular interests.

Source: An excerpt from Jarret S. Lovell (2002) *Media Power and Information Control: A Study of Police Organizations and Media Relations*. National Institute of Justice, Rockville, MD: GRP 2000-IJ-CX-0046, p. 3.

---

professionals who develop and publish news items look for headlines. As one reporter once noted, "If it does not bleed, it does not lead" (Box 1.7).

Punishing police misconduct

Police brutality is one of the most serious, enduring, and divisive human rights violations in the United States. The problem is nationwide, and its nature is institutionalized. For these reasons, the U.S. government—as well as state and city governments, which have an obligation to respect the international human rights standards by which the United States is bound—deserve to be held accountable by international human rights bodies and public opinion.

While there are a number of cases in which prosecutors have successfully prosecuted officers for misconduct, for the most part most allegations of police misconduct are not indicted or punished. This has been an area where prosecutors have exercised very selective prosecution. Numerous excuses have been given for not prosecuting police misconduct.[14] These include:

- That it is difficult to obtain a conviction because the judge or jury members tend to believe the officer and not the complaining citizen
- That prosecutors and the police work closely with each other, and prosecutors hesitate to prosecute

officers with whom they have a close working relationship
- Political pressures

Human Rights Watch (HRW) has noted that many critics have issues with local prosecution of police officer misconduct being left with the local prosecutor. One effort has been to direct the investigation and prosecution of alleged police misconduct away from prosecutors of general jurisdiction and the creation of civilian review boards as a means of alternate disposition of charges of police misconduct. This recommendation will be discussed in Chapters 7 and 9, when discussing the functions of civilian review boards.

The HRW recommended that the federal government compiles and publishes relevant, nationwide statistical data on police abuse to inform its own policy-making, maintain oversight of local data collection, and facilitate monitoring by both governmental and non-governmental entities. The HRW noted that the Justice Department should provide an annual report on the number of complaints alleging human rights violations against police officers received and investigated and the number of officers indicted or convicted under the federal criminal civil rights statutes. The report should contain an analysis of such issues as official acts of racial discrimination, trends in types of abuse, difficulties in prosecuting cases, and sources of information.

The HRW also noted that Congress should withhold federal grants to police departments that have failed to provide data on the use of excessive force. Congress has reportedly failed to provide adequate funding for data compilation on police use of excessive force and should do so without delay, provided that the research projects are refocused to fulfill the congressional mandate. Members of Congress should also monitor the Justice Department's efforts to compile these data and insist that use of excessive force data be produced immediately.

Are U.S. police too aggressive?

In 2015, a French editorial stated that "The sheer flagrance of police brutality against black Americans leaves one speechless." The editorial also noted that a single killing of an unarmed suspect in a European country would be unthinkable. The editorial opined that the police culture in the United States had gone mad.[15]

According to the May 15, 2015, issue of *The Week*, 458 people have been killed by police in the United States but many civic groups contend that the number is over twice that amount. It was noted that in Germany during that same period only eight individuals were killed by the police, and that with just 4.4% of the world's population, the United States has locked up 22% of the world's prisoners. According to Marie-Astrid Langer, a Swiss reporter, American police believe that the only way to deter crime is to jail potential criminals whereas European police are trained to defuse situations calmly.[16]

Some European researchers contend that, when the United States was first settled, pioneers relied on themselves and their neighbors, and law enforcement was called on only in severe cases, such as murder. Accordingly, Americans are used to police who regularly use excessive force, and have produced a system where authority can shoot or confiscate first and ask questions later.[16]

Ferguson effect

Michael Brown, an 18-year-old black male, was shot and killed on August 9, 2014, by a white Ferguson police officer. The circumstances surrounding the shooting are disputed. It appears that, shortly before the shooting, Brown stole several packages of cigarillos from a nearby convenience store. The police officer was notified of the robbery and given a description of Brown. When the officer confronted Brown, shots were fired and Brown died as the result. It is reported that the officer fired 12 shots at Brown, who was unarmed but moving toward the officer.

The killing of Brown caused unrest in the city of Ferguson. The protests, which included violence, continued for more than a week after the shooting. The Missouri governor ordered the local police agencies to cede most of their authority to the state highway patrol. The governmental response to the protests was criticized for their overly insensitive tactics and militarized response.

In November 2014, the St. Louis County grand jury decided not to indict the police officer, and in March 2015, the U.S. Department of Justice cleared the officer of civil rights violations in the shooting. In 2015, many news media outlets reported a rise in violent crime in major cities in the United States. The phrase "Ferguson effect" was coined as a popular description of the phenomenon. Many in the media blamed the Ferguson effect for the increase in crime.[17]

Apparently, the media failed to notice that most of the places that were cited as having a violent crime wave were experiencing an all-time low in crime, and that many of the places where increases in crime were reported were still the safest they had been in years or even decades. In addition, there was weak support for the claim that crime increases were the result of changes in policing; counterexamples indicated that retrenchment of low-level policing did not increase crime.[18]

A later study coauthored by Professors Justin Nix of the University of Louisville and Scott Wolfe of the University of South Carolina concluded that, while there was no "Ferguson effect," criticism from the incident has resulted in police officers being less motivated post-Ferguson. The professors concluded that officers are being less proactive on the job and less willing to engage directly with community members to solve problems. As one police supervisor noted, "We are not seeing the same level of self-initiated activity since Ferguson that we saw before Ferguson"[19] (Box 1.8).

Militarization of America's police forces

Mexico has used their army to supplement their police forces. A discussion with many human rights activists indicated that the citizens of Mexico are unhappy with their government's use of military troops to supplement the police. The United States has always drawn a firm line between the military and the police.[20] In a military boot camp, the trainees are taught to meet the enemy and destroy them, whereas in law enforcement recruitment training, the trainees are taught that the basic mission of law enforcement is to protect the public. There is a significant different between "meet the enemy and destroy them" and the mission to protect the public.

BOX 1.8   EXCERPTS FROM THE DREPARTMENT OF JUSTICE INVESTIGATION OF THE FERGUSON POLICE DEPARTMENT

In September 2014, the Department of Justice opened an investigation of the Ferguson Police Department (FPD) pursuant to the Violent Crime Control and Law Enforcement Act of 1994, the Omnibus Crime Control and Safe Streets Act of 1968, and Title VI of the Civil Rights Act of 1964. The investigation focused on allegations that Ferguson law enforcement engaged in a pattern or practice of violations of the Constitution and federal statutory law. On March 4, 2015, DOJ announced the results of the investigation, finding that FPD's police and municipal court practices systematically violate the First, Fourth and Fourteenth Amendments. DOJ determined that FPD's approach to law enforcement is unduly focused on revenue generation and that its practices both reflect and exacerbate existing race bias. As a result, Ferguson's law enforcement practices discriminate against African Americans and decrease trust between the Ferguson community and law enforcement, hampering FPD's ability to ensure public safety.

Ferguson has allowed its focus on revenue generation to fundamentally compromise the role of Ferguson's municipal court. The municipal court does not act as a neutral arbiter of the law or a check on unlawful police conduct. Instead, the court primarily uses its judicial authority as the means to compel the payment of fines and fees that advance the City's financial interests. This has led to court practices that violate the Fourteenth Amendment's due process and equal protection requirements. The court's practices also impose unnecessary harm, overwhelmingly on African-American individuals, and run counter to public safety.

POLICE PRACTICES

The City's emphasis on revenue generation has a profound effect on FPD's approach to law enforcement. Patrol assignments and schedules are geared toward aggressive enforcement of Ferguson's municipal code, with insufficient thought given to whether enforcement strategies promote public safety or unnecessarily undermine community trust and cooperation. Officer evaluations and promotions depend to an inordinate degree on "productivity," meaning the number of citations issued. Partly as a consequence of City and FPD priorities, many officers appear to see some residents, especially those who live in Ferguson's predominantly African-American neighborhoods, less as constituents to be protected than as potential offenders and sources of revenue.

This culture within FPD influences officer activities in all areas of policing, beyond just ticketing. Officers expect and demand compliance even when they lack legal authority. They are inclined to interpret the exercise of free-speech rights as unlawful disobedience, innocent movements as physical threats, and indications of mental or physical illness as belligerence. Police supervisors and leadership do too little to ensure that officers act in accordance with law and policy, and rarely respond meaningfully to civilian complaints of officer misconduct. The result is a pattern of stops without reasonable suspicion and arrests without probable cause in violation of the Fourth Amendment; infringement on free expression, as well as retaliation for protected expression, in violation of the First Amendment; and excessive force in violation of the Fourth Amendment.

Even relatively routine misconduct by Ferguson police officers can have significant consequences for the people whose rights are violated. For example, in the summer of 2012, a 32-year-old African-American man sat in his car cooling off after playing basketball in a Ferguson public park. An officer pulled up behind the man's car, blocking him in, and demanded the man's Social Security number and identification. Without any cause, the officer accused the man of being a pedophile, referring to the presence of children in the park, and ordered the man out of his car for a pat-down, although the officer had no reason to believe the man was armed. The officer also asked to search the man's car. The man objected, citing his constitutional rights. In response, the officer arrested the man, reportedly at gunpoint, charging him with eight violations of Ferguson's municipal code. One charge, making a False Declaration, was for initially providing the short form of his first name (e.g., "Mike" instead of "Michael"), and an address which, although legitimate, was different from the one on his driver's license. Another charge was for not wearing a seat belt, even though he was seated in a parked car. The officer also charged the man both with having an expired operator's license, and with having no operator's license in his possession. The man told us that, because of these charges, he lost his job as a contractor with the federal government that he had held for years.

Source: DOJ website at https://www.justice.gov/sites/default/files/opa/press-releases/attachments/2015/03/04/ferguson_police_department_report.pdf. Accessed on October 2, 2015.

The concept of keeping the military and police separated can be traced back to a civil war act, the Posse Comitatus Act. This act prohibits police from enlisting active-duty military personnel for civilian law enforcement. To skirt the provisions of this act, many police leaders and politicians have encouraged police officers to use the tactics and adopt the mind-set of military personnel.[21]

To a great extent, two trends have fostered the militarization of the police: the development of special weapons and tactics (SWAT) teams and the "war on drugs." Former Los Angeles police chief Daryl Gates is generally credited with establishing the first SWAT teams in early 1966. Gates was looking for ways to counter the guerrilla tactics used against the Los Angeles Police Department (LAPD). He developed the concept of assembling an elite unit of officers that were trained by the military in subjects such as crowd control and sniping. He wanted to name this new team the "Special Weapons Attack Team," but city officials objected to the use of the work "attack" and persuaded him to change its name to "Special Weapons and Tactics."[21] The first raid carried out by the SWAT team was a high-profile shootout with the city's Black Panther militia. His team was later involved in a celebrated standoff in 1974 against the Symbionese Liberation Army, which was carried out live on national television. By 1975, there were over 500 SWAT teams in the country.

The trend in the militarization process was President Nixon's declaration of the war on drugs. The Nixon administration influenced Congress to pass a bill authorizing no-knock raids for federal narcotics agents. While Congress repealed the no-knock law in 1974, the policy was established and continued. In addition, the administration rhetoric served to dehumanize drug offenders. It was during the term of President Reagan in 1980 when the war on drugs and the SWAT teams converged. President Reagan provided or encouraged new funding, equipment, and a more active drug policing role for the police SWAT teams. The Reagan administration took a more active role in the war on drugs and supported a more confrontational and militaristic approach to combat it. In 1989, President Bush created a series of regional task forces within the Department of Defense designed to bring together the police and the military for drug interdiction. In the 1990s, Congress created a reutilization program in order to provide police departments with military weapons.

President's Task Force On 21st Century Policing

"When any part of the American family does not feel like it is being treated fairly, that's a problem for all of us." —President Barack Obama

In December 2014, President Obama created the President's Task Force on 21st Century Policing. In establishing the task force, the president stated that

Trust between law enforcement agencies and the people they protect and serve is essential to the stability of our communities, the integrity of our criminal justice system, and the safe and effective delivery of policing services. http://www.cops.usdoj.gov/pdf/taskforce/Interim_TF_Report_150228_Intro_to_Implementation.pdf. Accessed on October 2, 2015.

In the summer of 2015, the task force submitted its report to the president. The report contained some important recommendations for improving policing and reducing police misconduct. Included in this section is the executive summary of their report. While it is too early to determine whether the task force recommendations will reduce police misconduct, the federal government should be applauded for their attempts.

The final report resulted in the announcement of the White House Police Data Initiative. The initiative is designed to ensure the release of information to the public of shows of force by officers and shootings in which police were involved. The initiative was designed to promote the use of open data to increase transparency, build community trust, and support innovation in the communities, using better technology, such as early warning systems, to identify problems, increase internal accountability, and decrease inappropriate uses of force. The initiative is credited with the increased use of body cameras by police officers.

The task force's results recommended that police departments be more transparent about serious events by communicating with citizens and the media. It also suggested initiating activities unrelated to enforcing the law to build trust with society.

The report also looked at issues regarding law enforcement involvement in immigration and the appearance of police officers when dealing with riots like those seen in Ferguson, New York, and Baltimore. Immediately after the report was released, a common concern voiced by many police researcher was that increased media coverage could make a police officer's job more dangerous. Probably only time will tell whether this concern is correct (Box 1.9).

Executive summary of task force report

Trust between law enforcement agencies and the people they protect and serve is essential in a democracy. It is key to the stability of our communities, the integrity of

BOX 1.9 EXECUTIVE ORDER

ESTABLISHMENT OF THE PRESIDENT'S TASK FORCE ON 21ST CENTURY POLICING

By the authority vested in me as President by the Constitution and the laws of the United States of America, and in order to identify the best means to provide an effective partnership between law enforcement and local communities that reduces crime and increases trust, it is hereby ordered as follows:

Section 1. Establishment. There is established a President's Task Force on 21st Century Policing (Task Force).

Sec. 2. Membership.

1. The Task Force shall be composed of not more than members appointed by the President. The members shall include distinguished individuals with relevant experience or subject-matter expertise in law enforcement, civil rights, and civil liberties.
2. The President shall designate two members of the Task Force to serve as Co-Chairs.

Sec. 3. Mission.

1. The Task Force shall, consistent with applicable law, identify best practices and otherwise make recommendations to the President on how policing practices can promote effective crime reduction while building public trust.
2. The Task Force shall be solely advisory and shall submit a report to the President by March 2, 2015.

Sec. 4. Administration.

1. The Task Force shall hold public meetings and engage with Federal, State, tribal, and local officials, technical advisors, and nongovernmental organizations, among others, as necessary to carry out its mission.
2. The Director of the Office of Community Oriented Policing Services shall serve as Executive Director of the Task Force and shall, as directed by the Co-Chairs, convene regular meetings of the Task Force and supervise its work.
3. In carrying out its mission, the Task Force shall be informed by, and shall strive to avoid duplicating, the efforts of other governmental entities.
4. The Department of Justice shall provide administrative services, funds, facilities, staff, equipment, and other support services as may be necessary for the Task Force to carry out its mission to the extent permitted by law and subject to the availability of appropriations.
5. Members of the Task Force shall serve without any additional compensation for their work on the Task Force, but shall be allowed travel expenses, including per diem, to the extent permitted by law for persons serving intermittently in the Government service (5 U.S.C. 5701-5707).

Sec. 5. Termination. The Task Force shall terminate 30 days after the President requests a final report from the Task Force.

Sec. 6. General Provisions.

1. Nothing in this order shall be construed to impair or otherwise affect
   a. The authority granted by law to a department, agency, or the head thereof; or
   b. The functions of the Director of the Office of Management and Budget relating to budgetary, administrative, or legislative proposals.
2. This order is not intended to, and does not, create any right or benefit, substantive or procedural, enforceable at law or in equity by any party against the United States, its departments, agencies, or entities, its officers, employees, or agents, or any other person.
3. Insofar as the Federal Advisory Committee Act, as amended (5 U.S.C. App.) (the "Act") may apply to the Task Force, any functions of the President under the Act, except for those in section 6 of the Act, shall be performed by the Attorney General.

our criminal justice system, and the safe and effective delivery of policing services.

In light of recent events that have exposed rifts in the relationships between local police and the communities they protect and serve, on December 18, 2014, President Barack Obama signed an executive order establishing the Task Force on 21st Century Policing. The president charged the task force with identifying best practices and offering recommendations on how policing practices can promote effective crime reduction while building public trust.

This executive summary provides an overview of the recommendations of the task force, which met seven times in January and February 2015. These listening sessions, held in Washington, DC; Phoenix, Arizona; and Cincinnati, Ohio, brought the 11 members of the task force together with more than 100 individuals from diverse stakeholder groups—law enforcement officers and executives, community members, civic leaders, advocates, researchers, academics, and others—in addition to many others who submitted written testimony to study the problems from all perspectives.

The task force recommendations, each with action items, are organized around six main topic areas or "pillars:" building trust and legitimacy, policy and oversight, technology and social media, community policing and crime reduction, officer training and education, and officer safety and wellness.

The task force also offered two overarching recommendations: that the president should support the creation of a national crime and justice task force to examine all areas of criminal justice and propose reforms and, as a corollary to this effort, the task force also recommended that the president support programs that take a comprehensive and inclusive look at community-based initiatives addressing core issues such as poverty, education, and health and safety.

Pillar one: Building trust and legitimacy

Building trust and nurturing legitimacy on both sides of the police/citizen divide is the foundational principle underlying the nature of relations between law enforcement agencies and the communities they serve. Decades of research and practice support the premise that people are more likely to obey the law when they believe that those who are enforcing it have authority that is perceived as legitimate by those subject to the authority. The public confers legitimacy only on those whom they believe are acting in procedurally just ways. In addition, law enforcement cannot build community trust if it is seen as an occupying force, coming in from the outside to impose control on the community. Pillar one seeks to provide focused recommendations on building this relationship. Law enforcement culture should embrace

a guardian—rather than a warrior—mind-set to build trust and legitimacy, both within agencies and with the public. Toward that end, law enforcement agencies should adopt procedural justice as the guiding principle for internal and external policies and practices to guide their interactions with rank-and-file officers and with the citizens they serve.

Law enforcement agencies should also establish a culture of transparency and accountability to build public trust and legitimacy. This is critical to ensuring that decision-making is understood and in accordance with stated policy.

Law enforcement agencies should also proactively promote public trust by initiating positive nonenforcement activities to engage communities that typically have high rates of investigative and enforcement involvement with government agencies. Law enforcement agencies should also track and analyze the level of trust that communities have in police, just as they measure changes in crime. This can be accomplished through consistent annual community surveys. Finally, law enforcement agencies should strive to create a workforce that encompasses a broad range of diversity including race, gender, language, life experience, and cultural background, to improve understanding and effectiveness in dealing with all communities.

Pillar two: Policy and oversight

Pillar two emphasizes that, if police are to carry out their responsibilities according to established policies, those policies must reflect community values. Law enforcement agencies should collaborate with community members, especially in communities and neighborhoods disproportionately affected by crime, to develop policies and strategies for deploying resources that aim to reduce crime by improving relationships, increasing community engagement, and fostering cooperation.

To achieve this end, law enforcement agencies should have clear and comprehensive policies on the use of force (including training on the importance of de-escalation), mass demonstrations (including the appropriate use of equipment, particularly rifles and armored personnel carriers), consent before searches, gender identification, racial profiling, and performance measures, among others such as external and independent investigations, prosecutions of officer-involved shootings, and other use-of-force situations and in-custody deaths. These policies should also include provisions for the collection of demographic data on all parties involved. All policies and aggregate data should be made publicly available to ensure transparency.

To ensure policies are maintained and current, law enforcement agencies are encouraged to periodically review policies and procedures, conduct nonpunitive peer reviews of critical incidents separate from criminal and administrative investigations, and establish civilian oversight mechanisms with their communities.

Finally, to assist law enforcement and the community to achieve the elements of pillar two, the U.S. Department of Justice, through the Office of Community Oriented Policing Services (COPS Office) and Office of Justice Programs (OJP), should provide technical assistance and incentive funding to jurisdictions with small police agencies that take steps toward interagency collaboration, shared services, and regional training. They should also partner with the International Association of Directors of Law Enforcement Standards and Training (IADLEST) to expand its national decertification index to serve as the national register of decertified officers, with the goal of covering all agencies within the United States and its territories.

Pillar three: Technology and social media

The use of technology can improve policing practices and build community trust and legitimacy, but its implementation must be built on a defined policy framework with its purposes and goals clearly delineated. Implementing new technologies can give police departments an opportunity to fully engage and educate communities in a dialogue about their expectations for transparency, accountability, and privacy. But technology changes quickly in terms of new hardware, software, and other options. Law enforcement agencies and leaders need to be able to identify, assess, and evaluate new technology for adoption, and to do so in ways that improve their effectiveness, efficiency, and evolution without infringing on individual rights.

Pillar three guides the implementation, use, and evaluation of technology and social media by law enforcement agencies. To build a solid foundation for law enforcement agencies in this field, the U.S. Department of Justice, in consultation with the law enforcement field, should establish national standards for the research and development of new technology including auditory, visual, and biometric data, "less than lethal" technology, and the development of segregated radio spectra such as FirstNet. These standards should also address compatibility, interoperability, and implementation needs, both within local law enforcement agencies and across agencies and jurisdictions, and should maintain civil and human rights protection. Law enforcement implementation of technology should be designed to consider local needs and align with these national standards. Finally, law enforcement agencies should adopt model policies and best practices for technology-based community engagement that increases community trust and access.

Pillar four: Community policing and crime reduction

Pillar four focuses on the importance of community policing as a guiding philosophy for all stakeholders. Community policing emphasizes working with neighborhood residents to coproduce public safety. Law enforcement agencies should therefore work with community residents to identify problems and collaborate on implementing solutions that produce meaningful results for the community. Specifically, law enforcement agencies should develop and adopt policies and strategies that reinforce the importance of community engagement in managing public safety.

Law enforcement agencies should also engage in multidisciplinary, community team approaches for planning, implementing, and responding to crisis situations with complex causal factors.

Communities should support a culture and practice of policing that reflects the values of protection and promotion of the dignity of all—especially the most vulnerable, such as children and youth most at risk for crime or violence. Law enforcement agencies should avoid using law enforcement tactics that unnecessarily stigmatize youth and marginalize their participation in schools (where law enforcement officers should have limited involvement in discipline) and communities. In addition, communities need to affirm and recognize the voices of youth in community decision making, facilitate youth participation in research and problem solving, and develop and fund youth leadership training and life skills through positive youth/police collaboration and interactions.

Pillar five: Training and education

As our nation becomes more pluralistic and the scope of law enforcement responsibilities expands, the need for expanded and more effective training has become critical. Today's line officers and leaders must be trained and capable of addressing a wide variety of challenges including international terrorism, evolving technologies, rising immigration, changing laws, new cultural mores, and a growing mental health crisis.

Pillar five focuses on the training and educational needs of law enforcement. To ensure the high quality and effectiveness of training and education, law enforcement agencies should engage community members, particularly those with special expertise, in the training process and provide leadership training to all personnel throughout their careers.

To further assist the training and educational needs of law enforcement, the federal government should support the development of partnerships with training facilities across the country to promote consistent standards for high-quality training and establish training innovation hubs involving universities and police academies. A national postgraduate institute of policing for senior executives should be created, with a standardized curriculum preparing participants to lead agencies in the twenty-first century.

One specific method of increasing the quality of training would be to ensure that Peace Officer and Standards Training (POST) boards include mandatory crisis intervention training (CIT), which equips officers to deal with individuals in crisis or living with mental disabilities as part of both basic recruit and in-service officer training, as well as instruction in disease of addiction, implicit bias and cultural responsiveness, policing in a democratic society, procedural justice, and effective social interaction and tactical skills.

Pillar six: Officer wellness and safety

The wellness and safety of law enforcement officers is critical, not only for the officers, their colleagues, and their agencies, but also for public safety. Pillar six emphasizes the support and proper implementation of officer wellness and safety as a multipartner effort.

The U.S. Department of Justice should enhance and further promote its multifaceted officer safety and wellness initiative. Two specific strategies recommended for the U.S. Department of Justice include (1) encouraging and assisting departments in the implementation of scientifically supported shift lengths by law enforcement and (2) expanding efforts to collect and analyze data, not only on officer deaths, but also on injuries and "near misses."

Law enforcement agencies should also promote wellness and safety at every level of the organization. For instance, every law enforcement officer should be provided with individual tactical first aid kits and training as well as antiballistic vests. In addition, law enforcement agencies should adopt policies that require officers to wear seat belts and bullet-proof vests and provide training to raise awareness of the consequences of failure to do so. Internal procedural justice principles should be adopted for all internal policies and interactions. The federal government should develop programs to provide financial support for law enforcement officers to continue to pursue educational opportunities. Finally, Congress should develop and enact peer-reviewed error management legislation.

Implementation recommendations

The administration, through policies and practices already in place, can start right now to move forward on the recommendations contained in this report. The president should direct all federal law enforcement agencies to implement the task force recommendations to the extent practicable, and the U.S. Department of Justice should explore public–private partnership opportunities with foundations to advance the implementation of the recommendations. Finally, the COPS Office and the OJP should take a series of targeted actions to assist the law enforcement field in addressing current and future challenges.

Conclusion

The members of the Task Force on 21st Century Policing are convinced that the concrete recommendations contained in this publication will bring long-term improvements to the ways in which law enforcement agencies interact with and bring positive change to their communities.

National decertification database

The NDD lists officers from member states who have lost their state certification due to criminal conviction or other misconduct disallowed by the reporting state. The database is administered by IADLEST, and each record indicates where an appropriate user may go to obtain more information on the decertified individual. Unfortunately, not all states are subscribed to the database, which was started in 1996 as part of an interstate communication system linking U.S. law enforcement agencies. The database is an effort to prevent "bad cops" from becoming "gypsy cops." As of August 2014, there were 29 states contributing to the database.[22]

A 2005 survey reported by the National Criminal Justice Reference Service indicated that, in 2004, over 2000 law enforcement officers had their certificates revoked for cause. The states with the highest number of revocations were California, Florida, and Georgia.[23]

Summary

- Skolnick and Fyfe have concluded that there are two Americas. One is urban, cosmopolitan, and multicultural and the other is suburban, relatively safe, relatively prosperous, and unicultural. The first suffers disproportionately from crime, gang violence, poverty, and homelessness. The second is predominantly white and middle class.
- Police misconduct is a complex and varied subject.
- There are over 12,000 law enforcement agencies in the United States alone, and close to one million people involved in law enforcement in one manner or another.

- The vast number probably makes law enforcement one of the largest professions in the world. Accordingly, in a profession this large, there will be some individuals who do not meet the expected professional standard expected of them.
- Police corruption is considered a form of police misconduct in which law enforcement officers seek personal gain, illegally discriminate against individuals, use excessive force, fail to respect the rights of individuals, or commit other criminal offenses.
- A subculture is a group of individuals who generally share attitudes, perceptions, assumptions, values, beliefs, ways of living, and traditions. Because police work entails so many experiences unique to the field, the police subculture can almost become stronger than the officer's family ties.
- Police corruption is an international problem. Historically, police misconduct has been a factor in the development of police institutions worldwide, but it is a particular problem in counterinsurgency and peacekeeping operations.
- The FBI considers police corruption as part of public corruption. According to the FBI, public corruption is a breach of trust by federal, state, or local officials—often with the help of private sector accomplices. It's also the FBI's top criminal investigative priority.
- Frequently, police misconduct is justified by the officers as "noble-cause corruption." where the illegal actions were undertaken to achieve acceptable and laudable ends. For example, an unauthorized search by a police officer designed to take illegal contraband off the market is justified by some as noble-cause misconduct.
- There are four different forms of police corruption. They are sale and organization, predatory forms, subversion of justice, and gifts and discounts.
- The President's Task Force on 21st Century Policing recommends that the police be more transparent in discussing these issues.

Practicum

A series of robberies took place in a Cincinnati neighborhood. After one of the robberies, a resident took down the license number of a car that was perceived to be moving about the neighborhood in a suspicious manner. The police traced the plate to a female citizen. A police officer determines that the citizen has three children. He goes to their school and arrests all three.

One of the minors is identified as RM. RM is driven to the police station where he is interrogated. The mother is not informed because the officer instructed the school personnel to not tell her. RM denies any involvement in the robberies. The officer tells RM that if he does not confess, the officer will arrest the mother and she will lose custody of the children. RM confesses.

The next day, the officer tells the school principal that he does not believe that RM was involved in the robberies. In addition, RM does not match the physical description of any of the robbers. Meanwhile, RM is retained in custody for 9 days before he is released by the prosecutor. When the prosecutor discovers that RM was in custody, she immediately orders his release and drops all charges.

As a member of the Cincinnati civil service board considering the misconduct of the officer, consider

- What are the specific acts of misconduct committed by the officer?
- What action should be taken against the officer?

Discussion questions

1. If you were the chief of police for Ferguson during the Brown killing, how would you have handled the situation?
2. What was the purpose of the President's Task Force on 21st Century Policing?
3. Why is it recommended that any complaints filed against a police officer be in writing?
4. Discuss the relationship of the media and the police and how the media may help to reduce police misconduct.
5. What rights should a police officer have when being investigated for official misconduct?

References

1. President's Task Force on 21st Century Policing. 2015. Report of the President's Task Force on 21st Century Policing. Washington, DC: Office of Community Oriented Policing Services.
2. Jerome H. Skolnick and James J. Fyre (1993) *Above the Law: Police and the Excessive Use of Force.* New York: Free Press.
3. Jerome H. Skolnick and James J. Fyre (1993) *Above the Law: Police and the Excessive Use of Force,* p. 8. New York: Free Press.
4. Stefan Harrendorf, Markku Heiskanen, and Steven Malby (eds.) (2010) International Statistics on Crime and Justice, HEUNI Publication Series, No. 64. Helsinki: United Nations.
5. Rich Martin (May, 2010) Police corruption: And analytical look into police ethics, *FBI Law Enforcement Bulletin,* Vol. 79 no. 5, 1–2.

6. Mark Carignan (March, 2013) Research forum: Misconduct allegations: Procedural vs. Distributional Justice, *FBI Law Enforcement Bulletin.* Vol. 82, No. 3.

7. David Bayley and Robert Perito (2011) Special report: Police corruption-what past scandals teach about current challenges. Washington, DC: United States Institute of Peace. Accessible at www.usip.org. Accessed on June 14, 2015.

8. FBI website at www.fbi.gov. Accessed on June 9, 2015.

9. As reported on Vanguard's website at http://www.vanguardngr.com/2015/06/of-all-institutions-in-nigeria-police-has-least-corrupt-officers-igp/. Accessed on June 9, 2015.

10. David Bayley and Robert Perito (2011) Special report: Police corruption–what past scandals teach about current challenges, p. 3. Washington, DC: United States Institute of Peace. Accessible at www.usip.org. Accessed on June 14, 2015.

11. At www.policeone.com. Accessed on June 11, 2015.

12. David Bayley and Robert Perito (2011) Special report: Police corruption–what past scandals teach about current challenges, p. 4. Washington, DC: United States Institute of Peace. Accessible at www.usip.org. Accessed on June 14, 2015.

13. David Griffith (March, 2015) Editorial: Fixing police training, *Police Magazine*, p. 4.

14. Allyson Collins (1998) *Shielded from Justice: Police Brutality and Accountability in the United States*. New York: Human Rights Watch.

15. As reported in the article (May 15, 2015) How they see us: Why the U.S. police are so aggressive, *The Week*, p. 4.

16. As reported in the article (May 15, 2015) How they see us: Why the U.S. police are so aggressive, *The Week*, p. 5.

17. "Investigation of the Ferguson Police Department" United States Department of Justice. USDOJ Civil Rights Division. Available at www.justice.gov March 4, 2015. Accessed on June 13, 2015.

18. E-mail from Professor Laura Dugan on behalf of the American Society of Criminology Policy Committee on June 13, 2015.

19. Philip M. Bailey (November 20, 2015) Study: Cops less motivated post-Ferguson, *USA Today*, p. 12A.

20. Robert Balko (Fall, 2013) *The Militarization of America's Police Forces Cato's Letter-a Quarterly Message on Liberty*. Washington, DC: Cato Institute.

21. Robert Balko (Fall, 2013) *The Militarization of America's Police Forces Cato's Letter: A Quarterly Message on Liberty*, pp. 2–3. Washington, DC: Cato Institute.

22. Florida Background Investigators Association website at http://www.flbia.org/archives/98. Accessed on October 1, 2015.

23. Raymond Franklin (2005) *Survey of Post Agencies Regarding Certification Practices*, NCJRS 213048. Rockville, MD: Bureau of Justice Assistance Clearinghouse.

chapter two

Historical analysis of police misconduct

Learning objectives

After studying this chapter, the reader should understand the following concepts and issues:

- How history has influenced the conduct of present American policing
- The development of modern policing
- The history of police corruption
- The history of police brutality

Introduction

Police misconduct is not a recent phenomenon. There have been reports of police misconduct from the beginning of the modern police force. Many of the early reports were of police brutality especially against striking workers. The reports include the Great Railroad Strike of 1877, the Pullman strike of 1894, the Lawrence textile strike of 1912, the Ludlow massacre of 1914, the steel strike of 1919, and the Hanapepe massacre of 1924. In each of these situations, the police brutally beat striking laborers. While racial profiling has been an issue with U.S. police departments, it is interesting to note that the first formal police units in America were the slave patrols.

According to Robin Kelly, the early policing of Black, Latino, and Native American communities in the United States was initially in the form of occupation, surveillance, and pacification. Even before formal police departments were established, the people in power relied on legal and extralegal violence and terrorism to pacify, discipline, and exploit minority communities.[1] Kelly points out that a 1705 Virginia statute allowed slave owners to burn, whip, dismember, or mutilate slaves as punishment for crimes. Kelly also notes that a 1723 Maryland law permitted the cutting off of the ears of Africans—slave or free—who struck a white person.

Kelly contended that lynching was an essential part in understanding the history and character of police violence in America because it revealed the sexual and gender dimensions of maintaining the color line and disciplining minorities (Boxes 2.1 and 2.2).

Development of police departments

Most researchers trace the origin of the modern police department to Alfred the Great of England during the ninth century. It started with the development of the shire-reeve system, which was the forerunner for the office of sheriff. In the thirteenth century, night watch systems developed in urban England to protect the streets during hours of darkness.

From the thirteenth century until the seventeenth century, there was minimal development in the concept of policing. During that period, it was presumed that each citizen had a duty to protect the laws of England. Often, this meant that citizens with resources used the law to enhance their own opportunities for enrichment.

By the seventeenth century, the chief law enforcement officials in the urban areas of England were the magistrates, who presided over the courts, ordered arrests, and investigated suspected criminal activities. In rural areas, the shire-reeves were responsible for maintaining law and order among the citizens.

Robberies flourished in England during the sixteenth and seventeenth centuries. In 1693, the English Parliament passed an act providing for rewards for the capture and conviction of any robbers. As a result of this act, the thief-takers emerged. The thief-takers were private individuals who were paid by the government on a piecework basis. They had no official status, and only the authority of private citizens to arrest. Many of the thief-takers were criminals themselves. As the number of thief-takers grew, a class of professional thief-takers developed. In many cases, they would encourage individuals to commit crimes and then arrest them for the rewards.

By the 1830s, there were over 3000 uniformed constables in the City of London. Henry Fielding, who wrote *Tom Jones*, was appointed as a magistrate in Westminster. Because his office was located on Bow Street, when he formed a small group of unofficial investigators they were known as the Bow Street Runners. The runners were not salaried and received their money under the standard reward system. Later, the government provided financial support for the runners.

When Henry Fielding stepped down because of poor health, his brother John Fielding was appointed

BOX 2.1 CORRUPTION AND PUBLIC RELIEF

In 1932, it was widely accepted in the United States that the administration of public relief was politically corrupt. Opponents of public relief often complained that the use of public relief was primarily for political purposes. By 1940, the criticisms of corruption and political manipulation had diminished considerably.[2] Wallis, Fishback, and Kantor explore the question of what had changed, and how the country entered the depression with a public welfare system that was riddled with political manipulation and emerged with one that was not. According to the authors, the president, Franklin Roosevelt, and other members of the executive branch gained little or nothing from the kind of local corruption involved in public relief. But they stood to incur enormous losses if the New Deal relief program was perceived as politically manipulative and corrupt by the voting public. Roosevelt and the Democrats brought relief to millions of families every month, and the gratitude of relief recipients was Roosevelt's political payoff.

Is this an approach our police departments should take?

BOX 2.2 DO WE PROMOTE POLICE SECRECY?

In September 2015, former tennis star James Blake was mistakenly arrested in New York City. Blake claimed he was brutalized during the arrest. When his attorney attempted to obtain the misconduct history of the arresting officer, he was denied access to the records.

A uniquely restrictive New York state law was used to deny access to the disciplinary history of the officer. Apparently, this law prevents disclosure of police officer discipline records, even if the officer is accused of violent crimes.

An editorial in the *New York Times* criticized this law, contending that the public had the right to be kept informed of police misconduct cases, especially at a time of heightened concern over police brutality. According to the editorial, the city's Civilian Complaint Review Board substantiated excessive force charges against the officer and released its findings to Blake's lawyer but barred him from making them available to the public.

The state law on officers' histories is the only one of its kind in the nation. It was enacted in 1976 to prevent criminal defense lawyers from using freedom-of-information laws to gain access to personnel records for information to use against officers in trials.

The law states that an officer's personnel record cannot be publicly released or cited in court without a judge's approval. But according to the editorial, municipalities and courts have since broadened the definition of "personnel record" to shield almost any information. As a result, police officers, who have more authority over the public than any other public sector employees, are the least accountable.[3]

as his successor. Since John was blind, he was often referred to as the Blind Beak. John received government funds to establish an eight-man horse patrol to patrol the streets of London at night. After less than a year, the patrol was disbanded.

In 1829, Sir Robert Peel—who was then serving as England's home secretary—convinced the English Parliament to pass an act for improving the police service in and near the metropolitan area. This act established the first permanent police force for London. The police force comprised over 1000 men and was established along military lines. Officers were required to wear distinctive uniforms so that citizens could recognize them and report any misconduct by the police. The police were not well received by the English citizens. Open battles often ensued between police officers, who were known as *Bobbies*, and the citizenry.

When the English settlers arrived in America they brought with them the English law enforcement structure. At the time, America was mostly rural and was policed by officers in the offices of constable and sheriff. Originally, crown-appointed governors appointed the constables and sheriffs. After the American Revolution, they were selected by popular vote. By 1936, Boston had established a night watchman system, and New York and Philadelphia established similar night watch systems soon thereafter.

The first modern police force in the United States was the slave patrols, which were established in the southern states. The slave patrols were intended to guard against slave revolts and to capture runaway slaves. For example, the Charleston, South Carolina, slave patrol had over 100 officers and was the largest police force in America at the time.

As the cities in America developed as a result of the Industrial Revolution, constables were unable to handle the increasing social disorder caused by migration to the urban areas so police departments were established in the large cities. For example, New York City was alleged at the time to be the most crime-ridden city in the world. The cities of Philadelphia, Baltimore, and Cincinnati were not far behind. Gangs of rowdy young criminals threatened to destroy the American reputation of respect for law. Against their misbehaviors and riots, the early police forces were often helpless.

The first organized metropolitan American police force was established in Philadelphia in 1833. The city government established a 24-man police force for day work and a 120-man night watchman force. The force was disbanded less than 2 years later. In 1838, Boston created a day police force to supplement its night watchman system.

In 1844, the state of New York passed legislation establishing a unified day and night police force for New York City and abolished its night watch system. In 1854, Boston consolidated its night watch with the day watch. By 1870, all of the large cities in America had full-time, uniformed, unified police forces.

The police forces were generally under the control of a chief of police who was appointed by the mayor. The mission of the early police departments was merely to keep the city clean and to keep everything quiet. Officer salaries were low and, to meet staffing requirements, personnel standards were compromised. The result was that many unqualified individuals were appointed as police officers. Most appointments were friends of either the mayor or the chief. For the most part, the appointments were based on political motives. In addition, promotions within the police departments were based on politics rather than ability (Box 2.3).

In Chicago in the 1850s, police officers were expected to give kickbacks out of their salaries to the controlling political party. In 1880, as a result of city elections in Cincinnati, a new political party gained control of the city administration and 219 of the 295 police officers were fired. At the next election, a different political party assumed power and 238 of the 289 line officers were fired.

In the late nineteenth century, in an effort to eliminate politics from the police forces, many cities established police administrative boards. These boards exercised control over the police department and were given responsibility for managing police affairs and appointing police administrators. For the most part, the boards were unsuccessful in eliminating political influences. One probable reason that the police boards were not successful was that they were not directly accountable to the citizens they served.[4]

In several states, state legislators assumed control over the police forces by requiring police administrators to be appointed by the state. The concept of state control was not uniformly applied and was directed mainly toward the larger cities. Friction often developed between the state-appointed administrators and the local citizens.

By the 1900s, most cities had regained control of their police forces. One city, St. Louis, Missouri, did not regain control of its police department until 2013. In August 2013, the Missouri state board of police commissioners held a ceremonial meeting at the St. Louis police headquarters to end the 152 years of state oversight of the city's police department. The state had gained control of the police department in 1861 to prevent Union sympathizers from influencing the police before the start of the Civil War.[5]

BOX 2.3 FORMER HEAD OF DALLAS CRIME STOPPERS SENTENCED ON CONSPIRACY AND TAX CONVICTIONS

On December 3, 2012, in Dallas, Texas, Theadora Ross, a former senior corporal with the Dallas police department, was sentenced to 46 months in prison and ordered to pay $274,304 in restitution. Ross pleaded guilty in August 2012 to one count of conspiracy to commit wire fraud and one count of willfully attempting to evade assessment of income taxes. According to court documents, Ross worked at the Dallas Crime Stoppers office from 2003 to May 2010, and was the head of that office from March 2006 to May 2010. The Dallas Crime Stoppers office is funded by the North Texas Crime Commission (NTCC). From February 2005 to May 2010, Ross and codefendant Malva R. Delley conspired to defraud the NTCC. Ross determined which tips would be listed and presented for cash reward approval. These lists contained both bogus tips that Ross created and legitimate cash reward tip numbers. Ross provided the bogus tip information to Delley, who then presented that information to the bank and collected cash rewards. Delley divided the cash with Ross. Ross admitted that, for the calendar years 2006, 2007, 2008, and 2009, she filed false federal income tax returns by omitting to declare nearly $175,000, the proceeds of her illegal scheme. Delley pleaded guilty in May 2011 and was awaiting sentencing at the time of writing.

Reform movement

Starting in the latter part of the 1800s, police forces grew in size and expanded their functions and attempts at reform, including the concept of merit employment and civil service. In 1895, Theodore Roosevelt, who was a member of the New York City board of police commissioners, attempted to raise recruitment standards and discipline among New York City police officers. Roosevelt's efforts were generally unsuccessful because the Tammany Hall political machine had returned to power in New York City in 1897.

The police reform movement started in 1900 and lasted until the 1960s. The reform movement resulted in an increased military-like structure of police departments and specialized police units such as traffic, juvenile, and vice. Starting from about 1900, there were several attempts to reform police departments by civic-minded reformers. For the most part, their efforts failed. Police officer salaries remained low and promotions continued to be based on the politics and personal preferences of the administrators.

In 1919, Boston police officers affiliated with the American Federation of Labor. In September of that year, the officers voted to strike for better working conditions.

Approximately 70% of the Boston officers went on strike. As a result of the strike, rioting and looting broke out in the city. Governor Calvin Coolidge mobilized the state police to handle the rioting and looting. The striking officers were fired and replaced with new employees. As a result of the firing of striking officers, Governor Coolidge became a hero and was later elected president.

In 1883, the federal government passed the first federal civil service act, the Pendleton Act. Under this act, which covered only federal employees, applicants were tested and appointed based on merit rather than for political reasons. Promotions were also required to be based on merit. Many local governments established similar acts in order to decrease the political influence on law enforcement (Figure 2.1) (Box 2.4).

History of police corruption

David Bayley and Robert Perito noted that, at the tactical level, police corruption is a contested phrase with narrow and broad meanings. Narrowly defined, police corruption refers to police personnel who use their position and authority for personal rather than public benefit. More broadly, police corruption refers to any violation of rules, even when there is no personal gain, as in

Figure 2.1 Young protestor being carried to a police patrol wagon during a demonstration in the 1960s in Brooklyn. (Photo courtesy of Library of Congress Prints and Photographs Division.)

BOX 2.4 HARD TRUTHS: LAW ENFORCEMENT AND RACE

With the death of Michael Brown in Ferguson, the death of Eric Garner in Staten Island, the ongoing protests throughout the country, and the assassinations of NYPD Officers Wenjian Liu and Rafael Ramos, we are at a crossroads. As a society, we can choose to live our everyday lives, raising our families and going to work, hoping that someone, somewhere, will do something to ease the tension—to smooth over the conflict. We can roll up our car windows, turn up the radio, and drive around these problems, or we can choose to have an open and honest discussion about what our relationship is today—what it should be, what it could be, and what it needs to be—if we took more time to better understand one another.

I worry that this incredibly important and incredibly difficult conversation about race and policing has become focused entirely on the nature and character of law enforcement officers, when it should also be about something much harder to discuss. Debating the nature of policing is very important, but I worry that it has become an excuse, at times, to avoid doing something harder.

Let me start by sharing some of my own hard truths:

First, all of us in law enforcement must be honest enough to acknowledge that much of our history is not pretty. At many points in American history, law enforcement enforced the status quo, a status quo that was often brutally unfair to disfavored groups. It was unfair to the Healy siblings and to countless others like them. It was unfair to too many people.

I am descended from Irish immigrants. A century ago, the Irish knew well how American society—and law enforcement—viewed them: as drunks, ruffians, and criminals. Law enforcement's biased view of the Irish lives on in the nickname we still use for the vehicles we use to transport groups of prisoners. It is, after all, the "paddy wagon."

The Irish had tough times, but little compares with the experience on our soil of black Americans. That experience should be part of every American's consciousness, and law enforcement's role in that experience—including in recent times—must be remembered. It is our cultural inheritance.

There is a reason that I require all new agents and analysts to study the Federal Bureau of Investigation's (FBI) interaction with Dr. Martin Luther King, Jr., and to visit his memorial in Washington as part of their training. And there is a reason I keep on my desk a copy of Attorney General Robert Kennedy's approval of J. Edgar Hoover's request to wiretap Dr. King. It is a single page. The entire application is five sentences long, it is without fact or substance, and is predicated on the naked assertion that there is "communist influence in the racial situation." The reason I do those things is to ensure that we remember our mistakes and that we learn from them.

One reason we cannot forget our law enforcement legacy is that the people we serve and protect cannot forget it, either. So we must talk about our history. It is a hard truth that lives on.

A second hard truth: Much research points to the widespread existence of unconscious bias. Many people in our white-majority culture have unconscious racial biases and react differently to a white face than a black face. In fact, we all, white and black, carry various biases around with us. I am reminded of the song from the Broadway hit, *Avenue Q*: "Everyone's a Little Bit Racist." Part of it goes like this:

Look around and you will find
No one's really color blind.
Maybe it's a fact
We all should face
Everyone makes judgments
Based on race.

You should be grateful I did not try to sing that.

But if we can't help our latent biases, we can help our behavior in response to those instinctive reactions, which is why we work to design systems and processes that overcome that very human part of us all. Although the research may be unsettling, it is what we do next that matters most.

But racial bias isn't epidemic in law enforcement any more than it is epidemic in academia or the arts. In fact, I believe law enforcement overwhelmingly attracts people who want to do good for a living—people who risk their lives because they want to help other people. They don't sign up to be cops in New York or

Chicago or Los Angeles to help white people or black people or Hispanic people or Asian people. They sign up because they want to help all people. And they do some of the hardest, most dangerous policing to protect people of color.

But that leads me to my third hard truth: something happens to people in law enforcement. Many of us develop different flavors of cynicism that we work hard to resist because they can be lazy mental shortcuts. For example, criminal suspects routinely lie about their guilt, and nearly everybody we charge is guilty. That makes it easy for some folks in law enforcement to assume that everybody is lying and that no suspect, regardless of their race, could be innocent. Easy, but wrong.

Likewise, police officers on patrol in our nation's cities often work in environments where a hugely disproportionate percentage of street crime is committed by young men of color. Something happens to people of good will working in that environment. After years of police work, officers often can't help but be influenced by the cynicism they feel.

A mental shortcut becomes almost irresistible and maybe even rational by some lights. The two young black men on one side of the street look like so many others that the officer has locked up. Two white men on the other side of the street—even in the same clothes—do not. The officer does not make the same association about the two white guys, whether that officer is white or black. And that drives different behavior. The officer turns toward one side of the street and not the other. We need to come to grips with the fact that this behavior complicates the relationship between the police and the communities they serve.

So why has that officer—like his colleagues—locked up so many young men of color? Why does he have that life-shaping experience? Is it because he is a racist? Why are so many black men in jail? Is it because cops, prosecutors, judges, and juries are racist? Because they are turning a blind eye to white robbers and drug dealers?

The answer is a fourth hard truth: I don't think so. If it were so, that would be easier to address. We would just need to change the way we hire, train, and measure law enforcement and that would substantially fix it. We would then go get those white criminals we have been ignoring. But the truth is significantly harder than that.

The truth is that what really needs fixing is something only a few, like President Obama, are willing to speak about, perhaps because it is so daunting a task. Through the "My Brother's Keeper" initiative, the President is addressing the disproportionate challenges faced by young men of color. For instance, data shows that the percentage of young men not working or not enrolled in school is nearly twice as high for blacks as it is for whites. This initiative, and others like it, is about doing the hard work to grow drug-resistant and violence-resistant kids, especially in communities of color, so that they never become part of that officer's life experience.

So many young men of color become part of that officer's life experience because so many minority families and communities are struggling, so many boys and young men grow up in environments lacking role models, adequate education, and decent employment—they lack all sorts of opportunities that most of us take for granted. A tragedy of American life—one that most citizens are able to drive around because it doesn't touch them—is that young people in "those neighborhoods" too often inherit a legacy of crime and prison. And with that inheritance, they become part of a police officer's life, and shape the way that officer—whether white or black—sees the world. Changing that legacy is a challenge so enormous and so complicated that it is, unfortunately, easier to talk only about the cops. And that's not fair.

Let me be transparent about my affection for cops. When you dial 911, whether you are white or black, the cops come, and they come quickly, and they come quickly whether they are white or black. That's what cops do, in addition to all of the other hard and difficult and dangerous and frightening things that they do. They respond to homes in the middle of the night where a drunken father, wielding a gun, is threatening his wife and children. They pound up the back stairs of an apartment building, not knowing whether the guys behind the door they are about to enter are armed, or high, or both.

I come from a law enforcement family. My grandfather, William J. Comey, was a police officer. Pop Comey is one of my heroes. I have a picture of him on my wall in my office at the FBI, reminding me of the legacy I've inherited and that I must honor.

He was the child of immigrants. When he was in the sixth grade, his father was killed in an industrial accident in New York. Because he was the oldest, he had to drop out of school so that he could go to work to support his mom and younger siblings. He could never afford to return to school, but when he was old enough, he joined the Yonkers, New York police department (NYPD).

Over the next 40 years, he rose to lead that department. Pop was the tall, strong, silent type, quiet and dignified, and passionate about the rule of law. Back during prohibition, he heard that bootleggers were running beer through fire hoses between Yonkers and the Bronx.

Now, Pop enjoyed a good beer every now and again, but he ordered his men to cut those hoses with fire axes. Pop had to have a protective detail, because certain people were angry and shocked that someone in law enforcement would do that. But that's what we want as citizens—that's what we expect. And so I keep that picture of Pop on my office wall to remind me of his integrity, and his pride in the integrity of his work.

Law enforcement ranks are filled with people like my grandfather. But, to be clear, although I am from a law enforcement family, and have spent much of my career in law enforcement, I'm not looking to let law enforcement off the hook. Those of us in law enforcement must redouble our efforts to resist bias and prejudice. We must better understand the people we serve and protect—by trying to know, deep in our gut, what it feels like to be a law-abiding young black man walking on the street and encountering law enforcement. We must understand how that young man may see us. We must resist the lazy shortcuts of cynicism and approach him with respect and decency.

We must work—in the words of New York City Police Commissioner Bill Bratton—to really see each other. Perhaps the reason we struggle as a nation is because we've come to see only what we represent, at face value, instead of who we are. We simply must see the people we serve.

But the "seeing" needs to flow in both directions. Citizens also need to really see the men and women of law enforcement. They need to see what police see through the windshields of their squad cars, or as they walk down the street. They need to see the risks and dangers law enforcement officers encounter on a typical late-night shift. They need to understand the difficult and frightening work they do to keep us safe. They need to give them the space and respect to do their work, well and properly.

If they take the time to do that, what they will see are officers who are human, who are overwhelmingly doing the right thing for the right reasons, and who are too often operating in communities—and facing challenges—most of us choose to drive around.

One of the hardest things I do as FBI Director is call the chiefs and sheriffs in departments around the nation when officers have been killed in the line of duty. I call to express my sorrow and offer the FBI's help. Officers like Wenjian Liu and Rafael Ramos, two of NYPD's finest who were gunned down by a madman who thought his ambush would avenge the deaths of Michael Brown and Eric Garner. I make far too many calls. And, there are far too many names of fallen officers on the National Law Enforcement Officers Memorial and far too many names etched there each year.

Officers Liu and Ramos swore the same oath all in law enforcement do, and they answered the call to serve the people, all people. Like all good police officers, they moved toward danger, without regard for the politics or passions or race of those who needed their help—knowing the risks inherent in their work. They were minority police officers, killed while standing watch in a minority neighborhood—Bedford–Stuyvesant—one they and their fellow officers had rescued from the grip of violent crime.

Twenty years ago, Bed-Stuy was shorthand for a kind of chaos and disorder in which good people had no freedom to walk, shop, play, or just sit on the front steps and talk. It was too dangerous. But today, no more, thanks to the work of those who chose lives of service and danger to help others.

But despite this selfless service—of these two officers and countless others like them across the country—in some American communities, people view the police not as allies, but as antagonists, and think of them not with respect or gratitude, but with suspicion and distrust.

We simply must find ways to see each other more clearly. And part of that has to involve collecting and sharing better information about encounters between police and citizens, especially violent encounters.

Not long after riots broke out in Ferguson late last summer, I asked my staff to tell me how many people shot by police were African-American in this country. I wanted to see trends. I wanted to see information. They couldn't give it to me, and it wasn't their fault. Demographic data regarding officer-involved shootings is not consistently reported to us through our Uniform Crime Reporting Program. Because reporting is voluntary, our data is incomplete and therefore, in the aggregate, unreliable.

I recently listened to a thoughtful, big city police chief express his frustration with that lack of reliable data. He said he didn't know whether the Ferguson police shot one person a week, one a year, or one a century, and that in the absence of good data, "all we get are ideological thunderbolts, when what we need are ideological agnostics who use information to try to solve problems." He's right.

The first step to understanding what is really going on in our communities and in our country is to gather more and better data related to those we arrest, those we confront for breaking the law and jeopardizing public safety, and those who confront us. "Data" seems a dry and boring word but, without it, we cannot understand our world and make it better.

How can we address concerns about "use of force," how can we address concerns about officer-involved shootings if we do not have a reliable grasp on the demographics and circumstances of those incidents? We simply must improve the way we collect and analyze data to see the true nature of what's happening in all of our communities.

The FBI tracks and publishes the number of "justifiable homicides" reported by police departments. But, again, reporting by police departments is voluntary and not all departments participate. That means we cannot fully track the number of incidents in which force is used by police, or against police, including nonfatal encounters, which are not reported at all.

Without complete and accurate data, we are left with "ideological thunderbolts." And that helps spark unrest and distrust and does not help us get better. Because we must get better, I intend for the FBI to be a leader in urging departments around this country to give us the facts we need for an informed discussion, the facts all of us need, to help us make sound policy and sound decisions with that information.

* * *

America isn't easy. America takes work. Today, February 12, is Abraham Lincoln's birthday. He spoke at Gettysburg about a "new birth of freedom" because we spent the first four score and seven years of our history with fellow Americans held as slaves—President Healy, his siblings, and his mother among them. We have spent the 150 years since Lincoln spoke making great progress, but along the way treating a whole lot of people of color poorly. And law enforcement was often part of that poor treatment. That's our inheritance as law enforcement and it is not all in the distant past.

We must account for that inheritance. And we—especially those of us who enjoy the privilege that comes with being the majority—must confront the biases that are inescapable parts of the human condition. We must speak the truth about our shortcomings as law enforcement, and fight to be better. But as a country, we must also speak the truth to ourselves. Law enforcement is not the root cause of problems in our hardest hit neighborhoods. Police officers—people of enormous courage and integrity, in the main—are in those neighborhoods, risking their lives, to protect folks from offenders who are the product of problems that will not be solved by body cameras.

We simply must speak to each other honestly about all these hard truths.

In the words of Dr. King, "We must learn to live together as brothers or we will all perish together as fools."

We all have work to do—hard work, challenging work—and it will take time. We all need to talk and we all need to listen, not just about easy things, but about hard things, too. Relationships are hard. Relationships require work. So let's begin that work. It is time to start seeing one another for who and what we really are. Peace, security, and understanding are worth the effort. Thank you for listening to me today.

Source: Excerpts from the speech of FBI Director James B. Corney on February 12, 2015, at Georgetown University in Washington, DC.

perjury, physical abuse of prisoners, sexual misconduct, robbery, and racial profiling.[6]

Police corruption in American police departments became widespread shortly after the formation of the first police departments in the mid-1800s. When the departments were founded, the municipal government and agencies were run by political parties. To be appointed as a police officer or public servant, you had to agree to follow the wishes of the political parties. Those wishes frequently required protecting illicit activities conducted or supported by members of the political elite. This environment of accepted corruption resulted in practices that monetarily benefited individual officers and their departments. Officers were given bribes to ignore criminal activity, such as prostitution. In addition, police officers expected to receive money for not reporting criminals such as pickpockets and con men.

George Kelling and Mark Moore noted that early American police were authorized by local municipalities.

Unlike their English counterparts, American police departments lacked the powerful, central authority of the crown to establish a legitimate, unifying mandate for their enterprise. American police derived both their authorization and resources from local political leaders, often ward politicians. They were, of course, guided by the law as to what tasks to undertake and what powers to utilize. But their link to neighborhoods and local politicians was so tight that they became adjuncts to local political machines. The relationship was often reciprocal: political machines recruited and maintained police in office and on the beat, while police helped ward political leaders maintain their political offices by encouraging citizens to vote for certain candidates, discouraging them from voting for others, and, at times, assisting in rigging elections.[6]

Efforts to clean up the police started at the end of the nineteenth century. The Progressives, upper-middle-class educated citizens, opposed the political control of police agencies. They sought to lessen this political control by the establishment of police commissions, the use of civil service exams, and legislative reforms. As the result of the progressive movement, widespread police corruption declined, but it still remained a large problem.

The political era of policing was so named because of the close ties between police and politics. This era began with the development of police departments during the 1840s, continued through the Progressive period, and ended during the early 1900s. The reform era developed in reaction to the political influence of the police departments. It started in the 1900s but only took hold during the 1930s. The era thrived during the 1950s and 1960s but began to erode during the late 1970s.[7]

Prohibition

Prohibition in the 1920s greatly increased the potential for corruption. Massive amounts of money were being made by bootleggers who in turn paid off police officers to allow their illegal activities to continue. The Wickersham Commission, organized by President Hoover in 1929, studied the problems associated with prohibition, found that it had caused a number of social and political problems, and recognized that it was unenforceable and carried a great potential for police corruption. The Wickersham Commission also provided an analysis of police misconduct, which led to systems being formed to protect against such misconduct.

Report on the Wickersham Commission

The production of the 1931 Report on Lawlessness in Law Enforcement by the Wickersham Commission was one of the most important events in the history of American policing. It was the first systematic investigation of police misconduct.

The report was one of the 14 reports published by the National Commission on Law Observance and Enforcement, known popularly as the Wickersham Commission. The commission conducted the first national study of the administration of justice in the United States. The commission was appointed by President Herbert Hoover on May 20, 1929, and published its reports in June 1930. Chaired by the former U.S. Attorney General George W. Wickersham, other members of the 11-member commission included Roscoe Pound, the dean of Harvard Law School, and Newton Baker, former secretary of war and a leading urban reformer. The commission was appointed as the result of

- The need to find a solution for problems caused by the enforcement of prohibition
- An expression of President Hoover's technocrat approach to governing
- The outgrowth of the crime commission movement that started in the 1920s

Many researchers of the Wickersham Commission have concluded that the commission's report was overtaken by events. First, the United States was, by 1931, in a great depression and the government was preoccupied with the problem of economic recovery. Second, prohibition was repealed in 1933. However, the report did have a significant long-term impact on the understanding of crime and the functions of the criminal justice system.

The report concluded that it was a widespread practice for police to use physical brutality, or other forms of cruelty, to obtain involuntary confessions or admissions. Specific tactics included protracted questioning, threats and methods of intimidation, physical brutality, illegal detention, and refusal to allow access of counsel to suspects. The report declared unequivocally that the third-degree methods used by police were secret and illegal.[8] The report also castigated the police for their general failure to detect and arrest criminals who had committed murders and robberies. It concluded that there was contempt among average citizens regarding corruption in the American police departments.

Kefauver hearings on organized crime

The Kefauver Committee hearings on organized crime were the direct result of a petition in 1949 by the American Municipal Association, which represents more than 10,000 cities nationwide. The hearings were chaired by the then first-term senator Estes Kefauver of Tennessee.

Figure 2.2 Illustration shows a police officer labeled "Platt" receiving "hush money" at the door of an "Insurance Co." from Richard A. McCurdy. Standing in the window of the building are James H. Hyde, Francis Hendricks, and John A. McCall, among others; another police officer labeled "Bliss" stands nearby holding a thick wad of "hush money." An insert labeled "Tenderloin Dive" shows police officers accepting a bribe. The drawing was created by Undo J. Keppler (artist, 1872–1956). This drawing was the centerfold of the December 13, 1905, issue of Pluck Magazine. (Photo courtesy of Library of Congress Prints and Photographs Division.)

The Kefauver Committee hearings remain the most widely viewed congressional investigation to date. An estimated 30 million Americans tuned in to watch the live proceedings in March 1951. The television broadcasts educated a broad audience about the complicated issues of interstate crime. "Television and radio make these events more vivid and alive to the general public than newspapers," explained one New York teacher. "I do not think any of you can possibly realize how much good it has done to have these hearings televised," wrote Mrs. Carl Johnson. "It has made millions of us aware of conditions that we would never have fully realized, even if we had read the newspaper accounts."[9]

The legislative results of the hearing were not significant. More important were the nonlegislative results of the investigation. By bringing public opinion to bear on the problems of interstate crime, the investigation helped local and state law enforcement and elected officials to aggressively pursue criminal syndicates. The hearings clearly demonstrated that some elected officials had facilitated and profited from criminal activities. In addition, the report concluded that gangsters were using legitimate business interests to curry favor with local law enforcement agencies. These dramatic hearings also made certain that television would play a large role in future Senate investigations (Figure 2.2).

History of police brutality

American history is replete with reports of police brutality, especially against striking workers. Apparently, the first use of the term *police brutality* by the media was in the *New York Times* in 1893. In an article printed on June 23, 1893, the *Times* reported that police officer Michael McManus of the East 22nd Street station was the latest police officer to get himself in trouble. According to the article, when one Michael Maher was arrested by Officer McManus for assault, Maher's face was almost fully concealed by several bandages. A witness stated that he heard the officer state "I will lock you up if I have to take you to the station in pieces." The article noted that "One of the more recent cases of police brutality came up in the Court of Special Sessions yesterday morning."[10] The article failed to report whether any action was taken against Officer McManus. A search of the *New York Times* archives revealed that, in May 1901, a police officer named Michael McManus was suspended for 3 months without pay for failure to provide support for his children.

As noted earlier, there are numerous reports of police brutality against striking workers and minority citizens. Included in the following subsections are a few of those instances.

Great Railroad Strike of 1877

The Great Railroad Strike of 1877, also known as the Great Upheaval, started in Martinsburg, West Virginia, on July 14 and continued for about 45 days. The strike may be described as spontaneous outbreaks of violence against the railroads in numerous cities. Unions were not involved. At the time, outside of agriculture, railroad companies were the largest employer of workers. The violence started in response to an announcement by the Baltimore and Ohio Railroad Company that they were cutting the wages of employees for the third time that year. The strike spread to Maryland, Pennsylvania, Illinois, and Missouri. It started to lose momentum when President Hayes sent federal troops from city to city to suppress the strikers.

The strikers were subjected to blood-soaked confrontations with the police and troops. In Chicago, the mayor requested help from 5000 vigilantes to restore order. In a confrontation with the police and the strikers in Chicago on July 25, approximately 20 strikers—but none of the law enforcement officers or troops—were killed.

As the result of the strike, many states enacted conspiracy statutes to combat similar strikes by organized workers. While the unions were not involved in the strike, they became better organized and more competent as a direct result of it. The business leaders took a more rigid stand against labor unions.[11]

Haymarket Square riot

In 1886, workers striked at the McCormick Harvesting Machine Company in Chicago, Illinois. The workers demanded an 8-h workday instead of a 60-h work week. The company then locked out the workers. On May 1, the workers protested at the May Day parade in Chicago, resulting in the death of a worker.

Outraged by this act of police violence, the leaders of the workers printed and distributed fliers calling for a rally at Haymarket Square. Printed in German and English, the fliers claimed that the police had murdered the striker on behalf of business interests and urged workers to seek justice.

On May 4, a crowd of about 1500 people gathered in Haymarket Square. A number of speakers protested what they regarded as brutality by the police. At first, the meeting was peaceful, but turned to violence when the police tried to disperse the crowd. As fights broke out, a bomb exploded in the crowd. Then, the police drew their weapons and began to fire into the panicking crowd. Seven policemen and four civilians were killed, most likely from the bullets fired in the chaos. More than 100 people were injured.

The rioting was blamed on the labor movement. A number of arrests were made and eight people were charged. All eight were tried and convicted. It was never determined who threw the bomb. Seven men were sentenced to death, four of whom were eventually hung. There were serious questions about the fairness of the trial and the reliability of the evidence. One of the eight killed himself in prison. In 1892, with the election of a new governor in Illinois, two of the prisoners had their sentences commuted to life in prison. The governor was criticized for commuting their sentences and was labeled a friend of anarchists. The governor was never elected to another office.[12,13]

Pullman strike of 1894

The Pullman strike of 1894 is considered a milestone in the history of labor unions. It was a widespread strike that was put down by federal troops. George Pullman originated the idea of making railcars with sleeping accommodation, and owned a company that made these passenger railcars. His cars became popular with the railroad companies. As his company grew, he built a town in the 1880s to house his workers. The town, Pullman, was located on the outskirts of Chicago.

After the economic downturn in 1893, the country suffered a severe financial depression. To offset the loss of sales from his cars, Pullman's company cut wages by one-third. Many of the workers were members of the American Railway Union, which at the time was the largest union in America. The union's national leaders decided to have the workers refuse to work on any train that had a Pullman car. About 260,000 workers joined in the boycott.

The U.S. attorney general was determined to crush the strike. On July 2, 1894, the federal government got an injunction in federal court to end the strike. The arrival of the military and the subsequent deaths of workers through violence led to further outbreaks of violence. During the course of the strike, 30 strikers were killed and 57 were wounded. Property damage exceeded $80 million.

As the result of the strike, Eugene Debs, one of the strike leaders, was arrested. Charges against him were later dropped. George Pullman suffered a heart attack and later died, and the Pullman Company was forced to divest itself from the town of Pullman since its corporation charter did not allow for ownership of the town. U.S. president Grover Cleveland, in an effort to conciliate labor after the strike and appease workers who were reacting to the harsh treatment of the military and law enforcement, designated the first Monday in September as a federal holiday, Labor Day.[14,15]

Harlem riot of 1943

On August 1, 1943, a black soldier was shot by a police officer. As a result of the shooting, widespread fighting, shooting, and looting took place on that Sunday night. Six persons were killed and over 500 were injured. There was an estimated loss of $5 million in property damage. Four days after the rioting, approximately 6000 city policemen, military policemen, and air raid wardens patrolled the streets of Harlem. In addition, 1500 civilian volunteers, most of whom were black, were armed with nightsticks and assigned to beats. Approximately 8000 members of the New York State National Guard were ordered on standby. The rioting, shooting, and looting lasted for 4 days.[16]

The 1943 riot broke out after white police officer James Collins shot and wounded Robert Bandy, a black American soldier, who had inquired about a woman's arrest for disorderly conduct and requested that she be released. Bandy reportedly hit the officer and was shot in the shoulder while trying to flee the scene. It was incorrectly reported that Bandy had been killed. During the riot, approximately 600 arrests were made, mostly of black citizens.

Prior to the 1943 riot, another riot had taken place on March 19, 1935. In that riot, 1 person was killed and 100 were injured. The rioting started after reports circulated that a 16-year-old boy caught stealing a penknife from a local store had been brutally beaten by the police.

Zoot Suit riots

The Zoot Suit riots were a series of riots that took place in Los Angeles in 1943, during World War II. Apparently the riots started when American sailors and Marines attacked Mexican American youths. The youths were recognized by the zoot suits that they wore. The sailors and Marines attacked the youths because they perceived them to be unpatriotic. At the time of the riots, the U.S. military had already forced the evacuation of more than 120,000 Japanese Americans, most of them native born, from the West Coast to internment camps. Although Mexican American men were overrepresented in the military in proportion to the population,

many European American servicemen resented the sight of these young Latinos wearing clothes that they considered extravagant and therefore unpatriotic.

As the violence escalated, thousands of white servicemen joined the attack, marching down city streets, entering bars and movie houses, and assaulting any young Latino males that they encountered. Although the police accompanied the rioting servicemen, they had orders not to arrest any of them. The police did, however, arrest more than 500 Latinos on charges ranging from rioting to vagrancy.[17]

Detroit riots of 1967

The Detroit Michigan race riots, in the summer of 1967, have been described as among the most violent urban revolts of the twentieth century. While they came as an immediate response to police brutality, there were underlying conditions that contributed to the riots including segregated housing and schools and rising black unemployment.

The riots started on Sunday evening, July 22, 1967, when Detroit police squad officers raided an after-hours licensed bar on 12th Street in the center of the city's oldest and poorest black neighborhood. A party was in progress at the bar to celebrate the return of two black servicemen from Vietnam. The officers had expected that only a few patrons would be inside, but they found and arrested 82 people who were attending the party. As they were being transported from the scene, a crowd of approximately 200 people gathered outside. At about 5:20 am, a bottle was thrown through the rear window of a police car. Shortly thereafter, additional police officers were sent to 12th Street to stop the growing violence.

By the next morning, 800 state police officers and 8000 national guardsmen had been ordered to the city by Governor George Romney. They were later augmented by 4700 paratroopers from the 82nd Airborne Division, ordered in by President Johnson. In the 5 days and nights of violence, 33 blacks and 10 whites were killed, 1189 citizens were injured, and over 7200 people were arrested.[18]

In 1967, the Detroit police department was administered directly by the mayor. The mayor's appointee, George Edwards, worked for reform. Edwards tried to recruit and promote black officers, but refused to establish a civilian police review board as had been requested by many black civic groups. In trying to discipline police officers accused of brutality, Edwards turned the police department's rank-and-file against him. Many white officers considered his policies to be too soft on crime. President Johnson's Kerner Commission determined that, prior to the riot, 45% of the police officers working in predominately black neighborhoods were extremely anti-black, and an additional 34% were prejudiced (Box 2.5).[19]

Future of policing considerations

Excerpts from the testimony of Robert Haas, Cambridge, M.A., Chief Police Commissioner before the President's Task Force on 21st Century Policing in America (January 13, 2015).

As is the case with all forms of sociological systems, things as we know them are subject to change and evolve. As society becomes more complex, those social systems in place that provide the underpinnings and basis of our societal structures will also become more increasingly complex. This is particularly true of the evolution of policing in this country.

Police departments across this country have been expected to evolve and reform its approaches as to how it responds to its own communal expectations and demands. In part, the type of policing that we see taking place, derived from the very same origins has taken on a myriad of approaches and individualistic styles that manifest themselves differently from one neighboring departments have

---

COMMENT: WHY A GOOD PERSON MAY COMMIT DEVIANT ACTS AS AN OFFICER?

Comments by Ryan Getty, PhD. California State University, Sacramento

[Ryan Getty, an associate professor at California State University, Sacramento (CSUS) (Figure 2.3), was an instructor of record and teaching associate at the University of Texas at Dallas, as well as a research fellow and instructor at the Dallas Police Department's Caruth police institute. He is a California and Georgia postgraduate. Currently, he is a master peace officer in the State of Texas where he has worked for over 25 years for small and large police departments in positions ranging from patrol supervisor to chief of police. His last full-time policing position, before going back to get his PhD, was as an investigator for a district attorney's office. While there, he investigated public integrity violations, major crimes, high-tech crimes, and juvenile crimes.]

To quote the movie *Forrest Gump*, "Life is like a box of chocolates. You never know what you are going to get." seems synonymous with wondering what type of police officer a jurisdiction will ultimately end up having. One often wonders when current media headlines are rife with officers' misconduct, "Why would that, or any officer do that?" This article will examine what we know, have experienced, and attempted to explain why a perfectly good person may commit deviant acts as an officer.

First, there is no magic answer or solution to fit every scenario as to why police commit deviant acts. If there were, we would be able to eliminate officers committing these acts. There would be researchers and consultants as rich as Warren Buffett. Second, it is reasoned that no one goes into policing with the attitude or belief that she or he wants to or even will commit criminal or deviant acts. In fact, there are many obstacles for civilians to pass in order to be the select few to become officers. So how is it that these chosen few end up being in highlight reel of what not to do? In order to understand how this happens, one should look at policing from a macro, systemic view and from a more personal, micro view. The macro view will explain why some departments seem to endure lots of scandals over time while the micro view will argue individual cases.

A brief history of policing is in order so that one understands why some departments and their personnel have perhaps not systemically evolved into the "professional era." Schmalleger and Worrall propose that there at least three policing eras.[20] The first era is the Political Era and is when police departments were formed. It is wrought with corruption and scandals mainly because of the officers' allegiance to the corrupt politicians who hired them.

Figure 2.3 Professor Ryan Getty.

BOX 2.5   EXCERPTS FROM THE REPORT OF THE NATIONAL ADVISORY COMMISSION ON CIVIL DISORDERS (KERNER REPORT)

[Please note that the report is written in 1960s language. Where the report refers to black Americans as Negros, they should be referred to as black Americans. Excerpts of the report are included in this text on police misconduct because a lot of the blame for the riots of 1967 and 1968 can be attributed to police misconduct.]

The summer of 1967 again brought racial disorders to American cities, and with them shock, fear and bewilderment to the nation. The worst came during a 2-week period in July, first in Newark and then in Detroit. Each set off a chain reaction in neighboring communities. On July 28, 1967, the President of the United States established this Commission and directed us to answer three basic questions:

- What happened? Why did it happen? What can be done to prevent it from happening again?
- To respond to these questions, we have undertaken a broad range of studies and investigations. We have visited the riot cities; we have heard many witnesses; we have sought the counsel of experts across the country.
- This is our basic conclusion: Our nation is moving toward two societies, one black, and one white— separate and unequal.*

Reaction to last summer's disorders has quickened the movement and deepened the division. Discrimination and segregation have long permeated much of American life; they now threaten the future of every American. This deepening racial division is not inevitable. The movement apart can be reversed. Choice is still possible. Our principal task is to define that choice and to press for a national resolution.

To pursue our present course will involve the continuing polarization of the American community and, ultimately, the destruction of basic democratic values. The alternative is not blind repression or capitulation to lawlessness. It is the realization of common opportunities for all within a single society. This alternative will require a commitment to national action—compassionate, massive and sustained, backed by the resources of the most powerful and the richest nation on this earth. From every American it will require new attitudes, new understanding, and, above all, new will. The vital needs of the nation must be met; hard choices must be made, and, if necessary, new taxes enacted.

Violence cannot build a better society. Disruption and disorder nourish repression, not justice. They strike at the freedom of every citizen. The community cannot—it will not—tolerate coercion and mob rule. Violence and destruction must be ended—in the streets of the ghetto1 and in the lives of people.

Segregation and poverty have created in the racial ghetto a destructive environment totally unknown to most white Americans. What white Americans have never fully understood—but what the Negro can never forget—is that white society is deeply implicated in the ghetto. White institutions created it, white institutions maintain, and white society condones it.

It is time now to turn with all the purpose at our command to the major unfinished business of this nation. It is time to adopt strategies for action that will produce quick and visible progress. It is time to make good the promises of American democracy to all citizens—urban and rural, white and black, Spanish-surname, American Indian, and every minority group.

Our recommendations embrace three basic principles:

- To mount programs on a scale equal to the dimension of the problems.
- To aim these programs for high impact in the immediate future in order to close the gap between promise and performance.
- To undertake new initiatives and experiments that can change the system of failure and frustration that now dominates the ghetto and weakens our society.

These programs will require unprecedented levels of funding and performance, but they neither probe deeper nor demand more than the problems which called them forth. There can be no higher priority for national action and no higher claim on the nation's conscience...

* The excerpts were reformatted by the author to make the report easier to read.

PART I: WHAT HAPPENED?

Chapter 1: Profiles of disorder

The Kerner report contains profiles of a selection of the disorders that took place during the summer of 1967. These profiles are designed to indicate how the disorders happened, who participated in them, and how local officials, police forces, and the National Guard responded. Illustrative excerpts follow.

NEWARK

…On Saturday, July 15, [Director of Police Dominick] Spina received a report of snipers in a housing project. When he arrived he saw approximately 100 National Guardsmen and police officers crouching behind vehicles, hiding in corners and lying on the ground around the edge of the courtyard.

Since everything appeared quiet and it was broad daylight, Spina walked directly down the middle of the street. Nothing happened. As he came to the last building of the complex, he heard a shot. All around him the troopers jumped, believing themselves to be under sniper fire. A moment later a young Guardsman ran from behind a building.

The Director of Police went over and asked him if he had fired the shot. The soldier said yes, he had fired to scare a man away from a window; that his orders were to keep everyone away from windows.

Spina said he told the soldier, "Do you know what you just did? You have now created a state of hysteria. Every Guardsman up and down this street and every state policeman and every city policeman that is present thinks that somebody just fired a shot and that it is probably a sniper."

A short time later more "gunshots" were heard. Investigating, Spina came upon a Puerto Rican sitting on a wall. In reply to a question as to whether he knew "where the firing is coming from?" the man said, "That's no firing. That's fireworks. If you look up to the fourth floor, you will see the people who are throwing down these cherry bombs."

By this time four truckloads of National Guardsmen had arrived and troopers and policemen were again crouched everywhere looking for a sniper. The Director of Police remained at the scene for 3 h, and the only shot fired was the one by the Guardsmen.

Nevertheless, at 6 o'clock that evening two columns of National Guardsmen and state troopers were directing mass fire at the Hayes Housing Project in response to what they believed were snipers….

DETROIT

…A spirit of carefree nihilism was taking hold. To riot and destroy appeared more and more to become ends in themselves. Late Sunday afternoon it appeared to one observer that the young people were "dancing amidst the flames."

A Negro plainclothes officer was standing at an intersection when a man threw a Molotov cocktail into a business establishment at the corner. In the heat of the afternoon, fanned by the 20–25 mph winds of both Sunday and Monday, the fire reached the home next door within minutes. As residents uselessly sprayed the flames with garden hoses, the fire jumped from roof to roof of adjacent two- and three-story buildings. Within the hour the entire block was in flames. The ninth house in the burning row belonged to the arsonist who had thrown the Molotov cocktail….

…Employed as a private guard, 55-year-old Julius L. Dorsey, a Negro, was standing in front of a market when accosted by two Negro men and a woman. They demanded he permit them to loot the market. He ignored their demands. They began to berate him. He asked a neighbor to call the police. As the argument grew more heated, Dorsey fired three shots from his pistol into the air.

The police radio reported "Looters, they have rifles." A patrol car driven by a police officer and carrying three National Guardsmen arrived. As the looters fled, the law enforcement personnel opened fire. When the firing ceased, one person lay dead. He was Julius L. Dorsey.

…As the riot alternatively waxed and waned, one area of the ghetto remained insulated. On the northeast side the residents of some 150 square blocks inhabited by 21,000 persons had, in 1966, banded together in the Positive Neighborhood Action Committee (PNAC). With professional help from the Institute of Urban Dynamics, they had organized block clubs and made plans for the improvement of the neighborhood….

When the riot broke out, the residents, through the block clubs, were able to organize quickly. Youngsters, agreeing to stay in the neighborhood, participated in detouring traffic. While many persons reportedly sympathized with the idea of a rebellion against the "system," only two small fires were set—one in an empty building.

* * *

...According to Lt. Gen. Throckmorton and Col. Bolling, the city, at this time, was saturated with fear. The National Guardsmen were afraid, the residents were afraid, and the police were afraid. Numerous persons, the majority of them Negroes, were being injured by gunshots of undetermined origin. The general and his staff felt that the major task of the troops was to reduce the fear and restore an air of normalcy.

In order to accomplish this, every effort was made to establish contact and rapport between the troops and the residents. The soldiers—20% of whom were Negro—began helping to clean up the streets, collect garbage, and trace persons who had disappeared in the confusion. Residents in the neighborhoods responded with soup and sandwiches for the troops. In areas where the National Guard tried to establish rapport with the citizens, there was a smaller response.

NEW BRUNSWICK

...A short time later, elements of the crowd—an older and rougher one than the night before—appeared in front of the police station. The participants wanted to see the mayor.

Mayor [Patricia] Sheehan went out onto the steps of the station. Using a bullhorn, she talked to the people and asked that she be given an opportunity to correct conditions. The crowd was boisterous. Some persons challenged the mayor. But, finally, the opinion, "She's new! Give her a chance!" prevailed.

A demand was issued by people in the crowd that all persons arrested the previous night be released. Told that this already had been done, the people were suspicious. They asked to be allowed to inspect the jail cells.

It was agreed to permit representatives of the people to look in the cells to satisfy themselves that everyone had been released. The crowd dispersed. The New Brunswick riot had failed to materialize.

Chapter 2: Patterns of disorder

The "typical" riot did not take place. The disorders of 1967 were unusual, irregular, complex, and unpredictable social processes. Like most human events, they did not unfold in an orderly sequence. However, an analysis of our survey information leads to some conclusions about the riot process.

In general: The civil disorders of 1967 involved Negroes acting against local symbols of white American society, authority and property in Negro neighborhoods—rather than against white persons.

Of 164 disorders reported during the first nine months of 1967, 8 (5%) were major in terms of violence and damage; 33 (20%) were serious but not major; 123 (75%) were minor and undoubtedly would not have received national attention as "riots," had the nation not been sensitized by the more serious outbreaks.

In the 75 disorders studied by a Senate subcommittee, 83 deaths were reported. Eighty-two percent of the deaths and more than half of the injuries occurred in Newark and Detroit. About 10% of the dead and 38% of the injured were public employees, primarily law officers and firemen. The overwhelming majority of the persons killed or injured in all the disorders were Negro civilians.

Initial damage estimates were greatly exaggerated. In Detroit, newspaper damage estimates at first ranged from $200 million to $500 million; the highest recent estimate is $45 million. In Newark, early estimates ranged from $15 to $25 million. A month later damage was estimated at $10.2 million, over 80% in inventory losses.

In the 24 disorders in 23 cities which we surveyed:

The final incident before the outbreak of disorder, and the initial violence itself, generally took place in the evening or at night at a place in which it was normal for many people to be on the streets.

Violence usually occurred almost immediately following the occurrence of the final precipitating incident, and then escalated rapidly. With but few exceptions, violence subsided during the day, and flared rapidly again at night. The night-day cycles continued through the early period of the major disorders.

Disorder generally began with rock and bottle throwing and window breaking. Once store windows were broken, looting usually followed.

Disorder did not erupt as a result of a single "triggering" or "precipitating" incident. Instead, it was generated out of an increasingly disturbed social atmosphere, in which typically a series of tension-heightening incidents over a period of weeks or months became linked in the minds of many in the Negro community with a reservoir of underlying grievances. At some point in the mounting tension, a further incident—in itself often routine or trivial—became the breaking point and the tension spilled over into violence.

"Prior" incidents, which increased tensions and ultimately led to violence, were police actions in almost half the cases; police actions were "final" incidents before the outbreak of violence in 12 of the 24 surveyed disorders.

No particular control tactic was successful in every situation. The varied effectiveness of control techniques emphasizes the need for advance training, planning, adequate intelligence systems, and knowledge of the ghetto community.

Negotiations between Negroes—including your militants as well as older Negro leaders—and white officials concerning "terms of peace" occurred during virtually all the disorders surveyed. In many cases, these negotiations involved discussion of underlying grievances as well as the handling of the disorder by control authorities.

The typical rioter was a teenager or young adult, a lifelong resident of the city in which he rioted, a high school dropout; he was, nevertheless, somewhat better educated than his non-rioting Negro neighbor, and was usually underemployed or employed in a menial job. He was proud of his race, extremely hostile to both whites and middle-class Negroes and, although informed about politics, highly distrustful of the political system.

A Detroit survey revealed that approximately 11% of the total residents of two riot areas admitted participation in the rioting, 20%–25% identified themselves as "bystanders," over 16% identified themselves as "counter-rioters" who urged rioters to "cool it," and the remaining 48%–53% said they were at home or elsewhere and did not participate. In a survey of Negro males between the ages of 15 and 35 residing in the disturbance area in Newark, about 45% identified themselves as rioters, and about 55% as "noninvolved."

Most rioters were young Negro males. Nearly 53% of arrestees were between 15 and 24 years of age; nearly 81% between 15 and 35.

In Detroit and Newark about 74% of the rioters were brought up in the North. In contrast, of the noninvolved, 36% in Detroit and 52% in Newark were brought up in the North.

What the rioters appeared to be seeking was fuller participation in the social order and the material benefits enjoyed by the majority of American citizens. Rather than rejecting the American system, they were anxious to obtain a place for themselves in it.

Numerous Negro counter-rioters walked the streets urging rioters to "cool it." The typical counter-rioter was better educated and had higher income than either the rioter or the noninvolved.

The proportion of Negroes in local government was substantially smaller than the Negro proportion of population. Only three of the 20 cities studied had more than one Negro legislator; none had ever had a Negro mayor or city manager. In only four cities did Negroes hold other important policy-making positions or serve as heads of municipal departments.

Although almost all cities had some sort of formal grievance mechanism for handling citizen complaints, this typically was regarded by Negroes as ineffective and was generally ignored.

Although specific grievances varied from city to city, at least 12 deeply held grievances can be identified and ranked into three levels of relative intensity:

First level of intensity

1. Police practices
2. Unemployment and underemployment
3. Inadequate housing

Second level of intensity

4. Inadequate education
5. Poor recreation facilities and programs
6. Ineffectiveness of the political structure and grievance mechanisms.

Third level of intensity

7. Disrespectful white attitudes
8. Discriminatory administration of justice
9. Inadequacy of federal programs
10. Inadequacy of municipal services
11. Discriminatory consumer and credit practices
12. Inadequate welfare programs

The results of a three-city survey of various federal programs—manpower, education, housing, welfare and community action—indicate that, despite substantial expenditures, the number of persons assisted constituted only a fraction of those in need.

The background of disorder is often as complex and difficult to analyze as the disorder itself. But we find that certain general conclusions can be drawn:

> Social and economic conditions in the riot cities constituted a clear pattern of severe disadvantage for Negroes compared with whites, whether the Negroes lived in the area where the riot took place or outside it. Negroes had completed fewer years of education and fewer had attended high school. Negroes were twice as likely to be unemployed and three times as likely to be in unskilled and service jobs. Negroes averaged 70% of the income earned by whites and were more than twice as likely to be living in poverty. Although housing cost Negroes relatively more, they had worse housing—three times as likely to be overcrowded and substandard. When compared to white suburbs, the relative disadvantage is even more pronounced.

A study of the aftermath of disorder leads to disturbing conclusions. We find that, despite the institution of some post-riot programs:

> Little basic change in the conditions underlying the outbreak of disorder has taken place. Actions to ameliorate Negro grievances have been limited and sporadic; with but few exceptions, they have not significantly reduced tensions.

In several cities, the principal official response has been to train and equip the police with more sophisticated weapons. In several cities, increasing polarization is evident, with continuing breakdown of inter-racial communication, and growth of white segregationist or black separatist groups....

PART II: WHY DID IT HAPPEN?

Chapter 4: The basic causes

In addressing the question "Why did it happen?" we shift our focus from the local to the national scene, from the particular events of the summer of 1967 to the factors within the society at large that created a mood of violence among many urban Negroes.

These factors are complex and interacting; they vary significantly in their effect from city to city and from year to year; and the consequences of one disorder, generating new grievances and new demands, become the causes of the next. Thus was created the "thicket of tension, conflicting evidence and extreme opinions" cited by the President.

Despite these complexities, certain fundamental matters are clear. Of these, the most fundamental is the racial attitude and behavior of white Americans toward black Americans.

Race prejudice has shaped our history decisively; it now threatens to affect our future.

White racism is essentially responsible for the explosive mixture which has been accumulating in our cities since the end of World War II. Among the ingredients of this mixture are:

- Pervasive discrimination and segregation in employment, education and housing, which have resulted in the continuing exclusion of great numbers of Negroes from the benefits of economic progress.

- Black in-migration and white exodus, which have produced the massive and growing concentrations of impoverished Negroes in our major cities, creating a growing crisis of deteriorating facilities and services and unmet human needs.
- The black ghettos where segregation and poverty converge on the young to destroy opportunity and enforce failure. Crime, drug addiction, dependency on welfare, and bitterness and resentment against society in general and white society in particular are the result.
- At the same time, most whites and some Negroes outside the ghetto have prospered to a degree unparalleled in the history of civilization. Through television and other media, this affluence has been flaunted before the eyes of the Negro poor and the jobless ghetto youth.

Yet these facts alone cannot be said to have caused the disorders. Recently, other powerful ingredients have begun to catalyze the mixture:

- Frustrated hopes are the residue of the unfulfilled expectations aroused by the great judicial and legislative victories of the Civil Rights Movement and the dramatic struggle for equal rights in the South.
- A climate that tends toward approval and encouragement of violence as a form of protest has been created by white terrorism directed against nonviolent protest; by the open defiance of law and federal authority by state and local officials resisting desegregation; and by some protest groups engaging in civil disobedience who turn their backs on nonviolence, go beyond the constitutionally protected rights of petition and free assembly, and resort to violence to attempt to compel alteration of laws and policies with which they disagree.
- The frustrations of powerlessness have led some Negroes to the conviction that there is no effective alternative to violence as a means of achieving redress of grievances, and of "moving the system." These frustrations are reflected in alienation and hostility toward the institutions of law and government and the white society which controls them, and in the reach toward racial consciousness and solidarity reflected in the slogan "Black Power."
- A new mood has sprung up among Negroes, particularly among the young, in which self-esteem and enhanced racial pride are replacing apathy and submission to "the system."

The police are not merely a "spark" factor. To some Negroes police have come to symbolize white power, white racism and white repression. And the fact is that many police do reflect and express these white attitudes. The atmosphere of hostility and cynicism is reinforced by a widespread belief among Negroes in the existence of police brutality and in a "double standard" of justice and protection—one for Negroes and one for whites.

To this point, we have attempted to identify the prime components of the "explosive mixture." In the chapters that follow we seek to analyze them in the perspective of history. Their meaning, however, is clear: In the summer of 1967, we have seen in our cities a chain reaction of racial violence. If we are heedless, none of us shall escape the consequences.

[Committee note: The term *ghetto* as used in this report refers to an area within a city characterized by poverty and acute social disorganization, and inhabited by members of a racial or ethnic group under conditions of involuntary segregation.]

Source: United States. Kerner Commission, Report of the National Advisory Commission on Civil Disorders (Washington: U.S. Government Printing Office, 1968)

their own differences, even if it resembles subtle differences in how policing is performed.

Policing has become increasing more complex, and the demands placed on policing have grown exponentially. All of these changes have taken place despite the primal mission of the police, which has been to focus primarily on the notions of public safety and public order. I would argue that along the way, the primary policing mission has changed substantially, and yet we continue to build reform upon the same fundamental constructs, which does not really fit with what communal demands and expectations that present themselves as challenges to modern policing. Arguably, public safety and public

order only represents a portion of the overall mission of policing (varying in scope and
magnitude depending upon the jurisdiction).

The next era was the Reform Era. Police were
introduced to various technologies of the time such
as fingerprinting, crude criminal data-basing, militaristic discipline within the ranks, education, and
other advancements to help deal with crime fighting.
However, many police departments still resisted the
change from the earlier spoils system.

As the government itself attempted to evolve, so too
did the various governments try to evaluate and reform
its policing. One of the earliest efforts to reform policing
was the 1929 Illinois Crime Survey.[21] Although mainly
addressing issues with the Chicago police and the
Illinois justice system, it was the first to directly confront
policing problems and systemic concerns. The next and
far more ambitious report was the Wickersham Report.

The 1931 National Commission on Law Observance
and Enforcement (more commonly known as the
Wickersham Commission) in volume 11 of their report
entitled "Report on Lawlessness in Law Enforcement,"
directly called attention to police corruption, poor
leadership and management, neglected education and
training, and need for the "divorce of enforcement from
politics" as well as other troubles within policing. The
report mentions "the third degree," disallowing access
to council, brutality, corruption, and other illegal practices.[22] The commission acknowledged these actions
had been going on for decades.

Since then, there has been no lack of governmental
committees to address what was first mentioned in the
1930s. The Knapp Commission in New York,[23] The LAPD
Rampart Scandal,[24] the NYPD Mollen Commission,[25]
and the LAPD Christopher Commission[26] are but a
partial mention of various committees to uncover
and report recommendations for change. For a more
comprehensive list of other less familiar committees,
Human Rights Watch organization has 14 cities listed
and their abuses listed.[27] Even the least committed
researcher can find several historical mentioning of
police deviance and subsequent recommendations.
Given the magnitude of systemic failure on the part of
governmental oversight, why haven't these plethora of
recommendations been implemented? The answer is
that some things do change but it is merely superficial
and not transformational.

As mentioned before, there are two different levels
to look at police deviance and behavior; one is the macro
level and one is the micro level. So far, this article has
been addressing the macro level thus, leading into organizational behavior and change. The New York City and
Los Angeles Police Departments are very large departments and have decades of organizational behavior upon

which to pass on. It is no easy task to change decades of
governmental behavior.

Currently, the panacea is to call in the U.S.
Department of Justice (DOJ) for a civil rights investigation. Most people from the current generation do not
seem to remember the lessons of the past. The DOJ has
been called in for most of the "incidents" to investigate,
make recommendations and coerce reform. As of the
last decade or so, the DOJ has provided "technical assistance" and/or investigated law enforcement agencies
in 20 states and the territories of Puerto Rico and the
Virgin Islands. According to their website, the DOJ has
or is involved in "helping" approximately 28 agencies.[28]

Bloomberg News gives a chilling account of just
how many and the cost of incidents precipitating DOJ
intervention.[29] The DOJ can initiate investigations, nego-
tiate with the government, come to a memorandum of
understanding/agreement or most invasive, a consent
decree. Some police departments are repeat offenders
and others are or were under some sort of DOJ supervision for more than 10 years. Most people can guess these
departments: Cleveland, Detroit, NYPD, LAPD, DC
police, New Jersey State Police, Portland, New Orleans,
and others.

How can this still be going on after so many commissions and intervention my DOJ? Organization
behavior is still the best answer. It is not just "one rotten
apple" or an "isolated incident" as many cities would
have one to believe. As I travel to different police organizations around the country and attend conferences,
I talk to the officers and trade "war stories." The one
thing I have noticed while taking to veterans from these
inglorious departments, they all say that they all say
that, "It's not like the old days." Certain key words and
phrases like suspects falling up the steps, using a "snot
lock" (choking), flashlight therapy (hitting with a flashlight) needing a "tune up," taking "corrective action"
for POP (pissin' off the police) or COP (contempt of cop)
with some "stick time" (using batons) seem to come up
when describing arrested or "abusive" citizens.

I was also introduced to a whole new lexicon for
people who the police didn't like or were not upstand-
ing. It varies regionally but terms such as *turds* or *float-
ers*, *perps*, *scumbags*, *ADFN* (another dumb f%$^ n^&%$),
Mope (a lazy person), *strawberry* (a young girl who
exchanges sex for drugs), *B girl* (prostitute), *badge bunny*
or *fender lizard* (girl cop-groupies) are just some of the
multitude of derogatory names police use to communicate disdain for the people they encounter.

For a decent "cop slang" listing, see policemag.com's
listing.[30] It is fairly accurate. If I were a normal "schmoe,"
this would lead me to wonder if other occupations had
their own words for people they encounter and dislike.
Although I've not studied that, I'm sure they do. But to
what degree would a salesperson describe a particularly

unpleasant person to their boss and more importantly, what she or he would have liked to do to them for wasting their precious time? Somehow I cannot envision a sales person telling their boss that a turd wasted their time and that they need to get the crap beat out of them for it.

To some, it might seem as if I have strayed from the subject. However, what has been evidenced is allowable organizational behavior that seems particularly harmless. Calling someone names and disrespecting citizens seems a long way from abuse of force and shooting people. Much like the DOJ investigations, I look for a "pattern of practices."

If management allows this type of behavior they are implicitly devaluing the citizens. If the citizens are not seen as husbands, wives, spouses, aunts, friends, and so on, for example, normal people who sometimes do bad things rather than just bad people, it is much easier to prejudge—as some are calling it now unconscious bias—and therefore, not respecting life and property.

Many people have made the astute observation that this does not seem to happen in the rich, white place in the jurisdiction. Correct. This is because the officers know through organizational behavior that they have a greater possibility of being complained about and having a legitimate chance of being investigated as well as possibly being sued. In order for this type of behavior to stop, police managers and supervisors need to pay close attention to how officers describe and interact with the public.

Officers know what type of behavior is permissible and in some instances, reinforced, and they will act accordingly. Sometimes the organizational behavior/culture has become so mismanaged, that change is required. This is not promoting another deputy chief from within the department because it is likely she or he is a conformer and enabler rather than a reformer.

A simple question for those mayors and committees who appoint from within is: What was that person doing to change the environment when they had the chance? If that person did nothing, he or she was just as complicit in creating or allowing that behavior and permissive organizational atmosphere as the person in charge. True change can only be accomplished by hiring an outside leader who has a proven track record along with some DOJ help. Having a leader with an unrelenting moral compass backed with the enforcement authority of the DOJ is a good starting point to (re) gaining legitimacy with the citizens and getting rid of noncompliant officers.

So far, much has been discussed about issues with police organizations and their behavior at the macro level. It is a matter of tradition, a lack of leadership and direction, and a permissive or unprincipled organizational behavior over time. There is no quick fix for these departments that have demonstrated unacceptable

police practices for decades. Much like habitual offenders in the criminal justice system, it is only a matter of time and opportunity before they offend again.

One can only mitigate the harm to the city and its people. I wish I could offer a rosier outlook but the years of proof in practice have led me to conclude that certain organizations are not going to change. However, there is hope at the micro level of police deviance and misconduct. This level is at the individual officer level and much more is known about what can be done to correct deficient officers.

There have been many theories posited as to why officers do bad things. In order to cover why individual officers, commit deviance, one must start from the beginning. People are not born police officers. At some point in a person's life, he or she decides they would like to become an officer.

For most departments, the steps from civilian to a sworn officer is a long an arduous one. As I suggested earlier, people who want to become officers do not believe they will be "that one" who becomes deviant or shoots someone illegally.

It's always the other officer; that "rotten apple." There is good cause to have this naïve attitude upon applying to become an officer. It's assumed that every applicant wants to "help" people and this is borne out in almost every applicant interview I've ever done. When asked why he or she wants to become an officer, the vast majority of applicants say, "I want to help people." or "I want to make a difference." Those two answers are by far the most popular answers. No one says that they want to drive fast, be above the law, and be allowed to shoot at people! So why do applicants change from wanting to help people to some wanting to hurt people?

Most applicants across the United States go through a set of minimum hiring processes mandated by their state and in some instances, additional "hoops" for certain departments. However, it was not so long ago that there were no standards for becoming an officer or even having a department.

Partially due to some factors in the 1960s, law enforcement and more specifically, training had to evolve. The first part of that evolution was The President's Commission on Law Enforcement and Administration of Justice.[31] Through much of the turbulent 1960s, people started seeing police officers at their worst during the civil rights movement.

During this time, it was decided several things needed to change. As a result, not only the police but also the entire criminal justice system was once again under a microscope. Hence, an entire chapter was devoted to policing. Within the several troubling concerns and recommendations confronted in the chapter on policing, two items seemed elementary and paramount to the professionalization of policing. The first was bringing all states to require minimum hiring standards and training. The second was to create a state-level organization to establish and oversee standards and training. This was the first attempt to create criteria for hiring and standards. These organizations are commonly referred to today as police officer standards and training or POST.

There are state variations on the name such as Texas's Texas Commission on Law Enforcement or TCOLE (formerly TCLEOSE) and Michigan's Commission on Law Enforcement Standards or MCOLES but essentially they all served the same functions. Those officers who were already employed were "grandfathered in" meaning, they were not required to go to an established basic academy. Ultimately they would have to attend periodic in-service training, but they were not required to attend an academy. In the first part of my career, we had several officers and even more supervisors who had never stepped foot inside an academy.

They seemed to hang on forever without even the basic knowledge of why they were doing what they were doing. They often explained to new officers— because they were training new officers!—we've done it that way forever and we're not changing now. So in essence, older, nontrained, senior officers were training new academy graduates.

There were no field-training programs or field-training officers in most departments. Training was haphazard and it was decided by senior officers talking to their supervisors who stayed and who was fired. The standards were if a recruit could handle himself (no females on patrol in most places) in a fight and would listen and follow orders.

To give you an idea of the times, Texas established TCLEOSE (POST) in 1965 but was not funded until 1967. Even then, it had four people to administrate a "voluntary program of certification" for the entire state.[32] The first mandated academy in Texas was not required until 1970 for new applicants and consisted of 140 h! The minimum education was a GED or high school diploma. If you will remember back to when this article mentioned all the committees dated as far back as 1931; every commission recommended some college education and basic hiring standards. It took more than four decades for some of these recommendations to take place. Several states also allowed for new hires to work as fully sworn officers for a year or more before they had to either be reassigned as nonsworn or go to an academy. It was a big deal in those days to send a person to an academy.

I was one of those who was hired as a civilian and worked in the police jail, a walking beat, and as a junior partner in a radio car for a year until the department sent me to a 240-h academy. However, I was still "trained" by a few senior officers and supervised by sergeants who had never been to an academy. That scenario was in the mid-80s in Georgia. Some states such as Texas had a 320-h academy by that time.[33] There was and still is no national standards of training and education!

Very slowly and painfully, older, less-trained officers and supervisors who were grandfathered started to retire around the 1980s. This was about the time POST starting having slightly more influence in basic standards for training and in-service. One element, education of officers, has been a subject of contention since the 1931 National Commission. It was suggested then and in every major commission since that officer at least have some college. Specifically, the President's Commission on Law Enforcement and Administration of Justice,[34] the National Advisory Commission on Criminal Justice Standards and Goals,[35] and the American Bar Association Project on Standards for Criminal Justice[36] all recommended college-educated police officers at the time.

One could easily argue, policing pioneers such as August Vollmer advocated as early as the turn of the twentieth century for an entrance requirement of at least some college.[37] As of 2013, 84% of the law enforcement agencies in the United States required only a GED or high school diploma as an entry-level requirement.[38]

To add insult to injury for those who seek higher standards, the federal government started the Office of Law Enforcement Assistance in 1966 specifically designed at "practically giving" a college education to officers. Several of the officers to whom I spoke remember those funds for college and remarked that the federal government paid for their college education and some actually made extra money by going to college! Yet few took advantage of "free college." In fact, there were few criminal justice programs back then.

Most officers majored in Sociology, Psychology, Social Work, Public Administration, and Business. If only one good thing came out of all the money spent to educate officers, universities had to (eventually) form a true criminal justice program because of the increased demand. However, it did little to increase the states' minimum requirements.

In fact, several studies and commissions on the effects of college-educated officers versus noncollege educated have not swayed the pendulum toward more education.[39] This issue is so controversial and there have been so many contradictory studies as to the effects of college and police/policing, it is far beyond the scope of this argument. It is worth noting however, there remains little progress since the early 1900s.

The minimum of a GED or high school diploma is but one of the typical requirements to become a police officer. Another, of course, is minimum age. All states agree that a minimum of 21-years old is the requirement. Some departments allow one to enter the academy at 20 but must be 21 at graduation. Again, there is too much literature as to the maturation of the average 21-year old to be properly discussed within the scope of this paper.

Departments must rely upon their individual screening process to assess if the applicant is "mature enough" at these younger ages. As a past background investigator, I can attest that the department trust such things as prior work history, credit history, driver's history, and drug use to better inform as to the maturity and acceptability of the applicant. Things such as multiple jobs, unusual terminations from jobs, poorly explained bad credit, several entries of traffic offenses and personal drug usage beyond experimenting with marijuana can be disqualifiers for a police job. Each department sets its threshold for all of these categories.

One department could overlook bad credit if it was the result of trying a small business unsuccessfully and having to file bankruptcy while another may not care and disqualify the applicant simply because of the bankruptcy entry. Another department may be alarmed at three traffic citations for speeding within a year whereas another looks at the speed over the limit as important. The most concerning point to all the inconsistencies is that an applicant can "shop around" for departments that have more lenient hiring practices.

Once hired, the officer has as many policing powers as another officer whose department has very stringent requirements. This may lead to the phenomenon known as gypsy cops. This is the problem where underqualified or rogue officers go from department to department without the state's intervention thereby causing liability for officers and their departments.[40] Few states have contingencies for gypsy cops.

Typically, after the applicants have successfully made it through the initial entrance exam and background, they may or may not have a polygraph or voice stress analysis to further verify what they have put in their background is truthful. Moreover, such practices of verification of truthfulness differ from department-to-department. While some use these devices as disqualifiers (a bad result), others may only use them to help inform their overall decision (inconclusive results). Others still, use no means to verify truthfulness other than the backgrounder's investigative skill in verifying the applicants' answers to their personal history. In any case, there is cause for concern at this stage.

Lie detectors are still not accepted as necessarily scientific and trustworthy while investigators are not usually trained in background investigations and personal interviews. As Lilienfeld and Landfiled put it, it is still a pseudoscience.[41]

If an applicant passes the entrance test, physical agility assessment, the background (with or without a polygraph), and typically a board of officers who question them regarding decision-making abilities, the applicant is given a "conditional offer of employment." This is condition that he or she passes a drug screen, a physical given by a medical doctor and a psychological test/interview given by a psychologist. If applicants pass these final hurdles, they are hired as cadets.

Some departments hire applicants and put them through their own academy while others (usually smaller departments) hire only applicants who have paid their own way through the academy and have passed. The most important part here is that to some extent, there has been some standardization of hiring. No department can get away with continually hiring unqualified candidates. Therefore, it is assumed that those who are hired meet a minimum standard and are mostly similar. The next stages, the academy and field training, are where I have noticed and hypothesized that most of the socialization into the police subculture and deviance begins.

Academies are usually divided into a "traditional" or militaristic academy where cadets are taught the curriculum while not questioning the chain of command, taught to follow orders, question little, and discipline. Punishments for adherence are pushups, extra duty, or ridicule. The other type of academy is called the academic academy or problem-based academy.

Although there are few studies as to the difference in effectiveness of their curriculum,[42] there is socialization taking place in various forms.[43] Particularly salient here are the recruits' concept of what is permissible and acceptable. Here is where use of force is taught as well as to some extent, verbal communication skills. Of particular notice is the use of time for instruction in these matters. I have begun to calculate the time for use of force lessons in state academies versus any forms of interpersonal communication and so far have come up with a ratio of about 5 to 1 for use of force.

For example, in Texas, classes such as firearms, baton training, "force options," and "professional police driving" topics devoted 104 h of the required 643 total academy hours while topics such as "multiculturalism and human relations," "professionalism and ethics," and racial profiling classes, totaled 22 h.[44]

The class with the most hours was traffic enforcement at 68 h. This is typical across states and in my opinion shameful and irresponsible. Management understands it is a liability issue and want their recruits to be fully versed in the use of force but to what degree do recruits need to be taught firearms training (48+ h) versus knowing how to talk to distressed people (8 h)? The vast majority of the job is being able to talk to a diverse set of citizens who are in some sort of crisis and yet that is not taught.

Some academies have scenarios such as answering a domestic disturbance but legal applications and allowable force is taught, not necessarily problem solving and de-escalation of force. Here is the first time civilians (essentially) are "taught" how to deal with stressful situations, uncooperative people, and force while using complex, split-second decision-making skills.

In my opinion and observations, police rely on what they have been taught: control the scene and officer safety. If they have been taught use force to control the scene and maintain officer safety, they will do so. If they have been taught to use their greatest "weapon" for example their wits and problem solving abilities, they will do so. This all directly relates to department standards and who the department hires. If the department does not have high hiring standards and the cadets are poorly or incorrectly trained, there should be no surprise that officers (re)act poorly on the street. After the academy stage, the department and his or her fellow officers still have a chance to weed out the "bad" officers or further socialize the "acceptable" ones.

I have often argued that the recruits who come out of the academy are trained similarly and socialized to a somewhat consistent standard—regardless of the content or adequacy of academy training. There is a field-training process between book learning (the academy) and being let loose alone on the unsuspecting public. I have advocated that phase is the most crucial part for an impressionable officer and sets their career trajectory.[45] I deemed this as the most pivotal part of an officer's socialization process, in that, the field-training officers (FTOs) are the most significant and influential people the officers will encounter during their career. (Remember that I had no field-training program or FTOs when I started law enforcements) I have asked countless 20+ year veteran officers who their supervisors or even chiefs were over their career and they had difficulty remembering them. When I asked who their FTOS were, the majority of them could recall at least one if not all of them—and still use them as a mentor. The FTO relationship is that influential. This influence can be positive or negative and I suggest, it is lasting.

In 1969, the San Jose Police Department (SJPD) hired a "likable, enthusiastic, but naïve, young recruit" who was judged by his peers and supervisors as "unacceptable police officer material," yet allowed to continue as a police officer, "although there were numerous areas in which he was judged to be 'in need of improvement' (judgment, safety consciousness, and work quality)."[46] A short after these observations, the officer killed a citizen in a traffic accident.

From this tragedy, the SJPD started what would become the nation's model training program initially called the Filed Training and Evaluation Program or FTO program for short. This FTO program bridged the gap from police academy graduates to solo officers. Through the years the program has morphed and

evolved and although there are other programs such as the Police Training Officer program or "Reno (Navada) Model" available, the basics remain the same: train the officer to become what the department expects for example socialize the officer.

The typical program (the San Jose model or the Reno model) essentially has phases whereby the officer progressively learns the "department's way of doing things" under the tutelage of prototypically ideal training officers. That is at least the concept in theory. In practice however, no program or training officer requirement or standardization exists. It varies by state and ultimately, by department.

Some departments have a very regimented program and strict selection processes for FTOs[47] while others still use "veteran" officers to train rookies. Still others may have a documented, strict, selection process but due to departmental issues such as a shortage of properly trained FTOs, substitutes are used. Such was the problem I encountered while studying the Dallas (Texas) Police Department's FTOs.

There had been some recent incidents where officers had violated policy and the officers were rookie officers. When questioned, the officers said they were trained in the proper way but shown various ways to get around policy. Some incidents were nationally publicized and shown the department in a less than favorable light. The tipping point where the chief asked what was going on with the "rookies" was after an officer attempted to pull over the driver of a car driven by a professional football player. The driver had committed a minor traffic and would not pull over. The officer "pursued" the driver—who was going the speed limit and stopping at stop signals—a short distance to the hospital.

Once the driver stopped, the young officer pointed a gun at the driver and lost control of the passengers. While the driver tried to explain that his mother-in-law was dying, he identified himself and pleaded to be released long enough to be at her dying bedside. The officer ignored the other passengers who simply walked away (officer safety issue) and told the driver, "I can screw you over." Another officer from a different jurisdiction arrived and tried to convince the Dallas officer to let him go. To no avail, the Dallas officer berated the driver further and caused him to miss his mother-in-law's last moments.[48]

The officer was fired in this case for violation of department policy. He had been on the department only a short time. Shortly after that incident, another rookie officer (less than 2 years) who was "in pursuit" of the driver of a motorcycle had a junior officer with him who had less than 20 months on the job. Both officers had just been released from the FTO program. The supervisor told the officers to stop the pursuit.

The officers not only did not stop the pursuit but exclaimed they were going to "...beat the [expletive] out of him." when they caught him. The in-car video captured this exchange between the officers and the subsequent beating of the motorcyclist as the cyclist begged the officers to "Please stop!"[49] While it may seem like I'm picking on the Dallas Police Department, these are only a glimpse of a much wider problem. I just happen to have personal knowledge of these incidents. A Google search of "rookie officer fired" yielded 8040 results. Much like the chief's question, I asked, "What's going on here?"

After researching the Dallas dilemma, I found that it was acceptable for division commanders (or lieutenants) to assign rookies to ride with rookies and even more troublesome, all senior corporals could be (and were) assigned as FTOs (I could not find a copy of the professed memorandum allowing this). This meant officers who had no training in how to be a trainer (an FTO) were in fact, training rookies. The standards were bent because of the lack of FTOs to trainees' ratio. What the department was experiencing were the repercussions from unqualified trainers influencing new officers. This form of socialization can stick with an officer throughout their career and easily manifest itself in poor judgment and deviance. The entire premise of the FTO program was to select a volunteer, model officer who is trained as an FTO to train rookies. This clearly was not happening.

Across the United States, FTOs are training rookie officers. No standards are required for FTOs by some departments and others are "drafted" into training without themselves being trained. There have been no studies about how officers were trained after incidents of abuse of force or other deviance. It is likely that those officers had poor training and/or supervision. Unfortunately, those incidents are usually settled through legal means and the *real* reason the officers misbehaved or committed illegal acts are not publicized.

Currently, there seems to be a media frenzy every time an officer shoots someone or uses force. I submit the officers' behavior is nothing new but rather, more publicized. In most cases, we will never know the real reason an officer used the force he or she thought necessary. Nevertheless, as responsible criminal justice practitioners or academics, we should find the root cause. I submit that these macro factors of organizational behavior that allows deviance and the micro level causes of bad recruitment and training are to blame for the majority of poor decisions.

As I have stated, people do not enter policing with the intent of violating someone's rights. They may not have the most altruistic reasons or they may be completely naïve, but no one has shown evidence yet that a model agency with properly trained and educated officers have displayed a pattern or practice of misconduct. It is time to raise that bar that August Vollmer proposed back in the 1900s and so many committees have recommended. If history has taught us nothing, we cannot expect different results given misguided management and supervision, poor officer selection, insufficient training and scant education. Why then are we surprised when things go bad?

Summary

- Police misconduct is not a recent phenomenon. There have been reports of police misconduct from the beginning of the modern police force.
- Many of the early reports were of police brutality, especially against striking workers.
- The early policing of black, Latino, and Native American communities in the United States was initially in the form of occupation, surveillance, and pacification.
- Lynching has had an essential part in understanding the history and character of police violence in America because it reveals the sexual and gender dimensions of maintaining the color line and disciplining minorities.
- Most researchers trace the modern police department's origin to Alfred the Great of England during the ninth century.
- By the seventeenth century, the chief law enforcement officials in the urban areas of England were the magistrates, who presided over the courts, ordered arrests, and investigated suspected criminal activities. In rural areas, the shire-reeves were responsible for maintaining law and order among the citizens.
- The thief-takers were private individuals who were paid by the government on a piecework basis. They had no official status and only the authority of private citizens to arrest. Many of the thief-takers were criminals themselves.
- When the English settlers settled in America, they brought with them the English law enforcement structure. At the time, America was mostly rural and was policed by officers in the offices of constable and sheriff.
- The first modern police force in the United States was the slave patrols, which were established in the southern states.
- The first organized metropolitan American police force was established in Philadelphia in 1833.
- The first police forces were generally under the control of a chief of police who was appointed by the mayor. The mission of the early police departments was merely to keep the city clean and to keep everything quiet.
- In the late nineteenth century, in an effort to eliminate politics from the police forces, many cities

established police administrative boards. These boards exercised control over the police department. The boards were given responsibility for managing police affairs and appointing police administrators.

- Starting with the latter part of the 1800s, police forces grew in size and expanded their functions, with attempts at reform including the concept of merit employment and civil service.
- Narrowly defined, police corruption refers to police personnel who use their position and authority for personal rather than public benefit. More broadly, police corruption refers to any violation of rules, even when there is no personal gain, as in perjury, physical abuse of prisoners, sexual misconduct, robbery, and racial profiling.
- Police corruption in American police departments became widespread shortly after the formation of the first police departments in the mid-1800s.
- The political era of policing was so named because of the close ties between police and politics. This era began with the development of police departments during the 1840s, continued through the Progressive period, and ended during the early 1900s.
- The reform era developed in reaction to politics. It started in the 1900s but only took hold during the 1930s. The era thrived during the 1950s and 1960s but began to be eroded during the late 1970s.
- Prohibition in the 1920s greatly increased the potential for corruption. Massive amounts of money were being made by bootleggers who in turn paid off police officers to allow their illegal activities to continue.
- The production of the 1931 Report on Lawlessness in Law Enforcement by the Wickersham Commission was one of the most important events in the history of American policing. It was the first systematic investigation of police misconduct.
- American history is replete with reports of police brutality, especially against striking workers. Apparently the first use of the term *police brutality* by the media was in the *New York Times* in 1893.
- There are numerous reports of police brutality against striking workers and minority citizens.
- The summer of 1967 again brought racial disorder to American cities, and with it shock, fear, and bewilderment to the nation.

Practicum

A criminal report was filed with the Brooklyn federal court charging a New York City Police Department detective, a 13-year veteran of the NYPD, with violating the civil rights of three women through sexual misconduct.

As alleged in court filings by the government, the officer arrested a woman identified in the information as Jane Doe 1 ("the victim") and her boyfriend on drug distribution charges following the execution of a search warrant at their apartment. During the arrest, the officer forced the victim to undress in front of him in the bedroom of the apartment. Later, the officer told the victim that she was going to jail and would lose her children unless she had sex with him. When the victim went to the restroom at the precinct, the officer followed her inside and made her perform oral sex. Upon the victim's release from custody, the officer told her that he expected her to have sex with him at a later time. Thereafter, the officer called the victim on numerous occasions. The victim subsequently reported the officer's misconduct to the NYPD's internal affairs bureau, which began an investigation. The officer was removed from active duty.

As further alleged in the government's court filings, the officer engaged in similar misconduct in connection with the arrest of another drug dealer. On that occasion, the officer coerced a female cousin of the drug dealer, identified in the information as Jane Doe 2, to engage in sex acts with him based on threats he made concerning the lengthy prison sentence faced by the drug dealer.

In a third incident, the officer allegedly engaged in lewd sexual behavior in front of a female arrestee and then forced her to raise her shirt to expose her upper body.

As a member of a police oversight board, what actions should the police department take to prevent future abuses such as those committed by this officer?

Discussion questions

1. Explain why the police in the United States have a history of brutality.
2. What were the problems with the early police departments?
3. What is the importance of the Wickersham Commission's report?
4. Why were the early labor strikes so violent?
5. Explain the role of race in early police misconduct.

References

1. Robin Kelly (2001) Slangin rocks...Palestinian style. In *Police Brutality*, ed. Jill Nelson, New York: Norton, pp. 21–59.
2. John Joseph Wallis, Price V. Fishback, and Shawn Kantor (2006) Politics, relief, and reform. In *Corruption and Reform: Lessons from America's Economic History* (National Bureau of Economic Research Conference Report), Chicago, IL: University of Chicago Press. Chapter 11, pp. 343–372.

3. A Law That Hides Police Misconduct From the Public. The Opinion Pages, an editorial. (October 12, 2015) *New York Times*, p. A18

4. Michael Birzer and Cliff Roberson (2007) *Policing: Today and Tomorrow*. Upper Saddle River, NJ: Pearson.

5. Blythe Bernhard (August 31, 2013) St. Louis takes control of police department from the state. *St. Louis Post-Dispatch*, p. A1.

6. David Bayley and Robert Perito (2011) *Police Corruption: What Past Scandals Teach about Current Challenges*. Washington, DC: United States Institute of Peace.

7. George L. Kelling and Mark H. Moore (1988) *The Evolving Strategy of Policing*. Washington, DC: National Institute of Justice.

8. Samuel Walker (1997) *Popular Justice: A History of American Criminal Justice*, 2nd edn., rev. New York: Oxford University Press.

9. The material for this section was adapted from the article "A History of Notable Senate Investigations" prepared by the U.S. Senate Historical Office, Washington, DC. GPO. The article may be accessed at http://www.senate.gov/artandhistory/history/common/investigations/pdf/Kefauver_Committee_fullcitations.pdf. Accessed on October 6, 2015.

10. Police officer in trouble: Charges against policeman McManus by his sergeant. *New York Times*, June 23, 1893. p. 5.

11. Sylvia Gillett (1991) Camden yards and the strike of 1877. In *The Baltimore Book: New Views of Local History*, eds. Elizabeth Fee, Linda Shopes, and Linda Zeidman. Philadelphia, PA: Temple University Press, pp. 11–14.

12. Janice L. Reiff (2005) The press and labor in the 1880s. In *Encyclopedia of Chicago*, ed. James Grossman. Chicago, IL: University of Chicago Press. pp. 687.

13. Richard Schneirov (1998) *Labor and Urban Politics: Class Conflict and the Origins of Modern Liberalism in Chicago, 1864–97*. Urbana, IL: University of Chicago Press.

14. David Ray Papke (1999) The Pullman case: The clash of labor and capital in industrial America. In *Landmark Law Cases and American Society*. Lawrence, Kansas: University Press of Kansas. pp. 35–37.

15. John R. Commons et al. (1918) *History of Labor in the United States* vol. 2. New York: Macmillan. p. 502.

16. Dommic Capeci, Jr. (1977) *The Harlem Riot of 1943*. Philadelphia, PA: Temple Books.

17. Kevin Johnson (2005) The forgotten "repatriation" of persons of Mexican ancestry and lessons for the "war on terror." *Pace Law Review*, 26(1), 1–26.

18. Kevin Boyle (2003) *After the Rainbow Sign: Jerome Cavanagh and 1960s*. Detroit, MI: Wayne State University Press.

19. United States (1968) *Kerner Commission, Report of the National Advisory Commission on Civil Disorders*. Washington, DC: U.S. Government Printing Office.

20. Frank Schmalleger and John L. Worrall (2010) *Policing Today*. Upper Saddle River, NJ: Prentice Hall.

21. Arthur V. Lashly (February, 1930) The Illinois crime survey. *American Institute of Criminal Law and Criminology*, 20(4). pp. 588.

22. National Commission on Law Enforcement Observance and Enforcement (1931) *Report on Lawlessness in Law Enforcement*. Washington, DC: National Commission on Law Enforcement Observance and Enforcement.

23. Knapp Commission (1973) *The Knapp Commission Report on Police Corruption: Commission to Investigate Allegations of Police Corruption and the Cities Anti-Corruption Procedures*. New York: George Braziller.

24. Board of Inquiry (2000) *Board of Inquiry into the Rampart Area Corruption Incident Public Report*. Los Angeles, CA: Los Angeles Police Department.

25. Milton Mollen (1994) *City of New York Commission to Investigate Allegations of Police Corruption and the Anti-Corruption Procedures of the Police Department*. Report issued by the City of New York.

26. Warren Christopher (1991) *Report of the Independent Commission on the Los Angeles Police Department*. Los Angeles, CA: The Commission.

27. Human Right Watch (2015) Shielded from justice. Statement to the Law Enforcement Equipment Working Group issued by Human Rights Watch.

28. U.S. Department of Justice (2015) Special litigation section cases and matters: Law enforcement agencies. Retrieved from http://www.justice.gov/crt/special-litigation-section-cases-and-matters0 - police. Accessed on December 11, 2015.

29. Bloomburg News (2015) A "pattern or practice" of violence in America. Retrieved from http://www.bloomberg.com/graphics/2015-doj-and-police-violence/. Accessed on December 11, 2015.

30. policemag.com (2015) Cop slang. Retrieved from http://www.policemag.com/cop-slang/list/browse/-.aspx. Accessed on December 10, 2015.

31. President's Commission on Law Enforcement and Administration of Justice (1967) *The Challenge of Crime in a Free Society*. Washington, DC: United States Government Printing Office.

32. Texas Commission on Law Enforcement (2015) Timeline of legislative and procedural changes. Retrieved from https://www.tcole.texas.gov/content/09011967. Accessed on December 13, 2015.

33. Texas Commission on Law Enforcement. (2008). *History of the BPOC Course*. Austin, TX: Texas Commission on Law Enforcement Standards and Education.

34. Presidents Commission on Law Enforcement and Administration of Justice (1967) *The Challenge of Crime in a Free Society*. Washington, DC: Government Printing Office.

35. United States of America (1973) *Report of the National Advisory Commission on Criminal Justice Standards and Goals*. Washington, DC: U.S. Department of Justice.

36. American Bar Association (1968) *American Bar Association Project on Standards for Criminal Justice*. Washington, DC: American Bar Association.

37. August Vollmer (1917) Police schools. *Journal of the American Institute of Criminal Law and Criminology*, 8(3), 463–464.

38. Bureau of Justice Statistics (2015) *Local Police Departments, 2013: Personnel, Policies, and Practices*. Washington, DC: U.S. Department of Justice.

39. Diane Burns (2010) Reflections from the one-percent of local police departments with mandatory four-year degree requirements for new hires: Are they diamonds in the rough? *Southwest Journal of Criminal Justice*, 7(1), 87–108.

40. Mathew Dolan (2014) Gypsy cops and agency liability. Retrieved from http://www.llrmi.com/articles/legal_

update/2014_dolan_gypsycops.shtml. Accessed on December 13, 2015.

41. Scott Lilienfeld and Kristin Landfield (2008) Science and pseudoscience in law enforcement: A user-friendly primer. *Criminal Justice and Behavior,* 35(10), 1215–1230.

42. Gregory P. Vander Kooi and Louann Bierlein Palmer (2014) Problem-based learning for police academy students: Comparison of those receiving such instruction with those in traditional programs. *Journal of Criminal Justice Education,* 25(2), 175–195.

43. Allison T. Chappell and Lonn L. Lanza-Kaduce (April, 2010) Police academy socialization: Understanding the lessons learned in a paramilitary-bureaucratic organization. *Journal of Contemporary Ethnography,* 39(2), 187–214; and Norman Conti and Patrick Doreian (December, 2014) From here on out, we're all blue: Interaction order, social infrastructure, and race in police socialization. *Police Quarterly,* 17(4), 414–447.

44. Texas Commission on Law Enforcement (2015) Basic peace officer. Retrieved from https://www.tcole. texas.gov/content/course-curriculum-materials-and-updates-0. Accessed on December 13, 2015.

45. Ryan M. Getty, John L. Worrall, and Robert G. Morris (2014) How far from the tree does the apple fall? Field training officers, their trainees, and allegations of misconduct. *Crime and Delinquency,* 1–19. doi:10.1177/0011128714545829

46. Sharon A. Moore and Aleda M. Womack (1975) A history of the San Jose police department field training program. Retrieved from http://michiganfto.com. Accessed on December 13, 2015.

47. City of Mesa. (2002) *Mesa Police Department Supplemental Manual: Field Training Officer Program.* Mesa, AZ: City of Mesa Police Department Retrieved from http://www. wftoa.org/manuals/Mesapd_fto_manual.pdf. Accessed on December 10, 2015.

48. Lynn Zinser, L (March 30, 2009) Ryan Moats and the Dallas police: Updated with apology accepted. *New York Times.* pp. A-4.

49. Rebecca Lopez (September 13, 2010) Dallas police consider next move in brutality probe. Retrieved from http://www.wfaa.com/news/crime/Police-Brutality-Investigation-102813284.html. Accessed on December 13, 2015.

chapter three

Excessive use of force

Learning objectives

After studying this chapter, the reader should understand the following concepts and issues:

- What constitutes the use of force
- When the use of force is excessive?
- When the police are legally permitted to use a taser
- What conduct is considered excessive use of force

Introduction

I am glad you asked that question [about allegations of police brutality toward minorities], but before I get into it, I might point out that in a study I once made of the factors that militate against public understanding of the police service, I said that two of the factors were the criticism of the police by certain minority groups in order to direct attention from the high incident of criminal activity within those groups and the practice of the press in magnifying police failures and in minimizing their successes or accomplishments. [A 1962 statement by Los Angeles Chief of Police William H. Parker[1]]

This quoted statement by the former chief of police of Los Angeles, California is reflective of the attitude of police supervisors in the 1960s whenever the police were accused of the excessive use of force.

That was in the 1960s; in October 2015, a former St. Louis prosecutor pleaded guilty to misprision of a felony. The ex-prosecutor admitted in federal court that she had failed to tell supervisors and a judge what she knew about the beating of a handcuffed suspect at the hands of a veteran police officer. She also admitted that she helped file a bogus charge against the man in custody. The term *misprision of a felony* relates to the crime of aiding someone to cover up a crime. In the ex-prosecutor's statement, she implicated several officers of having been aware of the beating in July 2014 and helping to cover it up.[2]

With the explosion of mass media, any incidents in which the police are alleged to have used excessive force will be extensively covered in the media. Officers need

to realize that, in present-day policing, they are working under the microscope of the media, and that any use of force will be examined in multiple different ways to see if the officer(s) used excessive force.

Law enforcement officers are authorized to use force in specific circumstances. They are trained to use the force under appropriate conditions. As noted by the National Institute of Justice, "Law enforcement officers should use only the amount of force necessary to mitigate an incident, make an arrest, or protect themselves or others from harm. The levels, or continuum, of force police use include basic verbal and physical restraint, less-lethal force, and lethal force."[3]

According to the International Association of Chiefs of Police (IACP), there is no universally agreed-upon definition of the use of force.[4] The IACP defines the use of force as the "amount of effort required by police to compel compliance by an unwilling subject." The IACP notes that no two situations are the same and that an officer should tailor his or her response to, and apply only that degree of force that is required for, the situation. The association noted that officers should be trained to judge when to use force, if necessary, to regain control of the situation, and the appropriate use of force (Figure 3.1) (Box 3.1).

Establishing excessive use of force

To establish an excessive use of force claim, a plaintiff must demonstrate an injury (injury must be more than a *de minimis* injury), which resulted directly and only from the use of force that was excessive to the need, and that the force used was objectively unreasonable.*

An interesting case of the excessive use of force is *Lockett v. New Orleans*.† In that case, a black American, as an arrestee, and his wife, as a bystander, brought civil action against the Louisiana governor, the mayor of New Orleans, officers of the Louisiana Air National Guard, a university police officer, and the New Orleans Police Department. Lockett alleged false arrest and the malicious use of power and sought injunctive relief against racial discrimination and profiling by the National Guard and the police. Lockett also contended that the defendants' multiple searches of his

---

* Glenn v. City of Tyler, 242 F.3d 307, 314 (5th Cir. 2001).
† Lockett v. New Orleans, 607 F.3d. 992 (5th Cir. 2010).

Figure 3.1 A June 11, 1887, cartoon by Eugene Zimmerman (artist, 1862–1935) depicting the citizens of New York City asking the mayor of the city to "Protect me from my protectors." This cartoon reflects the outcry of the citizens at that time against policemen engaged in brutality and corruption. (Photo courtesy of the Library of Congress Prints and Photographs Division.)

person constituted excessive use of force. However, Lockett failed to allege that an injury had resulted from the pat downs. The court of appeals affirmed the trial court's dismissal of the complaint of excessive use of force because Lockett had failed to prove that any injuries had resulted from the numerous searches or pat downs of his body. The court also held that a 1 hour detention of the arrestee, who had been stopped for speeding, was reasonable, and that the wife of the arrestee could not reasonably have been expected to have suffered severe, debilitating distress from seeing her husband in handcuffs and detained in a vehicle and in jail.

The *Lockett* case seems to imply that numerous searches and pat downs of the body cannot be considered as excessive force. The individual involved must show injury.

Assault and battery

Law enforcement officers are permitted to use appropriate force to accomplish their missions. But the use of excessive force by an officer is generally considered as a crime of assault or battery. Assault is the crime of threatening to commit a battery or an attempt to commit a battery, while the crime of battery is generally defined as the unlawful and offensive touching of another. Note that no injury is required for the crime of battery. Assault and battery are also civil torts, and the victim may sue in civil court for monetary damages.

> ## BOX 3.1 EXCERPTS FROM THE NATIONAL INSTITUTE OF JUSTICE REPORT "USE OF FORCE BY POLICE"
>
> ### WORKING DEFINITIONS[5]
>
> Police use of force is characterized in a variety of ways. Sometimes, these characterizations are functionally interchangeable so that one can be substituted for another without doing injustice to the factual interpretation of a statement. At other times, however, differences in terminology can be very consequential to a statement's meaning. For example, *deadly force* refers to situations in which force is likely to have lethal consequences for the victim. This type of force is clearly defined and should not be confused with other types of force that police use.
>
> In contrast, *police brutality* is a phrase used to describe instances of serious physical or psychological harm to civilians, with an emphasis on cruelty or savageness. The term does not have a standardized meaning; some commentators prefer to use a less emotionally charged term.
>
> In this report, the term *excessive force* is used to describe situations in which more force is used than is allowable when judged in terms of administrative or professional guidelines or legal standards. Criteria for judging excessive force are fairly well established. The term may also include within its meaning the concept of illegal force.
>
> Reference also is made to *excessive use of force*, a similar, but distinctly different, term. Excessive use of force refers to high rates of force, which suggest that police are using force too freely when viewed in the aggregate. The term deals with relative comparisons among police agencies, and there are no established criteria for judgment.
>
> "Illegal" use of force refers to situations in which use of force by police violated a law or statute, generally as determined by a judge or magistrate. The criteria for judging illegal use of force are fairly well established.
>
> *Improper, abusive, illegitimate,* and *unnecessary* use of force are terms that describe situations in which an officer's authority to use force has been mishandled in some general way, the suggestion being that administrative procedure, societal expectations, ordinary concepts of lawfulness, and the principle of last resort have been violated, respectively. Criteria for judging these violations are not well established.
>
> To varying degrees, all of the these terms can be described as transgressions of police authority to use force.

An "assault" is the apprehension of immediate, harmful, or offensive contact with the plaintiff's person, caused by acts intended to result in such contacts, or the apprehension of them, and directed at the plaintiff or a third person; thus, an essential element of the tort of assault is the apprehension of immediate harmful or offensive contact.[*]

As noted in the Florida case of *Long v. Baker*, to establish a civil cause of action for battery, a plaintiff must prove (1) the intent to cause a harmful or offensive contact with another person, and (2) an offensive contact as a direct or indirect result.[†] The intent required for a battery is not necessarily a hostile intent or a desire to do harm.

Right to resist unlawful arrest

In *John Bad Elk v. United States*,[‡] the U.S. Supreme Court stated that an illegal arrest was an assault and battery. A person restrained of his liberty has the same right to use force in defending himself as he would in repelling any other assault and battery. The *John Bad Elk* case is probably not valid in present-day America. As noted in a journal article, during the nineteenth and twentieth centuries almost every state, including Maryland, adopted the right to resist unlawful arrest. Since that time, however, the majority of states abolished the rule, claiming that it promoted violence. Ironically, the act once recognized by most American jurisdictions as an individual's right is now considered a criminal violation.[6]

As noted in the journal article, the modern trend among most jurisdictions has been to eliminate the common law right to resist arrest. At least 39 states abolished this right—23 by statute and 16 by judicial decision. These changing views are based largely on policy considerations. For example, many jurisdictions viewed the rule as anachronistic and dangerous, claiming it promoted violence. Several courts quoted Judge Learned Hand in their debate over whether to abrogate the rule. "The idea that you may resist peaceful arrest… because you are in debate about whether it is lawful or not is not a blow for liberty but on the contrary a blow for attempted anarchy."[§]

The article noted that the proposition that self-help caused graver consequences than an unlawful arrest was a valid concern (Box 3.2). It is highly unlikely that a

---

[*] Wynn v. City of Lakeland, 727 Fed Supp. 2nd. 1309 (MD, Fla. 2010).
[†] Long v. Baker, 37 Fed. Supp. 3d. 1243 (MD, Fla. 2014).
[‡] John Bad Elk v. United States, 177 U.S. 529 (1900).

[§] Rodgers v. State, 280 Md. 406, 373 A.2d 944, (1977) (quoting 1958 Proceedings, American Law Institute, at p. 254.

BOX 3.2   HAVE VIDEO CAMERAS RESULTED IN MORE OFFICERS BEING CHARGED?

Prior to 2015, the annual average was fewer than five officers charged each year with criminal charges in situations where a person had died. In 2015 alone, 15 were charged with criminal conduct regarding the use of force in the first 11 months of the year. Professor Phillip Stinson of Bowling Green University indicates that this sharp increase may be the result of increased use of body cameras. He noted that, over the past decade, roughly 1000 fatal shootings by on-duty officers were recorded. From the beginning of 2005 to 2014, 47 officers were charged and about half were convicted. Most experts predict that there will be more charges and more convictions because of the increased use of video cameras.[7]

BROWER V. INYO COUNTY 489 U.S. 593 (1989)

Was it excessive use of force for the police to park an 18-wheeled truck across the road behind a curve and shine bright lights toward a suspect's oncoming vehicle?

Brower's heirs brought suit under 42 U.S.C. § 1983 in the Federal District Court, claiming, *inter alia*, that the respondents, acting under color of law, had violated Brower's Fourth Amendment rights by effecting an unreasonable seizure using excessive force. Specifically, the complaint alleged that the respondents placed an 18-wheeled truck completely across the highway in the path of Brower's flight, behind a curve and with a police cruiser's headlights aimed in such fashion as to blind Brower on his approach. It also alleged that the fatal collision was a "proximate result" of this police conduct. The district court dismissed the case for failing to state a claim, concluding that the roadblock was reasonable under the circumstances, and the court of appeals affirmed this decision on the grounds that no "seizure" had occurred.

The U.S. Supreme Court held that

- Consistent with the language, history, and judicial construction of the Fourth Amendment, a seizure occurs when governmental termination of a person's movement is effected through means intentionally applied. Because the complaint alleges that Brower was stopped by the instrumentality set in motion or put in place to stop him, it states a claim of Fourth Amendment "seizure."
- Petitioners can claim the right to recover for Brower's death because the unreasonableness alleged consists precisely of setting up the roadblock in such a manner as to be likely to kill him. On remand, the court of appeals must determine whether the district court erred in concluding that the roadblock was not "unreasonable."

JUSTICE SCALIA delivered the opinion of the court:

> On the night of October 23, 1984, William James Caldwell (Brower) was killed when the stolen car that he had been driving at high speeds for approximately 20 miles in an effort to elude pursuing police crashed into a police roadblock. His heirs, petitioners here, brought this action in Federal District Court under 42 U.S.C. 1983, claiming, inter alia, that respondents used "brutal, excessive, unreasonable and unnecessary physical force" in establishing the roadblock, and thus effected an unreasonable seizure of Brower, in violation of the Fourth Amendment. Petitioners alleged that "under color of statutes, regulations, customs and usages," respondents (1) caused an 18-wheel tractor-trailer to be placed across both lanes of a two-lane highway in the path of Brower's flight, (2) "effectively concealed" this roadblock by placing it behind a curve and leaving it unilluminated, and (3) positioned a police car, with its headlights on, between Brower's oncoming vehicle and the truck, so that Brower would be "blinded" on his approach. Petitioners further alleged that Brower's fatal collision with the truck was the "approximate result" of this official conduct. The District Court granted respondents' motion to dismiss the complaint for failure to state a claim on the ground (insofar as the Fourth Amendment claim was concerned) that "establishing a roadblock was not unreasonable under the circumstances." A divided panel of the Court of Appeals for the Ninth Circuit affirmed the dismissal of the Fourth Amendment claim on the basis that no "seizure" had occurred. We granted certiorari to resolve a conflict between that decision and the contrary holding of the Court of Appeals for the Fifth Circuit in Jamieson v. Shaw, 772 F.2d 1205 (1985).

…. The complaint here sufficiently alleges that respondents, under color of law, sought to stop Brower by means of a roadblock and succeeded in doing so. That is enough to constitute a "seizure" within the meaning of the Fourth Amendment. Accordingly, we reverse the judgment of the Court of Appeals and remand for consideration of whether the District Court properly dismissed the Fourth Amendment claim on the basis that the alleged roadblock did not effect a seizure that was "unreasonable."

suspect can effectively escape or deter an arrest unless the suspect responds with equal or greater force. Thus, courts have attempted to end what amounted to "street justice" by eliminating this right and encouraging dispute resolution through the judicial process.

Use of tasers

In the first 10 months of 2015, at least 47 people in the United States died as the result of being tasered by law enforcement officers. In 43 of those reported cases, the victim was unarmed. Nearly 40% of the victims were black, and in 53% of the cases, the victim was displaying signs of intoxication before or after his or her death.

The *Guardian* surveyed 29 different police departments' guidelines and compared them with the U.S. Justice Department-funded research by the Police Executive Research Forum.[8] The *Guardian* noted that the following police guidelines did not comply with the research forum's recommendations. These included that

- 22 of the 29 departments did not instruct the officer to not use more than three shocks in all but exceptional circumstances.
- None of the department guidelines advised the officers that a mandated use of force investigation should be conduct where a taser was used for more than 15 seconds.
- Only 22 of the departments advised the officer to not use the taser if the only justification was that the suspect was fleeing.
- Only 15 of the departments advised the officer to not use a taser if the suspect was already in handcuffs and did not pose an exceptional threat.
- Eight departments did not require the officers to give a warning when possible before using a taser.

The Police Executive Research Forum (PERF), with support from the U.S. Department of Justice Office of Community Oriented Policing Services (COPS Office), produced a set of guidelines for the use of conducted energy devices (CEDs). The first set of guidelines was published in 2005 and revised in 2011. Many law enforcement agencies adopted the guidelines.[9]

In the updated guidelines, PERF changed the name of the weapons from CEDs to electronic control weapons (ECWs) to reflect the reality that these tools are less-lethal weapons meant to help control persons who are actively resisting authority or acting aggressively. ECWs are more commonly known as tasers. In the latest revision, PERF established seven guidelines for the use of ECWs:

- ECWs should be considered less-lethal weapons.
- ECWs should be used as a weapon of need, not a tool of convenience.
- Officers should not over-rely on ECWs in situations where more effective and less risky alternatives are available.
- ECWs are just one of a number of tools that police have available to do their jobs, and they should be considered one part of an agency's overall use-of-force policy.
- In agencies that deploy ECWs, officers should receive comprehensive training on when and how to use ECWs.
- Agencies should monitor their own use of ECWs and should conduct periodic analyses of practices and trends.
- Agencies should consider the expectations of their community when developing an overall strategy for using ECWs.

Under what circumstances is the use of a taser excessive force? In *Mattos v. Agrano*, the court held that an officer's use of a taser in drive-stun mode, three times over the course of less than 1 minute against a driver who refused to sign a traffic citation for driving at 32 mph in a 20 mph zone, constituted constitutionally excessive force; at no time did the driver verbally threaten the officers, she gave no indication of being armed and, being behind the wheel of her car, she was not physically threatening; at the time that the officer, who knew about and considered the driver's pregnancy before tasering her, applied the taser to the driver, she no longer posed even a potential threat to the officers' or others' safety.*

The electric discharge from a taser is extremely painful and overrides the body's nervous system, usually causing a suspect to fall down or otherwise cease

* Mattos v. Agarano, 661 F. 3rd. 433 (9th Cir. 2011).

resistance long enough for the officers to handcuff the suspect or otherwise regain control. Since the discharge of the taser can occur from a short distance away from a suspect, there is less of a need to get close enough to employ direct physical force, thus preventing more serious injuries both to the suspect and to the officers. However, police are frequently accused of misusing or overusing tasers where much less force was all that was necessary, or of using them on sick or otherwise sensitive individuals.[10]

The courts have traditionally used the rules set forth by the U.S. Supreme Court in *Graham v. Connor*, discussed in this chapter, to determine whether or not the use of a taser constituted excessive force. In *Graham*, the court held that the "reasonableness" of a particular use of force must be judged from the perspective of a reasonable officer on the scene, rather than with the 20/20 vision of hindsight. As in other Fourth Amendment contexts, however, the "reasonableness" inquiry in an excessive force case is an objective one; the question is whether the officers' actions are "objectively reasonable" in light of the facts and circumstances confronting them, without regard to their underlying intent or motivation.*

Tasers should not be used routinely or indiscriminately. Taser use is limited to situations where an officer's safety is a legitimate concern and less painful means of subduing difficult individuals are not available. In *Orsak v. Metropolitan Airports Commission Airport Police Department*, the court held that the pain and puncture marks inflicted by a taser were sufficient to represent some minimum level of injury.† In the *Orsak* case, the court applied the *Graham* test by first considering the nature and quality of the alleged intrusion and then the governmental interests at stake, by looking at

1. How severe the crime at issue is
2. Whether the suspect posed an immediate threat to the safety of the officers or others
3. Whether the suspect was actively resisting arrest or attempting to evade arrest by flight

In *Orsak*, a bicyclist brought an action in the state court against the Metropolitan Airports Commission and an airport police officer, alleging that the officer used excessive force, in violation of the bicyclist's Fourth Amendment right to be free from unreasonable seizures, when he ordered a fellow officer to deploy a taser against the bicyclist. Action was then moved to federal court. The federal court held that the bicyclist's claim for excessive force required the existence of an "actual

injury" to support a Fourth Amendment claim, and that the pain and puncture marks inflicted by a taser were sufficient to do so.

The court noted that a taser, when in dart mode, uses compressed nitrogen to propel a pair of "probes"—aluminum darts tipped with stainless steel barbs connected to the taser by insulated wires—toward the target at a rate of over 160 feet per second. Upon striking a person, the taser delivers a 1200 volt, low ampere electrical charge. The electrical impulse instantly overrides the victim's central nervous system, paralyzing the muscles throughout the body, and rendering the target limp and helpless.

When a taser is used in drive-stun mode, the operator removes the dart cartridge and pushes two electrode contacts located on the front of the taser directly against the victim. In this mode, the taser delivers an electric shock to the victim but does not cause an override of the victim's central nervous system as it does in dart mode. In drive-stun mode, the shock is "extremely painful." Tasers used in dart mode "constitute an intermediate, significant level of force."

The court in Mattos stated that, when determining whether the use of a taser constituted excessive force, the court would consider the governmental interests at stake and begin with (1) how severe the crime at issue was, (2) whether the suspect posed an immediate threat to the safety of the officers or others, and (3) whether the suspect was actively resisting arrest or attempting to evade arrest by flight.‡

In *McKenney v. Harrison*,§ a police officer used a stun gun in an attempt to stop a suspect, who was the subject of three misdemeanor arrest warrants, from fleeing through a second story window. The suspect, who was mentally ill, died as a result of the injuries he suffered during the encounter. The court held that the use of the stun gun was reasonable, despite the fatal consequences of the incident; the officer used only a single shock, the suspect attempted to escape through a window only 6–8 feet away, the alternative of tackling the suspect posed a risk to the safety of the officer and might not have ensured a successful arrest, the officers warned the suspect and one officer specifically said "you don't want to be tased;" the officer could have believed that the shock would incapacitate the suspect before he reached the window and not while he was in an "elevated position" and likely to fall from the second story window; and the officers did not know that the suspect was mentally retarded.

The Administrator for the McKenny estate in a 1983 action in federal district court federal district court against two police officers and the city alleging

---

* Graham v. Connor, 490 U.S. 386 (1989).
† Orsak v. Metropolitan Airports Com'n Airport Police Dept., 2009 WL 5030776 (D. Minn. 2009).

‡ Mattos v. Agarano, 661 F. 3rd. 433 (9th Cir. 2011).
§ McKenney v. Harrison, 635 F. 3rd 354 (8th Cir. 2011).

unlawful entry, excessive force, negligence, and a failure to train and supervise. The district court granted the officers and city's motion for a summary judgment. The U.S. Court of Appeals for the Eighth Circuit affirmed the decision and denied the appeal. The appellate court held that the use of force was reasonable by balancing "the nature and quality of the intrusion on the individual's Fourth Amendment interests against the countervailing governmental interests at stake." In so doing, the court stated "careful attention to the facts and circumstances of each particular case, including the severity of the crime at issue, whether the suspect poses an immediate threat to the safety of the officers or others, and whether [the suspect] is actively resisting arrest or attempting to evade arrest by flight." The court indicated that it may also consider the result of the force.

The appellate court stated that they must judge the reasonableness of the force "from the perspective of a reasonable officer on the scene, rather than with the 20/20 vision of hindsight," and that they must make "allowance for the fact that police officers are often forced to make split-second judgments—in circumstances that are tense, uncertain, and rapidly evolving—about the amount of force that is necessary in a particular situation." When the suspect made a sudden movement toward the window, which the officers reasonably interpreted as an active attempt to evade arrest by flight, the officers were entitled to use force to prevent his escape and effect the arrest. Despite the fatal consequences of the incident, the level of force employed was also not considered unreasonable.

Taser use in Great Britain

Most British police officers do not carry any kind of firearm. After a test run in 2007, 10,000 taser guns were ordered in 2008 to arm selected members of the U.K. law enforcement agencies. This action caused public concern in the United Kingdom. For example, Amnesty International U.K. described tasers as "potentially lethal electrical weapons" that deliver "50,000 volts of electricity into a person's body. The result is excruciatingly painful, causing a person to fall to the ground and, at times, lose control of his or her bodily functions."[11]

A British Broadcasting Corporation (BBC) news report in September 2013 noted that the police use of tasers in England and Wales more than doubled between 2009 and 2011. The report indicated that the devices were used by law enforcement 3328 times in 2009 and 7877 times in 2011. The report noted that, of the reported use, the tasers were actually fired about 26% of the time. Generally, the tasers were pointed or readied as a warning device. British officers are required to take a training course before being allowed to use a taser and they are told to only deploy them when threatened with violence. In 2013, there were about 14,000 British officers trained to use tasers in England and Wales.

According to the news report, incidents where a taser was used but "not discharged" included when the weapon was drawn and aimed; when it was "arced"—which means sparking it without having a target; and when it was "red-dotted"—which means using the targeting mechanism without firing. Most of the cases when a taser was "discharged" involved the taser being fired—where the probes are shot toward the target still attached to the weapon by copper wiring. It can also be used to "drive stun"—where it is held against the target's body.

In 2013, the Independent Police Complaints Commission (IPC) investigated 12 taser-related reports of misconduct, 3 of which involved death. The IPC noted that, in 2010, there were 68 complaints filed by citizens involving law enforcement use of tasers. That figure rose to 101 in 2011 but fell to 98 in 2013.[12]

One of the reported fatal cases involved a 23-year-old man. On July 11, 2013, the Manchester police were call to Beard Road in Gorton after receiving reports of a man with a knife. After he was tasered, he stopped breathing and was taken to a hospital where he died. The deceased's employer, who observed the scene, described the officers at the scene as being "quite aggressive" and he believed that the death was preventable. The incident occurred shortly after the deceased had finished his work shift at an ice-cream factory. The employer stated that he was driving his ice-cream van when he saw his employee outside a terraced house with the police. The deceased waved to him and tried to explain to the police that the employer was his boss. The employer drove off before the incident escalated. The employer stated that the deceased had worked for the company for about 4 years and was a very efficient, good worker. This was the tenth death that had occurred in Britain after police had used a stun gun. One report indicated that, on average, an officer will draw a taser twice a year and discharge it every 4 years.

The Police Superintendents' Association of England and Wales, President of the Police Irene Curtis, said that using tasers could mean that fewer officers and members of the public were hurt. Curtis stated: "'A taser used appropriately can reduce the amount of time that officers need to have off because it reduces injuries. It reduces harm to the public because if there's a dangerous individual, they can be restrained more quickly.[12]

"And sometimes the only other option is firearms. A Taser isn't a gun. A Taser can in some circumstances cause less harm than striking someone with a baton.'"

Legal guidelines on use of force

U.S. Supreme Court via Graham v. Connor, 490 U.S. 86 (1989), stated that force at arrest must be "...objectively reasonable in view of all the facts and circumstances of each particular case..."

In the 1989 case of *Graham v. Connor*, the U.S. Supreme Court established the rules that are used to determine the legality of law enforcement's use of force.* Graham, a diabetic, asked his friend Berry, to drive him to a convenience store to purchase some orange juice to counteract an insulin reaction. When Graham entered the store, he noticed that there was a line of customers ahead of him. He hurried out of the store and requested that Berry drive him to a friend's house. Connor, a city police officer, became suspicious after seeing Graham leave the store in a hurry.

Connor followed Berry's car and made an investigative stop. Connor ordered Graham and Berry to wait while he checked to find out what happened in the store. Backup officers arrived and, ignoring Graham's attempts to explain, handcuffed him. Later, Graham lost consciousness.

Several officers lifted Graham up from behind, carried him over to Berry's car, and placed him face down on the hood. Regaining consciousness, Graham asked the officers to check in his wallet for a diabetic decal that he carried. In response, one of the officers told him to "shut up" and shoved his face down against the hood of the car. Four officers grabbed Graham and threw him headfirst into the police car.

A friend of Graham's brought some orange juice to the car, but the officers refused to let him have it. Finally, Officer Connor received a report that Graham had done nothing wrong at the convenience store, and the officers drove him home and released him.

During the encounter, Graham suffered multiple injuries. At some point during his encounter with the police, Graham sustained a broken foot, cuts on his wrists, a bruised forehead, and an injured shoulder; he also claimed to have developed a loud ringing in his right ear that continues to this day.

Graham filed a 42 U.S.C. 1983 action in the federal district court. The district court dismissed the case, using the test that in determining when excessive force was used, the court should consider whether the force was applied in a good-faith effort to maintain and restore discipline or was maliciously and sadistically used for the purpose of causing harm.

The U.S. Supreme Court reversed the ruling and stated that claims that law enforcement officials have used excessive force—deadly or not—in the course of an arrest, investigatory stop, or other seizure of a free citizen should be analyzed under the Fourth Amendment's "objective reasonableness" standard rather than the

substantive due process standard that the district court had used.

The court stated that, where the excessive force claim arises in the context of an arrest or investigatory stop of a free citizen, it is most properly characterized as one invoking the protections of the Fourth Amendment, which guarantees citizens the right to be secure in their person against unreasonable seizures of the person.

The court noted, in its decision in *Tennessee v. Garner* that the court held that the use of deadly force to apprehend a fleeing suspect who did not appear to be armed or otherwise dangerous violated the suspect's constitutional rights, notwithstanding the existence of probable cause to arrest.[†] The court stated that it analyzed the constitutionality of the challenged application of force solely by reference to the Fourth Amendment's prohibition against unreasonable seizures of the person, holding that the "reasonableness" of a particular seizure depends not only on when it is made, but also on how it is carried out.

The court opined:

> Today we make explicit what was implicit in Garner's analysis, and hold that all claims that law enforcement officers have used excessive force—deadly or not—in the course of an arrest, investigatory stop, or other "seizure" of a free citizen should be analyzed under the Fourth Amendment and its "reasonableness" standard, rather than under a "substantive due process" approach. Because the Fourth Amendment provides an explicit textual source of constitutional protection against this sort of physically intrusive governmental conduct, that Amendment, not the more generalized notion of "substantive due process," must be the guide for analyzing these claims.[‡]
>
> Determining whether the force used to effect a particular seizure is "reasonable" under the Fourth Amendment requires a careful balancing of "the nature and quality of the intrusion on the individual's Fourth Amendment interests" against the countervailing governmental interests at stake. Our Fourth Amendment jurisprudence has long recognized that the right to make an arrest or investigatory stop necessarily carries with it the right to use some degree of physical coercion or threat thereof to effect it. Because "the test of reasonableness under the Fourth Amendment is not capable of precise

---

* Graham v. Connor, 490 U.S. 386 (1989).

† Tennessee v. Garner, 490 U.S. 386 (1985).
‡ Graham v. Connor, at p. 395.

definition or mechanical application, however, its proper application requires careful attention to the facts and circumstances of each particular case, including the severity of the crime at issue, whether the suspect poses an immediate threat to the safety of the officers or others, and whether he is actively resisting arrest or attempting to evade arrest by flight. "The question is "whether the totality of the circumstances justifies a particular sort of seizure."

In 2014, the Supreme Court affirmed the guidance in the *Graham v. Connor* decision. The court's ruling in *Plumhoff v. Rickard** further embedded the *Graham v. Connor* mandate: that any analysis of force under the Fourth Amendment must be viewed from the perspective of a reasonable officer at the scene, rather than with the 20/20 vision of hindsight.

Donald Rickard was stopped by a West Memphis, Arkansas police officer because Rickard's car had only one operating headlight. After Rickard refused to give up his driver's license when asked, and the officer had noticed Rickard's nervous appearance and damage to the car consistent with vehicle theft, the officer ordered Rickard to step out of the vehicle. Rather than comply, Rickard sped away.

The ensuing pursuit, ultimately involving six police cruisers, lasted some 5 minutes, exceeded speeds of 100 mph, and came within close proximity to other motorists on the road, including swerving through traffic at high speeds. Eventually, Rickard lost control of his vehicle, "spun out" into a parking lot, and collided with one of the pursuing officer's vehicles. Now cornered, Rickard put his car into reverse in an attempt to escape but collided with another officer's vehicle. At that point, two officers got out of their cars and approached Rickard's car, with one of the officers drawing his pistol and ordering Rickard to stop and get out while knocking on his passenger window. Once again, instead of complying, Rickard slammed on the accelerator in an apparent attempt to push through the sitting police cruiser blocking his car's escape. At this point, one of the officers fired three shots into Rickard's car. Rickard then reversed in a "180° arc," narrowly avoiding a diving officer, and managed to maneuver onto a side street and began to speed away. Other officers on scene then fired 12 shots into the car. Rickard crashed shortly thereafter, and both he and his passenger died.

As for the 15 shots fired, the court noted that it stands to reason that, if police officers are justified in firing at a suspect in order to end a severe threat to public safety, the officers need not stop shooting until the threat has ended. And this is exactly what occurred, as during the 10 second span when all the shots were fired, Rickard never abandoned his attempt to flee. The court noted that, had the officers initiated a second round of shots after an initial round had clearly incapacitated Rickard and ended any threat of continued flight, or if Rickard had clearly given himself up, it may have been a different result. The court dismissed Rickard's daughter's 1983 action, holding that the officers acted reasonably.

Mullenix v. Luna

In 2015, the U.S. Supreme Court, by an 8-1 vote, made it harder to sue police officers for use of deadly force against fleeing suspects. The court stated that police officers are immune from lawsuits unless it was beyond doubt that a shooting was unjustified and clearly unreasonable. The case involved a Texas police officer who ignored a warning by his supervisor and took a high-powered rifle to a highway overpass to shoot at an approaching car. The officer apparently intended to stop the car, but he killed the driver.

The Supreme Court said that the benefit of the doubt in such cases always goes to the police officer who sees a potential deadly situation. It is easy to agree with Justice Sonia Sotomayor, who dissented. She stated in her dissent that the court adopted a "shoot first and think later" approach to policing.

It was noted that the decision was announced a few days after two officers killed a 6-year-old boy in Louisiana. It also came at a time when there was growing concern over the police's use of deadly force. The case started when Leija fled from a drive-in restaurant as the police tried to arrest him. He was considered drunk, and believed to be carrying a gun. He led officers on a chase that reached 110 mph. Texas Trooper Mullenix heard about the chase and drove to the spot where the officers were putting down a strip of spikes to puncture Leija's tires.

According to the news reports, Mullenix had been criticized for not reacting decisively in the past. Apparently, he decided to take decisive action, even though his supervisor advised him against it. He fired six shots. It was later determined that Leija had been killed by Mullenix's shots, four of which struck his upper body. There was no evidence that any of Mullenix's shots hit the car's radiator, hood, or engine block.

The Luna family sued, and the federal trial judge ruled that the case could go to the jury to decide whether Mullenix was reckless or reasonable under the circumstances. The U.S. Court of Appeals for the Fifth Circuit agreed and said that the officer was not entitled to immunity.

Justice Sotomayor, in her dissent, stated that the actions of the court "renders the protections of the

---

* Plumhoff v. Rickard, 572 U.S. ___ (2014).

Fourth Amendment hollow" by sanctioning the officer's "rogue conduct." She noted he had not been trained to shoot at a moving car, and was not told to shoot before the vehicle encountered the spikes across the highway. According to Justice Sotomayor, "When Mullenix confronted his superior officer after the shooting, his first words were, 'How is that for proactive?' She noted, "The glib comment seems to me revealing of the culture this court's decision supports when it calls even reasonable— or even reasonable use of deadly force for no discernible gain and over a supervisor's express order to standby."

Apparently, Mullenix was more worried about what people thought of him than the fact that he had just killed a man for no reason.

The court stated that the doctrine of qualified-immunity shields officials from civil liability so long as their conduct "does not violate clearly established statutory or constitutional rights of which a reasonable person would have known." And a clearly established right is one that is "sufficiently clear that every reasonable official would have understood that what he is doing violates that right."

Justice Scalia, concurring in judgment, stated: "It is conceded that Trooper Mullenix did not shoot to wound or kill the fleeing Leija, nor even to drive Leija's car off the road, but only to cause the car to stop by destroying its engine. That was a risky enterprise, as the outcome demonstrated; but determining whether it violated the Fourth Amendment requires us to ask, not whether it was reasonable to kill Leija, but whether it was reasonable to shoot at the engine in light of the risk to Leija. It distorts that inquiry, I think, to make the question whether it was reasonable for Mullenix to apply deadly force."

According to Justice Sotomayor, "When confronting a claim of qualified immunity, a court asks two questions. First, the court considers whether the officer in fact violated a constitutional right. Second, the court asks whether the contours of the right were 'sufficiently clear that a reasonable official would [have understood] that what he is doing violates that right.' This Court has rejected the idea that 'an official action is protected by qualified immunity unless the very action in question has previously been held unlawful.' Instead, the crux of the qualified immunity test is whether officers have 'fair notice' that they are acting unconstitutionally."

Research on police use of force

The National Institute of Justice has funded numerous studies on the use of force by police officers. The one that will be discussed in this section is the William Terrill, Eugene Paoline, and Jason Ingram report of 2012.[13] The report noted that it was difficult to identify a standard practice used by police departments across the country. While some departments are quite restrictive in terms of

allowing officers to use more severe forms of force only on actively aggressive suspects, other agencies are quite liberal and place a large amount of discretion in officers hands by allowing them to use nearly all types of force against nearly all types of resistance faced, short of extreme imbalance (e.g., allowing a baton strike to a compliant suspect).

The report noted that Colorado Springs relied on a "Situational Force Model" (alternatively referred to as a "wheel" model) as its means of a force continuum in teaching officers when to use force. This model graphically depicted an officer standing in the middle of a circle with various force options surrounding him or her. The force options are placed in random order to indicate that there is no natural progression of force (e.g., deadly force is placed next to soft hand tactics). There is no graphical depiction of citizen resistance as to which types of force are most appropriate, given different types of resistance. The researchers noted that Colorado Springs had the lowest rate of force in relation to workload. The Colorado Springs Police Department, however, had the highest rate of citizen complaints for improper force/discourtesy of the police.

Columbus, Ohio, used a linear design referred to as the Action–Response to Resistance/Aggression (Use of Force) Model in training their officers, which did not graphically depict a force continuum but simply laid out eight levels of force (soft hands, chemical spray, electronic devices, hard hands, impact weapon, canine, less-lethal munitions, and deadly force). Columbus officers used the least amount of force relative to citizen resistance. However, Columbus had the second highest rate of citizen complaints for improper force/discourtesy.

Charlotte–Mecklenburg used a linear design, although their policy directive specifically stated that it is "not designed to be a step-by-step progression." The model graphically depicted six levels of citizen resistance in linear fashion (cooperative, verbal and nonverbal, passive, defensive, active aggression, and aggravated active) on a horizontal axis above another horizontal axis that depicted seven levels of force in linear fashion (professional presence and verbal dialogue and commands, soft hands, chemical spray, hard hands, conducted energy devices, impact weapon, and deadly force). Charlotte–Mecklenburg had the highest amount of citizen injuries.

As can be seen by a review of the cities' responses examined in the report, no uniform measures were used by the police departments in training officers on the use of force. The researchers concluded that, what was abundantly clear from the many analyses and rankings conducted, was that there was no ideal (or flawed) policy approach across all outcomes. The Terrell *et al.* study used the matrixes set forth in Figures 3.2a–d to illustrate the use of force and citizen resistance matrixes.

Police departments generally use one of the matrixes shown in Figure 3.2 to teach officers the appropriate use

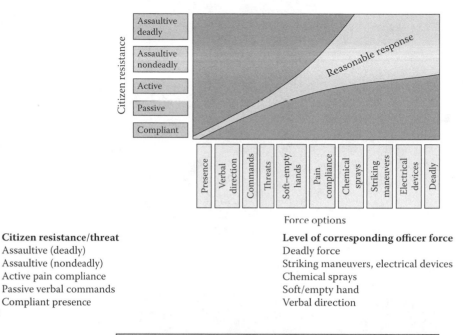

Citizen resistance/threat
Assaultive (deadly)
Assaultive (nondeadly)
Active pain compliance
Passive verbal commands
Compliant presence

(a)

Level of corresponding officer force
Deadly force
Striking maneuvers, electrical devices
Chemical sprays
Soft/empty hand
Verbal direction

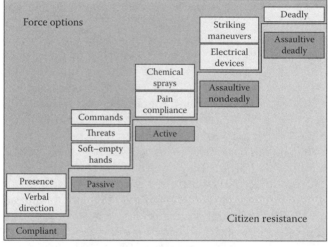

(b)

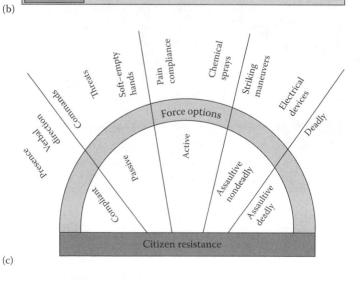

(c)

Figure 3.2 Matrixes of the possible use of force by police officers. (b) Linear design (e.g., step, ladder, FLETC model) with graphic representation. (c) Half wheel example. (d) Wheel example.

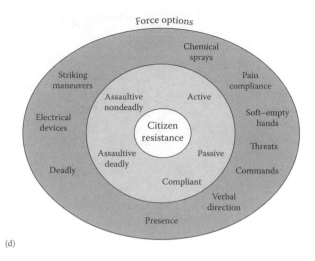

(d)

Figure 3.2 (Continued)

PROGRESSIVE DISCIPLINE AND ACCOUNTABILITY IN POLICE AGENCIES

Comments by Matthew O'Deane, PhD[14]

Officers and employees of law enforcement agencies have the responsibility to provide service to the public in an appropriate manner. They are, therefore, expected to exercise judgment and discretion and observe established and accepted standards of personal behavior in the performance of duties and responsibilities. However, as we all see on almost a daily basis in media reports, the issues of unacceptable job performance, misconduct, and violations of department policies and procedures occur in agencies all across the nation. These incidents must be properly addressed, and when found to be true, may result in disciplinary action ranging from a simple warning up to termination or in some rare cases criminal prosecutions.

Progressive discipline is characterized by addressing unacceptable job performance or conduct with a corrective and rehabilitative (rather than punitive) approach, by addressing unacceptable job performance or conduct with informal disciplinary action appropriate to the situation, and by addressing continuing or repeated instances.

It is the policy of most police agencies to motivate its officers and employees to perform efficiently and effectively through positive encouragement and recognition for satisfactory, above standard and outstanding job performance.

There are two major categories of discipline I hope to describe and discuss in this article, they include Informal and Formal. As we discuss the various options, consider the scenarios involving Officer Smith listed below. Based on the facts presented, if you were the supervisor what actions you would take, what level of discipline you would think is appropriate based on the facts you have been provided.

Scenario 1

Officer Smith accepted a free cup of coffee from the clerk at the local 7/11 store. The Chief made an announcement to the entire department the week before that officers are not to accept gratuities of any kind, and if they do they will be disciplined. Officer Smith was present in the room when the Chief made the announcement. What level (Informal or Formal) and what action in the category would you take, and explain why?

Scenario 2

Officer Smith backed his patrol car into a light pole in a parking lot denting the bumper. Officer Smith parked the car at the end of the shift and never reported the damage. When asked about the damage from his Sergeant, Officer Smith said he did not know anything about it. The next day a citizen walked into the lobby and had a cell phone video of the officer hitting the pole, getting out of the car and looking at the damage, then driving away. What level (Informal or Formal) and what action in the category would you take, and explain why?

Scenario 3

Officer Smith backed his patrol car into a light pole in a parking lot denting the bumper. He immediately called his supervisor and reported the damage and completed all of the required reports. Officer Smith had a similar accident three months before which he attributed to inattention while driving. Officer Smith received a counseling for the prior accident which was documented in his file. What level (Informal or Formal) and what action in the category would you take, and explain why?

Scenario 4

Officer Smith was seen going into the evidence room of the police facility after hours. When he exited the supervisor asked what he was doing and could see that Officer Smith had an item of evidence sticking out of his gym bag. The evidence was a kilo of cocaine that had been impounded and was not checked out by Officer Smith and Officer Smith had no reason for having the evidence. What level (Informal or Formal) and what action in the category would you take, and explain why?

Progressive discipline: Informal

- Counseling
- Oral warning
- Written warning

Counseling and oral and written warnings are the most widely used methods of maintaining appropriate standards and are the first steps in progressive discipline. Counseling is the most common, and usually the most positive and timely means of addressing unacceptable performance. Counseling should be characterized by a clear statement of the unacceptable aspects of the employee's job performance or conduct, using a tone of inquiry rather than accusation.

There should be an opportunity for the employee to provide an explanation and presentation of mitigating circumstances if he or she feels that they are relevant. A restatement of expected standards of job performance should be conducted with confidentiality and privacy, with respect to the location and subject of discussion.

For some supervisors, the process of meeting with their officers and disciplining them is a bit uncomfortable, or they are not well-versed as to how this process should be conducted. The following is a suggested process of what a supervisor can do before, during, and after a meeting with an employee in informal discipline situations.

Progressive discipline: The meeting process

Before the meeting

- Inform your chain of command and employee relations officer.
- Arrange to meet with the employee privately.
- Do not discipline an employee in public or in front of other workers.
- Prepare for the meeting by reviewing your notes and files on the specific incident(s) and The problem(s) in question and any past discipline taken, either verbal or written.
- Bring any resources or tools that will assist the employee.

During the meeting

- Explain to the employee why you have called the meeting (if the employee doesn't know already).
- State the specific problem in terms of actual performance and desired performance.
- Explain the impact on others or on the department.
- Review your progressive discipline policy/program with the employee, and Explain what steps have already been taken, and what the next step is.
- Give the employee a chance to respond, explain, and defend his or her actions.
- Acknowledge the employee's story and be sure to include it in your notes of the discipline session.
- Tell the employee that you expect his or her behavior to change. Give specific examples and suggestions.
- Indicate your confidence in the employee's ability and willingness to change the behavior.

- Have the employee repeat back to you or otherwise confirm that he or she understands the problem and is clear on what changes are expected.
- Reassure the employee that you value his or her work and that you want to work with the employee to make sure that he or she can continue to work at your business.

After the meeting

- Using your notes from the session, write a memo or other documentation that summarizes the conversation.
- Give the employee a copy of the document no later than the end of the day following the conversation.
- If the employee has other supervisors, distribute copies to them but emphasize that the information is confidential and not to be shared with anyone else.
- Monitor the employee's behavior and performance to make sure that the problem has been corrected.
- Meet with the employee, as appropriate, to discuss progress and provide any additional feedback or tools.

Progressive discipline: Verbal warnings

Despite the fact that the warning is a verbal one, this does not mean that it should not be documented. Verbal warnings are a building block to more formal warnings in the future. All documentation should include

- The employee's name
- The date of the verbal warning
- The specific offense or rule violation
- The date(s) of the incident
- A specific statement of the expected performance
- An explanation given by the employee, or other information that is significant

Progressive discipline: Written warning

A written warning is more serious than a verbal warning and represents a progression in the progressive discipline process. In documenting a written warning, include

- The employee's name
- The date of the conversation
- The specific offense or rule violation
- References to previous conversations and verbal warnings about the problem
- A specific statement of the expected performance
- An explanation given by the employee or other information that is significant
- A statement indicating your confidence in the employee's ability to perform properly in the future
- The employee's signature; if the employee refuses to give it, include a note on the signature line indicating your attempt to get the employee to sign and his or her refusal to do so

Progressive discipline: Formal

- Reprimand
- Transfer to another position in the same class
- Suspension without pay or with reduced pay
- Demotion (reduction in rank or pay)
- Termination (removal)

The more severe forms of disciplinary action, that is, written reprimand, suspension, demotion, and termination, must be administered appropriately according to established county rules and regulations. It is essential that the appointing authority or his or her designee carefully assesses each instance of unacceptable performance or conduct in a precise and thorough manner, consulting their departmental human resources officer and/or group human resources director, as necessary.

Serious instances of unacceptable job performance or conduct may require formal disciplinary action at the outset to provide an appropriate remedy or to protect the agency or other employees.

The patient, diligent, consistent, equitable, and appropriate application of department rules and regulations is the foundation for exercising effective discipline.

An appointing authority who is considering disciplinary action and who desires additional guidance on the applicable policies or procedures should contact their Internal Affairs, Labor Relations Division, or Department of Human Resources for assistance.

Supervising members of police agencies (sergeants, lieutenants, and captains) should avoid, as far as circumstances warrant, censuring a subordinate in the presence of others, and should support a subordinate when that member is acting within their rights.

Performance reports are not considered a disciplinary device. However, ratings of "improvement needed" or "unsatisfactory" performance or conduct on a regular or supplemental report can support disciplinary action.

Formal discipline procedures and processes require police supervisors to have a solid understanding of police officer rights to ensure that the discipline is administered in a fair and equitable manner. Formal incidents are typically investigated by a police agency internal affairs division, as opposed to a line supervisor, but this may not be the case in all agencies.

When investigating a complaint against an officer which may result in formal discipline, it is critical that the police supervisor establish the truth, maintain integrity, and remain fair during the investigative process.

of force. There is no correct or ideal continuum design in existence. Rather, agencies across the country simply prefer one design over another. These designs are basic examples of some of the continuum designs currently in use. An agency's continuum may vary to some extent in terms of the number and location of resistance/force options.

Summary

- With the explosion of mass media, any incidents in which the police are alleged to have used excessive force will be extensively covered in the media.
- Officers need to realize that, in present-day policing, they are working under the microscope of the media.
- Any use of force will be examined in multiple different ways to see if the officer(s) used excessive force.
- Law enforcement officers are authorized to use force in specified circumstances. They are trained to use force under appropriate conditions.
- According to the IACP, there is no universally agreed-upon definition of the use of force. It defines the use of force as the amount of effort required by the police to compel compliance by an unwilling subject.
- *Police brutality* is a phrase used to describe instances of serious physical or psychological harm to civilians, with an emphasis on cruelty or savageness.
- The term *excessive force* is used to describe situations in which more force is used than is allowable, when judged in terms of administrative or professional guidelines or legal standards.

- *Improper, abusive, illegitimate,* and *unnecessary* use of force are terms that describe situations in which an officer's authority to use force has been mishandled in some general way.
- To establish an excessive use of force claim, a plaintiff must demonstrate an injury (injury must be more than a *de minimis* injury), which resulted directly and only from the use of force that was excessive to the need, and where the force used was objectively unreasonable.
- The use of excessive force by an officer is generally considered a crime of assault or battery.
- Assault is the crime of threatening to commit a battery or an attempt to commit a battery.
- The crime of battery is generally defined as the unlawful and offensive touching of another person.
- The electric discharge of a taser is extremely painful and overrides the body's nervous system, usually causing a suspect to fall down or otherwise cease resistance long enough for the officers to handcuff the suspect or otherwise regain control.
- The courts have traditionally used the rules set forth by the U.S. Supreme Court in *Graham v. Connor* to determine whether or not the use of a taser has constituted excessive force.
- In *Graham*, the court held that the "reasonableness" of a particular use of force must be judged from the perspective of a reasonable officer on the scene, rather than with the 20/20 vision of hindsight.
- While some departments are quite restrictive in terms of allowing officers to use more severe forms of force only on actively aggressive suspects, other

agencies are quite liberal and place a large amount of discretion in officers' hands by allowing them to use nearly all types of force against nearly all types of resistance faced, short of extreme imbalance (e.g., allowing a baton strike to a compliant suspect).

Practicums

Practicum one

Kenneth Siler filed a suit against the Crestview Police Department and several of the police officers alleging the excessive use of force and battery. It appeared that Siler refused to obey an officer's order to move from an area where an ambulance and its crew were attending to an injured person. The officer placed his hand on Siler's chest to make him back away.

As trial judge how would you rule regarding the excessive force and the battery claims?

[See: Siler v. Floyd, 476 Fed. Appx. 710 (11th cir. 2012)]

Practicum two

On the evening of October 17, Koeiman entered the 44th precinct station house in the Bronx. Police Officer Mondello approached Koeiman, who was under the influence of alcohol, and asked whether he could assist him. Koeiman, without provocation or warning, punched Officer Mondello in the face. Officer Mondello took a step back before attempting to restrain Koeiman by grabbing his shoulders. Another police officer, Officer Carson, who witnessed Koeiman punch Officer Mondello, "jumped" on both Koeiman and Officer Mondello. Officer Carson took this action because he wanted to get Koeiman on the floor as quickly as possible, which would allow the officers to restrain Koeiman and prevent him from punching either of the officers. Notably, both officers testified that Koeiman was resisting Officer Mondello's efforts to subdue him. As a result of Officer Carson's action, the three men fell to the floor, thus permitting the officers to handcuff Koeiman. The officers then picked Koeiman up off the floor. Both officers insisted that neither of them punched, kicked, or otherwise struck Koeiman. The entire incident—from the moment Koeiman struck Officer Mondello to the moment the officers picked Koeiman up off the floor—lasted between 5 and 15 seconds.

After getting Koeiman to his feet, Officer Carson noticed that one of Koeiman's legs was injured. The officers escorted Koeiman to another room in the precinct and summoned an ambulance for Koeiman. Emergency medical technicians arrived at the precinct, immobilized the decedent's injured leg, and transported him to a local hospital. Koeiman was diagnosed with a comminuted fracture of the left femur.

Did the officers' treatment of Koeiman constitute excessive force?

[See Koeiman v. City of New York, 829 N.Y.S. 2nd 24 (2007)]

Practicum three

RIVERSIDE, CA—A former officer with the San Bernardino Police Department (SBPD) was sentenced today to 300 months in federal prison for violating the civil rights charges of two women he forced to perform sex acts while he was in uniform.

Jose Jesus Perez, 47, of Menifee, received the sentence from U.S. District Judge Virginia A. Phillips.

Perez was found guilty by a federal jury in May of two felony counts and one misdemeanor count of deprivation of rights under color of law for sexually assaulting two victims in 2011. The jury determined that both felony offenses involved aggravated sexual abuse and that one attack involved a kidnapping and bodily injury.

The evidence presented during a week-long trial showed that Perez groped a woman and coerced her to perform oral sex on him by using force against her on April 25, 2011.

The jury also found that Perez had unlawful sexual intercourse with another woman on two occasions in August 2011.

The testimony at trial indicated that the two victims, who worked as prostitutes in the City of San Bernardino, engaged in the sex acts demanded by Perez out of fear of arrest because he was a police officer. One victim testified that he forced her to perform oral sex on him in his patrol car, and the other victim testified that he forced her to have intercourse with him next to his patrol car in a vacant lot and again in motel rooms.

A third woman testified that Perez had aggressively solicited sex from her while he was in uniform when he found her stranded in San Bernardino. The three women each testified that they feared repercussions if they did not comply with Perez's demands.

Perez "has a long and escalating history of inappropriate sexual behavior towards women," prosecutors wrote in a sentencing brief that noted a lengthy history of misconduct toward women. "Although defendant is no longer a police officer and is no longer able to abuse a position of public authority to his own criminal ends, he remains the same person—someone who lacks basic respect for the humanity and autonomy of women. Unfortunately, sexual predators in this county do not lack for means of carrying out their crimes, and a badge is unnecessary for their purposes. Defendant poses a greater danger than most sexual predators; although he lacks a badge, he retains his police tactical training and knowledge of police investigative methods. Defendant remains a threat to the public regardless of his employment."

Perez became a police officer in 1997, when he was hired by the Los Angeles Police Department (LAPD). Perez worked for the LAPD until 2008, when he went to work for the SBPD. Perez was released from employment by the SBPD in December 2012 and has been in custody since he was arrested in September 2013 in Texas.

The investigation into Perez was conducted by the SBPD and the Federal Bureau of Investigation (FBI).

What actions should be taken to reduce a city's chances of hiring and retaining officers such as Perez?

Discussion questions

1. What constitutes "excessive force"?
2. Explain the meaning of "qualified immunity."
3. When is it permissible for a police officer to use a taser?
4. Explain the use of force matrixes.
5. When may a police officer use force to arrest a person for a minor offense?
6. Explain the Graham Rule.

References

1. As reported by Jerome H. Skolnick and James J. Fyre (1993) *Above the Law: Police and the Excessive Use of Force.* New York: Free Press, p. 1.
2. Christine Byers (October 28, 2015) Former St. Louis prosecutor admits covering up officer's assault on handcuffed suspect. *St. Louis Post Dispatch*, p. A-1.
3. Matthew J. Hickman (2006) Citizen complaints about police use of force. Bureau of Justice Statistics Special Report, Washington, DC: Bureau of Justice Statistics, p. 1.
4. International Association of the Chiefs of Police (2001) *Police Use of Force in America.* Alexandria, VA: IACP.
5. National Institute of Justice Report "Use of Force by Police" (1999) Report NCJ 176330, p. 4.
6. Kimberly T. Owens (Fall, 2000) Maryland's common law right to resist unlawful arrest: Does it really exist? *University of Baltimore Law Review*, 30, 213.
7. Don Baldwin (November 4, 2015) Video cited as more officers face charges in killings. *St. Louis Post Dispatch*, p. C-1.
8. The *Guardian* website at http://www.theguardian.com/us-news/2015/nov/05/police-tasers-deaths-the-counted. Accessed on November 5, 2015.
9. Police Executive Research Forum (March, 2011) *2011 Electronic Control Weapon Guidelines.* Washington, DC: Police Executive Research Forum. pp. 11–15.
10. Jay Zitter (2009) When does use of taser constitute violation of constitutional rights. 45 American Law Reports, 6th ed.
11. As reported by CNN Website at http://edition.cnn.com/2008/WORLD/europe/11/24/britain.tasers/index.html. Accessed on October 12, 2015.
12. As reported on BBC News Website at http://www.bbc.com/news/uk-24029706. Accessed on October 12, 2015.
13. William Terrill, Eugene Paoline, and Jason Ingram (2001) Final technical report draft: Assessing police use of force policy and outcomes. Document No. 237794. Washington, DC: DOJ.
14. Matthew O'Deane currently works for the San Diego County, California District Attorney Office. This article was written especially for this text.

chapter four

Use of deadly force

Learning objectives

After studying this chapter, the reader should understand the following concepts and issues:

- How frequently law enforcement officers use deadly force in the United States compared with other countries.
- The rules on the use of deadly force by law enforcement officers.
- When is the use of deadly force justified?
- The Federal Bureau of Investigation (FBI) policy on the use of deadly force.
- The guidelines issued by the U.S. Supreme Court in *Tennessee v. Gardner*.

Introduction

An article published by *Economist* magazine, shortly after the Ferguson shooting, indicated that "last year, in total, British police officers actually fired their weapons three times." The number three resonated when the private autopsy of Michael Brown, the teenager killed by Ferguson, Missouri, police officer Darren Wilson concluded that Brown was shot at least six times. Many tweets contrasted the numbers, saying Wilson had fired more shots at Brown than British police officers had discharged in all of 2013.[1] The article noted that, even after adjusting for the smaller size of Britain's population, British citizens are about 100 times less likely to be shot by a police officer than American citizens. The article also pointed out that, between 2010 and 2014, the police force of Albuquerque, New Mexico, shot and killed 23 citizens. This was seven times more than the number of British killed by all of England and Wales 43 police forces. According to the article, in 2012, British officers actually fired their weapons only one time whereas the FBI reported that 410 Americans were justifiably killed by the police.

The article also noted that American police officers are also far more likely to be killed than British police officers. For example, in 2013, 30 American police officers were shot and killed in the line of duty compared with none in the England and Wales police forces. The article stated: "Add to that a hyper-militarized police culture and a deep history of racial strife and you have

the reason why so many civilians are shot by police officers. Unless America can either reduce its colossal gun ownership rates or fix its deep social problems, shootings of civilians by police—justified or not—seem sure to continue." (Box 4.1).

When is the use of deadly force justified?

The leading case on when the police may use deadly force is the U.S. Supreme Court case of *Tennessee v. Garner*.* In the *Garner* case, a father, whose son was shot by a police officer as he was fleeing from the burglary of an unoccupied house, brought a wrongful death action under the federal civil rights statute against the police officer who fired the shot, the police department, and others. The U.S. District Court rendered judgment for the defendants, and the father appealed. The court of appeals reversed and remanded. The Supreme Court, Justice White, when writing the majority opinion held that

1. Apprehension by use of deadly force is a seizure, subject to the Fourth Amendment's reasonableness requirement.
2. Deadly force may not be used unless it is necessary to prevent escape and the officer has probable cause to believe that the suspect poses a significant threat of death or serious physical injury to the officer or others.
3. The Tennessee statute under authority of which the police officer fired the fatal shot was unconstitutional insofar as it authorized the use of deadly force against an apparently unarmed, nondangerous fleeing suspect.
4. The fact that the unarmed suspect had broken into a dwelling at night did not automatically mean that he was dangerous.

Justice White noted that the Tennessee statute is unconstitutional insofar as it authorizes the use of deadly force against, as in this case, an apparently unarmed, nondangerous fleeing suspect; such force may not be used unless necessary to prevent escape and where the officer has probable cause to believe that the

---

* Tennessee v. Garner, 471 U.S. 1 (1985).

BOX 4.1   WHAT IS THE FBI'S POLICY ON THE USE OF DEADLY FORCE BY ITS SPECIAL AGENTS?

FBI special agents may use deadly force only when necessary—when the agent has a reasonable belief that the subject of such force poses an imminent danger of death or serious physical injury to the agent or another person. If feasible, a verbal warning to submit to the authority of the special agent is given prior to the use of deadly force.

suspect poses a significant threat of death or serious physical injury to the officer or others.

In this case, Justice White stated that, whenever an officer restrains the freedom of a person to walk away, he has seized that person. While it is not always clear exactly when minimal police interference becomes a seizure, there can be no question that apprehension by the use of deadly force is a seizure subject to the reasonableness requirement of the Fourth Amendment.

The court noted that a police officer may arrest a person if he or she has probable cause to believe that that person committed a crime. Petitioners and appellants argue that, if this requirement is satisfied, the Fourth Amendment has nothing to say about how that seizure is made. This submission ignores the many cases in which the court, by balancing the extent of the intrusion against the need for it, has examined the reasonableness of the manner in which a search or seizure is conducted. To determine the constitutionality of a seizure, a court must balance the nature and quality of the intrusion on the individual's Fourth Amendment interests against the importance of the governmental interests alleged to justify the intrusion. The court has described "the balancing of competing interests" as "the key principle of the Fourth Amendment." Because one of the factors is the extent of the intrusion, it is clear that reasonableness depends not only on when a seizure is made, but also on how it is carried out.

Applying these principles to particular facts, the court held that governmental interests did not support a lengthy detention of luggage and an airport seizure not "carefully tailored to its underlying justification, or detention for fingerprinting without probable cause." On the other hand, under the same approach, it has upheld the taking of fingernail scrapings from a suspect, administrative housing inspections without probable cause to believe that a code violation will be found, and a blood test of a drunk-driving suspect. In each of these cases, the question was whether the totality of the circumstances justified a particular sort of search or seizure.

The court held that, notwithstanding probable cause to seize a suspect, an officer may not always do so by killing him or her. The intrusiveness of a seizure by means of deadly force is unmatched. The suspect's fundamental interest in his or her own life need not be elaborated on. The use of deadly force also frustrates the interest of the individual, and of society, in the judicial

determination of guilt and punishment. Against these interests range governmental interests in effective law enforcement.

The court noted the argument that overall violence would be reduced by encouraging the peaceful submission of suspects who know that they may be shot if they flee. Effectiveness in making arrests requires a resort to deadly force, or at least the meaningful threat thereof. "Being able to arrest such individuals is a condition precedent to the state's entire system of law enforcement."

The court stated that, without in any way disparaging the importance of these goals, they are not convinced that the use of deadly force is a sufficiently productive means of accomplishing them to justify the killing of nonviolent suspects. The use of deadly force is a self-defeating way of apprehending a suspect and so setting the criminal justice mechanism in motion. If successful, it guarantees that that mechanism will not be set in motion. And while the meaningful threat of deadly force might be thought to lead to the arrest of more live suspects by discouraging escape attempts, the presently available evidence does not support this thesis. The fact is that a majority of police departments in this country have forbidden the use of deadly force against nonviolent suspects. If those charged with the enforcement of the criminal law have abjured the use of deadly force in arresting nondangerous felons, there is a substantial basis for doubting that the use of such force is an essential attribute of the arrest power in all felony cases. Petitioners and appellants have not persuaded us that the shooting of nondangerous fleeing suspects is so vital as to outweigh the suspect's interest in his or her own life.

The court stated that the use of deadly force to prevent the escape of all felony suspects, whatever the circumstances, was constitutionally unreasonable. The court stated that it was not better that all felony suspects die than that they escape. Where the suspect poses no immediate threat to the officer and no threat to others, the harm resulting from failing to apprehend him or her does not justify the use of deadly force to do so. It is no doubt unfortunate when a suspect who is in sight escapes, but the fact that the police arrive a little late or are a little slower afoot than the suspect does not always justify killing the suspect. A police officer may not seize an unarmed, nondangerous suspect by shooting him or her dead. The Tennessee statute is unconstitutional insofar as it authorizes the use of deadly force against such fleeing suspects.

The court stated that, where the officer has probable cause to believe that a suspect poses a threat of serious physical harm, either to the officer or to others, it is not constitutionally unreasonable to prevent escape by using deadly force. Thus, if the suspect threatens the officer with a weapon or there is probable cause to believe that he or she has committed a crime involving the infliction or threatened infliction of serious physical harm, deadly force may be used if necessary to prevent escape if, where feasible, some warning has been given. As applied in such circumstances, the Tennessee statute would pass constitutional muster.

The court disagreed with the principle that the Fourth Amendment must be construed in light of the common-law rule, which allowed the use of whatever force was necessary to effect the arrest of a fleeing felon, though not a misdemeanant.

The court noted that there is an additional reason why the common-law rule cannot be directly translated to the present day. The common-law rule was developed at a time when weapons were rudimentary. Deadly force could be inflicted almost solely in a hand-to-hand struggle during which, necessarily, the safety of the arresting officer was at risk. Handguns were not carried by police officers until the latter half of the 1900s. Only then did it become possible to use deadly force from a distance as a means of apprehension. As a practical matter, the use of deadly force under the standard articulation of the common-law rule now has an altogether different meaning—and harsher consequences—than in past centuries (Box 4.2).

Probable cause

In *Price v. Sery*,* Gwen Price, as the personal representative of a deceased motorist, brought suit against the City of Portland and others. The deceased was shot by a city police officer during a routine traffic stop. Price alleged improper use of deadly force by the officer.

Portland Police Bureau (PPB) policy, training, and discipline practices, with respect to the use of lethal force, are relevant to the constitutional claims. The use of deadly force is governed by PPB General Order (GO) § 1010.10, the relevant part of which reads as follows:

* 513 F.3rd 962 (2008).

The Bureau recognizes that members may be required to use deadly force when their life or the life of another is jeopardized by the actions of others. Therefore, state statute and Bureau policy provide for the use of deadly force under the following circumstances:

1. Members may use deadly force to protect themselves or others from what they reasonably believe to be an immediate threat of death or serious physical injury.
2. A member may use deadly force to effect the capture or prevent the escape of a suspect where the member has probable cause to believe that the suspect poses a significant threat of death or serious physical injury to the member or others.
3. If feasible, some warning has been given.

Specifically, Price argued that the city's policy, expressed in G.O. § 1010.10, where an officer reasonably believes that a suspect poses an immediate threat of serious physical injury or death falls short of the probable cause requirement set forth in the *Tennessee v. Garner* case. Price claimed that the city's policy only requires that the officer reasonably believes that he or she is confronted by an immediate threat. Price argues that reasonable belief is of a different, and lesser, standard than probable cause.

The appellate court held that it was satisfied that the case law did not support Price's contention that reasonable belief is of a lesser standard than probable cause, as a matter of law. Both standards are objective and depend on the circumstances confronting the officer rather than on the officer's mere subjective beliefs or intentions, however sincere. The case law requires that a reasonable officer under the circumstances believes himself or herself, or others, to face a threat of serious physical harm before using deadly force. Moreover, as the Supreme Court has stated, the touchstone of the inquiry is "reasonableness," which does not admit an "easy-to-apply legal test." The city's policy requires that an officer has a reasonable belief in an "immediate threat of death or serious physical injury," and thus comports with the requirement.

Who is killed by the police?

According to writer Al Vicens, Native Americans get shot by cops at an astonishing rate and the media rarely mentions it. Vicens uses as an example the killing of

Paul Castaway, a Lakota Sioux, in July 2015 in downtown Denver. According to the reports, the police stated that a man was coming toward an officer with a knife, but the man's family and witnesses at the scene disputed those claims and stated that he was pointing the knife at himself. Witnesses at the scene stated that he was holding the knife to his own throat and was not threatening the officers.[2]

He was shot four times and died later that night. Castaway's mother had called 911 after her son caused a disturbance at her apartment, which was about a block away from the mobile home park where he was shot. She said that her son suffered from a mental illness and an addiction, and that she had called the police for help because he was experiencing some sort of mental episode. His mother reported that Castaway struggled with schizophrenia and alcoholism.

According to the writer, Castaway's death brings up a rarely discussed aspect of the ongoing conversation around police brutality in the United States–Native Americans are more likely than most other racial groups to be killed by police. According to the Center on Juvenile and Criminal Justice, a nonprofit organization that studies incarceration and criminal justice issues, police kill Native Americans at a higher rate than any other ethnic group.[3]

The center's analysis relied on data from the Centers for Disease Control and Prevention and the National Center for Health Statistics. It found that Native Americans, making up just 0.8% of the population, are the victims in 1.9% of police killings. When the numbers are broken down further, they reveal that Native Americans make up three of the top five age groups killed by law enforcement. According to the center, the following groups are most likely to be killed by law enforcement:

- African Americans aged 20–24: 7.1 per million population per year
- Native Americans aged 24–35: 6.6 per million population per year
- Native Americans aged 35–44: 5.9 per million population per year
- African Americans aged 25–34: 5.6 per million population per year
- Native Americans aged 20–24: 4.6 per million population per year
- Latinos aged 20–24: 4.4 per million population per year
- Latinos aged 25–34: 3.2 per million population per year
- African Americans aged 35–44: 3.0 per million population per year
- African Americans aged 15–19: 2.9 per million population per year
- Average, all races and ages: 1.2 per million population per year

According to the center, the five states or jurisdictions where a person is most likely to be killed by law enforcement are New Mexico, Nevada, District of Columbia, Oregon, and Maryland. California ranks sixth from the top. Alabama, North Carolina, New Jersey, Massachusetts, and New York are the safest (or, perhaps, the worst at reporting).[3]

The center reports that the major counties and urban jurisdictions with the highest rates of law enforcement killings are Wyandotte County (Kansas City); Denver County, Baltimore (city), Norfolk (city); and Anderson County, South Carolina; interestingly, Harris County (Houston) has the lowest reported rate. Fresno, Riverside, Kern, San Bernardino, and San Diego have the highest rates in California; Contra Costa has the lowest.

The racial group most likely to be killed by law enforcement is Native Americans, followed by African Americans, Latinos, whites, and Asian Americans. Latinos are victimized by police killings at a level 30% above average and 1.9 times the rate of white, non-Latinos.

One-fourth of those killed by law enforcement are under the age of 25, 54% are aged 25–44, and nearly one-fourth are aged 45 and older. Teenagers comprise only 7% of all police killings. The risk of an older teen aged 15–19 being killed by police is about the same as for a 50 year old; for a younger teen aged 10–14, the risk is about the same as for an 80 year old.

It is interesting to note that police killings of African Americans aged 25 years and older have declined by 61% from the late 1960s, but that the rates for younger African Americans are still 4.5 times higher than for other races and ages.

An attorney with the Lakota People's Law Project stated "You can tell they're shooting out of fear. If it's not out of hate, for some reason they're pulling the trigger before determining what the actually is. Something does need to happen. Somebody does need to take a look and we need help."[2]

Deaths that caused public outcry

According to a *Washington Post* analysis on police use of deadly force, only a small number of shootings involving deadly force by the police occur under circumstances that raise doubts and draw public outcry. The *Post* states that the vast majority of individuals shot and killed by police officers were armed with guns and were killed after attacking police officers or civilians or making other direct threats.[4] It also claimed that Jim Pasco, the executive director of the National Fraternal Order of Police, confirmed the *Post*'s finding.

The *Post* reported that, in 74% of all fatal police shootings, the victims had already fired shots, brandished a gun, or attacked a person with a weapon or with their bare hands. Also, 16% of the shootings happened after incidents that did not involve firearms or active attacks but featured other potentially dangerous threats. These shootings were mostly of individuals who brandished knives and refused to drop them. The majority of the 5% of cases that caused public outcry involved victims who failed to follow police orders, made sudden movements, or were accidentally shot. In 4% of the total number of shootings, the *Post* stated that their analysis was unable to determine the circumstances of the shooting because of limited information or ongoing investigations.

The *Post* stated that it would track all fatal shootings by the police while on duty, and reported that both the FBI and the U.S. Attorney General acknowledged the need to more thoroughly collect data on fatal police shootings.

In the *Post*'s study of 595 fatal police shootings in the partial year 2015, in which a person fired a gun, brandished a gun, or attacked an officer or individual with a weapon or bare hands

- The most common encounter (242 cases) occurred when individuals pointed or brandished a gun but had not fired a weapon at a person.
- The next largest group (224 cases) involved situations where the victim was firing a gun at an officer or a bystander. In 87% of these cases, the gunfire was directed at the officer.
- In 129 cases, the individuals had attacked police officers or civilians but had no gun. They were armed instead with weapons such as knives, hatchets, chemical agents, and vehicles. Seventy percent of these attacks were directed toward the police.

During the period of time covered by the *Post*'s research, there were 205 cases in which no opinions could be formed regarding the circumstances of the killing because of a lack of information or because of an ongoing investigation (Box 4.3).

Deaths where the police were held liable in civil court

As noted in a journal article by H. Lee and M.S. Vaughn, the police use of deadly force is a significant concern for municipal policymakers and law enforcement agencies.[6] Police agencies and municipal entities may be held civilly liable under Section 1983 for force that is not objectively reasonable; for failure to train; and for policies, customs, and practices that cause constitutional injury. Lee and Vaugh analyzed 86 cases from the U.S. District Courts and the U.S. Courts of Appeals on Section 1983 liability regarding police use of deadly force. Their research focused specifically on police firearm use in deadly force situations, highlighting how managerial disorganization and administrative breakdown impacts departmental decision-making.

The researchers noted that federal courts are more likely to find the police liable when they use deadly force against unarmed, nonviolent, and nonthreatening fleeing suspects. They noted that oftentimes, long and dangerous high-speed chases and foot pursuits make police officers frustrated because of "adrenalin overload," which leads to the application of excessive force. Police must not use deadly force against suspects who are surrendering. While most police–citizen encounters begin with misdemeanor or nonviolent crimes, police officers sometimes believe that their safety is threatened

---

BOX 4.3   WHEN COPS KILL: THE PSYCHOLOGY OF DEADLY-FORCE ENCOUNTERS

LAURENCE MILLER

According to a research study by Dr. Laurence Miller, 85 percent of the police officers killed in the line of duty never discharged their service weapons. He concludes that this indicates that officers are far from being trigger-happy gunslingers, many police officers hesitate in using justifiable deadly force, even when it puts their own safety in jeopardy.

Dr. Miller notes that police culture is still important. According to him, all things being equal three factors have found to be associated with fewer police deadly force encounters in a community. Those are:

- The higher overall educational level of the rank and file patrol force.
- Higher investment in mental health response and verbal crisis intervention training.
- Greater efforts at police-community relationship building.

If these three factors reduce police deadly force, why are more police departments not using these factors to reduce the use of deadly force? [5]

when it is not, thus creating conditions for unnecessary deadly force.

Cases where they identified that the individual officer was liable were classified under the following classes:

- Use of deadly force against suspects who were surrendering to police authority
  - Failure of the officer to control adrenalin overload resulting from a hot pursuit
  - Street justice
- Deadly use of force against uncooperative suspects
  - Failure to handle "suicide by cop" situations
  - Failure to consider a suspect's intoxication
  - Abuse of authority
  - Injuring a citizen by failure to apply "knock and announce" procedures
  - Killing a suspect while chasing a fleeing suspect on foot
  - Killing a suspect who refused to open a door
  - Killing a suspect who was holding a pipe
  - Killing a suspect 90 seconds after contact
  - Killing a citizen after a private altercation
- Reckless use of deadly force
  - Misidentification of a suspect
  - Friendly fire

The researcher noted that the code of silence frequently hampers an investigation into an officer-involved deadly incident. The researchers noted that the code of silence can be defined as unwillingness to report official police misconduct to protect colleagues. Unusually strong solidarity in police work, formulated by low predictability and potential danger, drives police to maintain a code of silence that emphasizes loyalty to the department and to other officers and makes officers reluctant to report unethical behavior to the proper authorities. In addition, federal courts have found that maintaining a code of silence may cause the police to turn a blind eye to serious police wrongdoing.

Arrest-related deaths (ARD) program

The Arrest-Related Deaths (ARD) program is an annual national census of persons who die either during the process of arrest or while in the custody of state or local law enforcement personnel. The Bureau of Justice Statistics (BJS) implemented the ARD program in 2003 as part of the Deaths in Custody Reporting Program (DCRP). The DCRP was initiated to fulfill the data collection requirement of the Deaths in Custody Reporting Act of 2000 (DICRA, P.L. 106-247). It collects in-depth information on deaths during arrest and incarceration and provides national-level information on the deaths

of suspects and offenders from their initial contact with law enforcement personnel through to the time that they are incarcerated in jail or prison.[7]

ARD data are collected to quantify and describe the circumstances surrounding civilian deaths that take place during an arrest or while in the custody of law enforcement. These data describe the prevalence and incidence of arrest-related deaths across the nation, identify the circumstances or activities that contribute to these deaths, and reveal trends in the causes and circumstances of these deaths in custody at national and state levels. These data can be used to inform specific policies that may increase the safety of law enforcement officers and citizens, identify training needs in law enforcement agencies, and assist in developing prevention strategies.

The current ARD program relies on state reporting coordinators (SRCs) in each of the 50 states and the District of Columbia to identify and report all eligible cases of arrest-related deaths. The BJS compiles data from the states to produce national-level statistics on deaths that occur in the process of arrest by, or while in the custody of, state and local law enforcement personnel. When the DICRA reporting requirements ended in 2006, the BJS undertook efforts to understand the variability between and within SRCs over time, in terms of data collection methodologies and available resources. This variability has led to concerns about definitions, data quality, and undercoverage error.

Highlights of the program

- The ARD program collects information on deaths that occur in the process of arrest.
- An arrest-related death is defined as any death (e.g., gunshot wound, cardiac arrest, or drowning) that occurs during an interaction with state or local law enforcement personnel, including those that occur
  - During an attempted arrest or in the process of arrest
  - While the person is in law enforcement custody (before transfer to jail)
  - Shortly after the person's freedom to leave is restricted.
- Exclusions include
  - Deaths of bystanders, hostages, and law enforcement personnel
  - Deaths occurring during an interaction with federal law enforcement agents
  - Deaths of wanted criminal suspects before police contact
  - Deaths by vehicular pursuits without any direct police action

Methodology

Centralized SRCs operate the state-level ARD data collection. The ARD program has three main tasks:

- To identify arrest-related deaths
- To acquire information about arrest-related deaths
- To submit the CJ-11 form, *Quarterly Summary of Arrest-Related Deaths* (or summary of incidents) and the CJ-11A form, *Arrest-Related Death Report* (or incident report)

SRCs use one or more of the following sources to identify eligible ARD cases:

- Law enforcement
- Medical examiner or coroner
- Prosecutor's office
- Uniform crime reports (UCRs)
- National Violent Deaths Reporting System (NVDRS)
- Open-source media search

Perceptions of deadly force

Shannon Bohrer and Robert Chaney contend that police investigations of the use of deadly force can influence perceptions and outcomes.[8] The authors note that the law enforcement profession spends considerable time and resources in training officers to use firearms and other weapons and to understand the constitutional standards and agency policies concerning when they can employ such force. Society expects this effort because of the possible consequences of officers not having the skills they need if and when they become involved in a critical incident.

The authors recommend that, in addition to receiving instruction about the use of force, officers should be taught investigative techniques. They must reconstruct the incident, find the facts, and gather evidence to prosecute the offenders. Historically, they have done this extremely well. But the authors questioned whether the same amount of attention is paid to examining the investigative process of the use of deadly force and how this can affect what occurs after such an event. The authors conclude that there are many reasons why the police should approach the investigation of an officer-involved shooting differently. To help answer these questions, the authors present an overview of perceptions about these events and some elements that law enforcement agencies can incorporate into investigations of officer-involved shootings to help ensure fair and judicious outcomes. The authors point out that, just because the officer had the right to shoot and the evidence supports the officer's actions, a positive, or even a neutral, reception from the public may not be guaranteed.

The authors point out that public perceptions of officer-involved shootings are usually as wide and diverse as the population, often driven by media coverage, and sometimes influenced by a long-standing bias and mistrust of government. Documented cases of riots, property damage, and loss of life have occurred in communities where residents have perceived a police shooting as unjustified. Some members of the public seem to automatically assume that the officer did something wrong before any investigation into the incident begins. Conversely, others believe that if the police shot somebody, the individual must not have given the officer any choice.

Departmental perceptions can also prove diverse and difficult to express according to the authors. They point out that, when interviewed, one chief of police advised that "it is sometimes easier to go through an officer being killed in the line of duty than a questionable police shooting." The chief was referring to the public's response, including civil unrest, to what was perceived as an unjustified police shooting. At various levels, however, administrators may feel that a full and fair investigation will clear up any negative perceptions by the public. While not all-inclusive, departmental perceptions include many instances where an officer-involved shooting was viewed with clear and objective clarity before, during, and after the investigation.

The authors recommend six elements for correctly investigating officer-involved shootings. While the elements are not meant to be all-inclusive or broad enough to cover every conceivable situation, they appear to be useful as a guide. The six elements are

- Investigators need to have correct and neutral attitudes. Not all officers are suited to conducting police-shooting investigations.
- There must be an appropriate response to and protection of the crime scene. Homicide or criminal investigators should protect the site.
- The officers involved should be removed from the scene as soon as possible and taken to a secure location away from other witnesses and media personnel.
- The investigators need to gain the confidence and respect of civilian witnesses. After all, they need their assistance. In most cases, investigators should handle witnesses the same way as the officers involved.
- The need to have these cases vetted through the criminal justice process as soon as possible is critical for the involved officers, their families, and their employing agencies.

- The department's public information officer should contact the media before their representatives approach the agency. In the early stages of the investigation, the department should demonstrate that it wants to cooperate with the media. By informing the public through press releases and interviews, the agency shows that it is investigating the incident and that as soon as information can be released, it will be. Departments should remember that the proverbial "no comment" often gives the impression that the police are hiding something.

Duty to provide medical assistance

According to one news report, a man shot by an off-duty Houston, Texas, police officer lay bleeding from two gunshots in his abdomen for 15 minutes as the responding officers stood by without providing first aid. At one point, the victim, a 53-year-old black man, raised his head and an officer used his foot to keep the man's face on the pavement. From the time the episode was first reported, it took more than an hour for the man to arrive at an emergency room. An hour after his arrival at the hospital in an ambulance, he was dead. The length of time that the dying man was left unassisted for has angered his relatives and has been criticized by two witnesses to the episode and by law enforcement officials.

"He was shot twice, bleeding, and nobody did anything," said his mother. She also stated: "I don't think that if he was white they would have just left him like that. A dog would have gotten more attention than he did."

It is unclear if the victim, a former computer programmer, would have survived if the officers had rendered aid before the paramedics arrived. But experts on police procedure and law enforcement officials who examined the video said that the off-duty officer and his colleagues should have done more to assist him.

He was shot by an off-duty Harris County deputy constable after getting into a confrontation with the officer at an apartment complex northwest of Houston. A video shows the dying man sprawled in a parking lot before an ambulance arrives, as officers put up crime scene tape and put him in handcuffs. They talk to him and walk by him, but at other times they leave him alone, bleeding, and are not in view of the camera.[9]

This appears to be an issue in need of attention. For example, some police agencies require officers who use force to perform first aid on injured suspects. For instance, one police department has a policy stating that "the involved officer will render first aid to the individual until the arrival of E.M.S. unit." Many departments, however, only place a duty on the officer to ensure that paramedics are notified.

In *Wilson v. Meets,** the U.S. Court of Appeals for the Tenth Circuit commented on the duty of a law enforcement officer to render medical aid after the suspect had been shot by the officer: "We have found no authority suggesting that the due process clause establishes an affirmative duty on the part of police officers to render CPR in any and all circumstances." The district court erred in holding that it was a police officer's duty to provide medical treatment in all situations. The appellate court held that there was no duty to give, as well as summon, medical assistance, even if the police officers are trained in CPR. The district court here cited no other authority for the duty to render medical aid or for guidance on what circumstances would mandate action.

Nevertheless, the appellate court noted that there is a difference between medical aid and first aid. Few citizens would be likely to want police officers to render medical aid. Such steps are best left to the qualified and highly trained personnel who act as paramedics or emergency medical technicians (EMTs). However, anyone can render first aid. The goal of first aid is to sustain life until those who can render medical aid arrive. As the plaintiffs suggested, first aid attends to the patient's "ABC"—airway, breathing, and circulation, and is a limited form of intervention with the immediate goal of preventing death. The appellate court stated that they did not hold that police officers never have a duty to give first aid.

The court further noted that this was a case of both malfeasance and nonfeasance. The court denied the city's request for a summary judgment, with the statement that "Taking the facts as most favorable to plaintiffs, defendants took deliberate actions that may have aggravated the dying person's medical needs."

In *Howard v. Dickerson,*† a police officer arrested a woman in her home following a hit-and-run accident. The officer handcuffed the woman, despite her statements that she had recently undergone neck surgery and that handcuffing her hands behind her back would be painful. Ms. Howard was wearing a neck brace when she was arrested. The court held that Ms. Howard had stated a cause of action under section 1983 for failure of the police to render first aid.

Excited delirium syndrome

Excited delirium syndrome (ExDS) is a serious and potentially deadly medical condition involving psychotic behavior, elevated temperature, and an extreme fight-or-flight response by the nervous system. Failure to recognize the symptoms and involve emergency medical services (EMS) to provide appropriate medical

---

* Wilson v. Meeks, 52 F.3rd 1547 (10th Cir. 2004).
† Howard v. Dickerson, 34 F.3d 978 (10th Cir. 1994).

treatment may lead to death. Fatality rates of up to 10% have been reported in ExDS cases.

According to medical researchers Brian Roach, Kelsey Echols, and Aaron Burnett, law enforcement officers have repeatedly seen cases of ExDS in the last 20 years.[10] The researchers cite several cases that involved in-custody deaths from ExDS. One occurred in West Palm Beach, Florida, when a police officer found a shirtless and distraught man stumbling on the road and attempting to stop vehicles. The officer instructed the man to relax, but he kept gesticulating wildly with vehicles stopping to avoid him. After a struggle, the officer placed him in a prone position and handcuffed him. Other officers arrived, helped to move the man out of the street, and further restrained him by hog-tying his legs and hands. The man later became unconscious. Responding paramedics failed to resuscitate him. The chief medical examiner for Palm Beach County determined that the cause of death was "sudden respiratory arrest following physical struggling restraint due to cocaine-induced ExDS."

Another case discussed by the researchers involved an ExDS death after taser use in Dallas, Texas. The police found a 23-year-old male subject in his underwear, screaming and holding a knife on a neighbor's porch on April 24, 2006. The man ignored English and Spanish instructions and came at the officers with the knife. One officer fired a taser, which failed to connect. A second shot did, causing electrical shock. A third was reportedly fired. After being handcuffed to an ambulance backboard, the subject stopped breathing and was pronounced dead at hospital. The Dallas County medical examiner attributed the death to "excited delirium."

The researchers noted that reports of presentations consistent with ExDS occurred as early as the 1840s. They noted that, in 1849, Massachusetts psychiatrist Dr. Luther Bell described an acute, exhaustive mania in which patients developed hallucinations, profound agitation, and fever, which were often followed by death.

The American College of Emergency Physicians has recognized ExDS as a unique clinical syndrome amenable to early therapeutic interventions. According to the researchers, although cocaine use is associated with ExDS, postmortem cocaine levels in those who have died from ExDS are similar to those of recreational cocaine users and lower than in individuals who have died from heart attacks or other nonExDS causes after cocaine use. They concluded that the findings suggest that cocaine intoxication alone does not cause ExDS, and that a degree of cellular or genetic susceptibility may exist that leads some cocaine users to develop ExDS while others do not.

The researchers noted that dopamine is a neurotransmitter with many functions. It plays a role in the brain's perception of reward and temperature regulation. Increased dopamine levels result in fast heart rates, feelings of euphoria, and hallucinations. Highly addictive drugs, specifically cocaine and methamphetamine, increase the level of dopamine in the brain. Schizophrenia also results in elevated levels of dopamine in the brain, and antipsychotics work to treat hallucinations by blocking dopamine on a cellular level. In chronic cocaine abusers who have died of ExDS, research has shown the loss of a crucial protein that eliminates dopamine from the brain. This loss results in increased dopamine levels and chaotic signaling in the brain. The elevated dopamine levels help to explain some of the similarities between ExDS and schizophrenia (e.g., hallucinations and paranoia) but do not account for the high rates of sudden cardiac arrest seen in the former but not the latter condition.

The researchers recommend that law enforcement agencies undertake a concerted effort to increase awareness of ExDS among officers by providing information to help identify symptoms and establishing protocols to engage the medical community. With this information, officers should be in a better position to engage EMS for urgent evaluation, treatment, and transport to the hospital.

Report of the use of deadly force

Many states have enacted statutes requiring detailed reports on the use of deadly force by law enforcement officers. Connecticut General Statutes Section 51-277a requires such a report. The following are excerpts from a report submitted by the Chief State's Attorney as required under the statute. A copy of these reports should be available under a state's freedom of information statutes. If not, a court order should force the state to provide an interested party with a copy of the report.

This report is being filed with the Chief State's Attorney as required under Connecticut General Statutes Section 51-277a(c).

On Saturday, May 7, 2005, at approximately 1930 hours, Officer Robert Lawlor, a sworn member of the Hartford, Connecticut Police Department, while on duty, was involved in an incident pertaining to the use of deadly force. Officer Lawlor shot Brandon Henry (date of birth August 26, 1983) and Jashon Bryant (date of birth December 9, 1986). Brandon Henry was shot in the chest and Jashon Bryant was shot twice in the top of the head, causing his death. At the time of the shooting Officer Lawlor was working in plainclothes as part of a joint City of Hartford and Federal Gun Task Force known as The Violent Crime Impact Team (VCIT). With Officer Lawlor, at the time of the shooting, was U.S. Alcohol, Tobacco and Firearms Special Agent Daniel Prather.

The initial investigation into the use of deadly force by Officer Robert Lawlor was conducted by the Hartford

Police Department and subsequently by the Office of the State's Attorney for the Judicial District of Hartford. That investigation continued until June 2, 2005 when the State's Attorney for the Judicial District of Hartford, James Thomas, requested, pursuant to Connecticut General Statutes Section 51-277a, that Chief State's Attorney, Christopher Morano, designate a prosecutorial official from another judicial district to investigate the use of deadly force. On June 2, 2005, the investigation was assigned to the Waterbury State's Attorney's Office.

Upon the State's Attorney's office for the Judicial District of Waterbury assuming the investigation, inspectors from said office, along with a special inspector appointed pursuant to Connecticut General Statutes Section 51-277a(b) received from members of the Hartford Police Department: physical evidence, written statements, photographs, videotapes, and recorded communications which transpired before, during and after the time of the use of deadly force by Officer Lawlor. These materials were reviewed, along with the autopsy report of Jashon Bryant and the interviews of various witnesses.

The investigation of the use of deadly physical force by Officer Robert Lawlor, upon Jashon Bryant and Brandon Henry was conducted by members of the State's Attorney's Office for the Judicial District of Waterbury with the assistance of members of the Hartford Police Department, Connecticut State Police, Connecticut Forensic Science Laboratory and Office of the Chief Medical Examiner.

After having exhausted normal investigative means into the use of deadly physical force by Hartford Police Officer Robert Lawlor on May 7, 2005, State's Attorney John A. Connelly filed an application on September 13, 2005 pursuant to Connecticut General Statutes Section 54-47c, for an investigation into the commission of a crime or crimes, and on October 4, 2005, the Investigatory Grand Jury Panel approved said application. The Honorable George N. Thim was appointed as Grand Juror to conduct an investigation into all events and circumstances relating to the use of deadly force by Hartford Police Officer Robert Lawlor on Saturday, May 7, 2005 resulting in the death of Jashon Bryant and serious injury to Brandon Henry.

The Grand Juror held eleven sessions during which forty-eight witnesses testified and two hundred and four exhibits were submitted into evidence.

On March 31, 2006, the Grand Juror, pursuant to Connecticut General Statutes Section 54-47g, filed a report with his findings, in which he stated:

> On October 12, 2005, I was appointed by the Chief Court Administrator as an investigatory grand juror for the purpose of

conducting an investigation that was authorized by the Grand Jury Investigatory Panel upon its approval of an application submitted by John A. Connelly, State's Attorney, Judicial District of Waterbury. The Investigatory Grand Jury Panel defined the scope of the investigation as follows: "All events and circumstances relating to the use of deadly force by Hartford Police Officer Robert Lawlor on Saturday, May 7, 2005, resulting in the death of Jashon Bryant and serious injury to Brandon Henry." I have gathered and reviewed all the relevant evidence. The investigation has been completed.

> I conclude that there is probable cause to believe that a crime or crimes have been committed. This finding is based on the credible and legally admissible evidence revealed in the course of the investigation and is made with knowledge that, should there be a prosecution, the state will be required to prove beyond a reasonable doubt that Officer Robert Lawlor acted without legal justification.

Circumstances of the incident

On May 7, 2005 at approximately 7:15 p.m., Officer Lawlor and Special Agent Prather were interviewing an unknown white male at the corner of Main and Nelson Streets in Hartford, directly in front of Olga's Market. Lawlor noticed a black Maxima across the street, in the parking lot of 2374 Main St., which is at the rear of the Ideal Market. Said market is located at the corner of Main and Sanford Streets. On the far side of the Maxima, Lawlor saw a black male (Jashon Bryant), outside of the vehicle, handling what Lawlor believed to be a semi automatic handgun. Prather did not notice anyone outside the Maxima, nor did he see anyone with a gun. Lawlor turned his attention from the unknown white male, nodded across the street and began walking across Main St. toward the parking lot of 2374 Main St., which is at the rear of the Ideal Market. A black male later identified as Brandon Henry exited the Ideal Market and began walking to the parking area at the rear of the building. Henry subsequently entered the driver's seat of the black Maxima, and Bryant got into the front passenger's seat. Prather proceeded to follow Lawlor across the street. While walking Lawlor asked Prather if he had his badge showing. Prather then produced the badge he was wearing around his neck, and Lawlor pulled out his service weapon, a .45 caliber automatic. Lawlor began shouting commands at Henry, "police shut the vehicle off." When they reached the parking lot, Prather walked straight to the driver's side of the vehicle, while Lawlor angled north and approached from in front of the vehicle. Lawlor now pointed his weapon at Henry. Henry began to slowly back the vehicle up. After commands from Lawlor to turn the vehicle off, Henry complied, raising his hands above the steering wheel. The Maxima was now facing north-northwest. Lawlor then walked from the front of the Maxima and approached the passenger side of the vehicle and began talking to Bryant. Bryant's window was partially down. Prather remained on the driver's side of the vehicle and began conversing with Henry. Lawlor ordered Prather to call for back up. Prather radioed fellow VCIT members at 7:21 p.m., and requested assistance. Fellow VCIT members acknowledged Prather and indicated that they were responding to his location. At this point Prather saw Henry lower his hands, and he ordered him to raise them. Henry did, resting them on the steering wheel. Prather, now standing aside the front tire, drew his service weapon, and held it down by his side. Prather turned to look for fellow VCIT members, heard a noise, and turned back to see Henry begin to drive off. Prather stated he then heard "four pops." Said pops were in fact (5) gunshots fired by Lawlor. Brandon Henry was shot in the chest and Jashon Bryant was shot twice in the head (fatally). At 7:23 p.m., Prather radioed "shots fired, shots fired."

After being shot, Henry then drove the vehicle forward, over grass and curb, creating his own exit out of the parking lot, onto Main Street. Fellow VCIT officers pursued the vehicle. Henry then drove his vehicle north on Main Street approximately 2110 feet to the intersection of Westland Street. Henry turned left onto Westland and drove west approximately 1600 feet to the intersection of Westland and Clark Streets where his vehicle collided with another car. Henry then ran from the Maxima, while Jashon Bryant remained in the car. A short time later Henry was apprehended hiding underneath a porch.

Bryant was transported by ambulance to St. Francis Hospital where he was pronounced dead. His clothing was seized as evidence by the Hartford Police, and his hands were bagged prior to his removal to the Office of the Chief Medical Examiner.

Based on the evidence recovered at the scene (shell casings), and an examination of Officer Lawlor's service weapon, it was determined that five shots were fired, all from Officer Lawlor's weapon.

Immediately after the shooting at 7:25 p.m., Officer Lawlor made a radio transmission in which he warned other officers, "be careful 83s in the car." Signal 83 is Hartford Police Department code for a gun or firearm.

None of the officers that pursued the Maxima ever saw anything thrown from the car during the pursuit. Following the capture of Brandon Henry, the Maxima was searched. A bag of cocaine was found under the driver's seat. Nothing was found under the passenger's seat where Bryant was seated. On May 7, 2005, the police conducted a massive search of the area, shooting scene and Henry's direction of travel. No weapon was found. Two subsequent searches were conducted on May 8, 2005 during daylight hours, and again no weapon was found.

The Hartford Police Evidentiary Services Division processed the shooting scene at 2374 Main Street, the accident scene at the intersection of Westland and Clark Streets, and the Brandon Henry apprehension scene at 68 Elmer Street. Photographs of the Nissan Maxima show that the driver's side windows, front and rear, and the passenger's front window were all partially down. The passenger's rear window was shot out.

Raphael Melendez witnessed the shooting from across the street at Olga's Market. Melendez was familiar with Officer Lawlor having previously been arrested by him. According to Melendez, immediately following the shooting, Lawlor came to the edge of the road and said "I can't believe he pulled a gun on me."

Officer Lawlor in an I-call radio transmission to Detective William Rivera at 7:31 p.m., had the following conversation:

Lawlor: Hey. …what's going on with these two? Did, did
   I hit anybody that tried to just kill me and this guy?
Rivera: Yeah ya hit somebody bro. I'll let ya know in a
   second.
Lawlor: Is he dead?
Rivera: I'll let ya know in a second
Lawlor: Alright
Rivera: Say, ya all right?
Lawlor: No, I'm not. F…… guy almost hit me and f……
   pulled a gun on me. No, I'm not all right. I'm pissed.

Hartford Police Sergeant Mack Hawkins was the supervisor assigned to the Intelligence Division overseeing the VCIT, and was the first officer to respond to the shooting scene. Officer Lawlor told Hartford Police Sergeant Mack Hawkins that Bryant pulled up a gun, and that when he saw the gun, he jumped back from the passenger's door and fired four to five shots. Hawkins did not ask Prather what transpired, nor did Prather volunteer any information regarding the shooting. That all the information Hawkins ever ascertained came solely from Robert Lawlor.

On May 9, 2005, Special Agent Prather submitted to an interview conducted by ATF Shooting Review Coordinator Robert A. Schmitt. On May 11, 2005, Special Agent Prather was interviewed at the Hartford Police Department. Present were Special Agent Dennis Turman (ATF Agent in Charge), James T. Cowdery (Prather's attorney), Lieutenant Achilles Rethis (Commander of Major Crimes), Detective Patricia Beaudin (lead investigator) and Detective Timothy Shaw (assistant investigator). Agent Prather did not provide a written statement nor allow the interview to be videotaped or orally recorded. Said interview was memorialized by notes of Detective Beaudin. On June 1, 2005, Attorney James T. Cowdery submitted a signed unsworn statement of Special Agent Dan Prather to Lieutenant Achilles Rethis, Commander of the Major Crimes Division of the Hartford Police Department.

On January 10, 2006, Special Agent Prather testified before the Grand Jury. His testimony included the following information: While speaking to the unknown white male at the corner of Main and Nelson Streets, Prather saw Lawlor nod toward the parking lot across Main Street and then begin crossing the street. Prather did not recall Lawlor saying anything to him. When they got to the opposite side of Main Street, Prather heard Lawlor tell him to take out his badge. Prather testified to the following:

> Question: And did Officer Lawlor at that time indicate to you that there was a weapon in the car while you were standing by the car and he's crouched down on the side of the passenger door?
> Answer: I don't recall him saying that.
> Q: He doesn't say; Dan, watch out. There's a gun, or anything like that?
> A: I don't recall that.
> Q: Do you know the signal for gun in Hartford Police dispatch language?
> A: I believe it was 83.
> Q: Did you hear him say; Dan, 83?
> A: I don't recall.
> Q: Did he tell you; Dan, take out your weapon. Or; Dan watch out?
> A: I don't recall any of that.

Prather testified that at no time while he was at the car with Officer Lawlor did he believe his life was in danger, nor was Officer Lawlor's. Prather indicated he saw Lawlor approach the passenger side of the car and at one point Lawlor was crouched down on the passenger side of the car. Prather indicated he stayed on the driver's side of the Maxima throughout the entire incident, approximately one foot from the car, between the front tire and the driver's door.

Prather testified that while he was at the car with the two men in the car, he was not aware of any activity that would lead to probable cause to make any type of an arrest. Prather did not see any criminal activity by Bryant or Henry at any time.

Prather testified the shots were fired while the car was moving forward. Prather testified that a few moments after the shooting Lawlor said "something wasn't right" but at no point, before, during or after the

shooting did Lawlor ever indicate to Prather that either person in the Maxima had a gun.

Prather testified that although he spoke to Sergeant Hawkins when he first arrived on the scene after the shooting, Prather did not tell him what had occurred.

None of Prather's four oral or written statements indicated that he saw either person in the Maxima in possession of a gun.

Brandon Henry was shot in the chest, fled from the police, and when apprehended, was taken to the hospital for treatment of the gunshot wound. A subsequent search of the vehicle revealed there was no weapon in the car. No gun was recovered in the car nor in the course of the escape route, however there were drugs found under the driver's seat where Henry was seated. Based on the finding of drugs under the seat where Henry was sitting he was arrested for Possession of Narcotics and Interfering with Police. He was subsequently arrested for Violation of Probation. Both cases are now pending in the Judicial District of Hartford.

Brandon Henry's medical records were produced at the Grand Jury, and subsequently disclosed to the Connecticut Forensic Laboratory for use in their reconstruction. Brandon Henry was shot in the chest. According to Dr. John Welch, his attending physician, Henry had two wounds in his chest, which appeared to be one entry and one exit wound. One wound was over the center of the chest over the sternum. The second was to the right near Henry's right nipple. Dr. Welch concluded that the bullet entered one of these wounds, traveled horizontally along the front of his body, hit some structure and exited out the other wound. Dr. Welch described Henry's injury as nonlifethreatening.

On May 9, 2005, Associate Medical Examiner Ira Kanfer, M.D., performed a postmortem examination on the body of Jashon Bryant at the Office of the Chief Medical Examiner. Dr. Kanfer concluded Mr. Bryant died of multiple gunshot wounds to the head, and described the gunshots wounds of the head as follows:

> Gunshot wound "A" is an entry type gunshot wound located approximately at the top of the head, located 1-1/2 inches to the right of the midline. It is a 1.5 cm., somewhat irregular hole without soot or stippling associated with the wound.

> Gunshot wound "B" is also located at the top of the head, somewhat posterior. It is also 1-1/2 inches to the right of midline. It is a 0.5 cm irregular hole. Associated with the entry wounds are one copper jacketed bullet recovered in the base of the cranial vault and the 2nd bullet is recovered in the soft tissue posterior to the mandible. The bullets

are large caliber, copper jacketed bullets. The paths of the bullets are from back to front, right to left and downward. The brain is markedly disrupted and pulverized.

In addition to the gunshot wounds there is a 2 cm defect of the right thumb with hemorrhage surrounding the defect. According to Dr. Ira Kanfer, Jashon Bryant died instantly from the wounds to his head.

On September 6, 2005, Dr. Kanfer, indicated to State's Attorney John Connelly and Inspector James Bart Deeley that, to a reasonable degree of medical certainty, the grazed wound type injury to the deceased's right thumb is consistent with a defensive wound, which would indicate that at the time of the shooting, at least one of Bryant's hands was on his head.

According to Jashon Bryant's grandmother Betty Bryant, with whom he resided, Jashon Bryant was right-handed.

Five bullets were discharged from Lawlor's weapon, and all of the bullets were subsequently recovered. Two bullets were recovered from the head of Jashon Bryant. One bullet was found on the ground outside the driver's door at the site of the collision. One bullet was found in the driver's door map holder. The last bullet was recovered inside the rear passengers' door panel.

Dr. Henry C. Lee of the Connecticut Forensic Laboratory conducted a reconstruction of the shooting. Based on the review of documentation, results of examination of physical evidence, reconstruction of the scene and location of physical evidence at the scene, Dr. Lee determined that:

The vehicle was moving from a location near the center of the parking lot toward Main Street in a northwest direction from the shooting incident.

Based on the location of the spent casings and the location of the tire marks on the parking lot, all five shots were discharged from the passenger side of the vehicle.

The locations of the fired shell casings and glass fragments and the conditions of the tire marks indicate that both the vehicle and the shooter were moving at the time of the shooting.

The most likely sequence of events was:

1. The first two shots were fired from the front passenger side toward the front driver's side. One of the bullets grazes the chest area of the driver. The trajectories of these shots were from right to left. The driver appears to have been in an upright position at the time when this bullet impacted him.
2. Next a shot was fired from the back passenger side toward the front passenger side. The bullet impacted the rear passenger's window and subsequently entered the right side of the passenger

headrest and exited the front of the passenger headrest and then entered the passenger's head to cause one of his head wounds. The bullet trajectory was from back to front, right to left, approximately 36 degree angle and 5 degrees downward.
3. The next shot was fired from the back passenger side through the broken window toward the front passenger side. The bullet trajectory is back to front, right to left, approximately 50 degree angle, and 14 degrees downward. This bullet impacted the back side of the passenger's head.
4. The last shot was fired from the back of the passenger side. This bullet impacted the rear passenger's door and did not exit the door. The trajectory of this shot is from back to front, right to left, approximately 23 degree angle and 3 degrees downward.

Dr. Lee testified on January 17, 2006 in accordance with his report's conclusions.

On November 13, 2005 the Connecticut Forensic Laboratory submitted a report of the instrumental analysis on the Scanning Electron Microscopy tabs taken by the Hartford Police Evidentiary Services Division to test for the presence of gunshot residues. The three elements found in gunshot residue are lead, barium and antimony. The analysis detected the presence of lead on samples from the: driver's door exterior, passenger's door exterior, passenger's door rear, left sleeve of Brandon Henry's jacket, passenger's side and driver's side headliner, sunroof cover and driver's floor, but did not detect the additional elements of barium and antimony on any of these samples.

The November 13, 2005 report from the Connecticut Forensic Laboratory on instrumental analysis failed to detect the presence of lead, barium or antimony (gunshot residue) on samples from the: steering wheel, gearshift, passenger's door interior, driver's side rear door exterior, driver's door interior, passenger's floor and the bags from Bryant's hands.

On June 7, 2005, the Connecticut Forensic Laboratory submitted a report of the analysis of a gunshot residue kit from the hands of Jashon Bryant. The analysis failed to detect the presence of the elements of lead, barium or antimony (gunshot residue).

On June 14, 2005, the Stuart Somers engineering firm surveyed the parking lot and intersection at Main and Nelson Streets. The lot at 2374 Main Street in Hartford was paved, but undeveloped, without designated parking spaces. Based on Lawlor and Prather's information as to their initial location on Main Street, the distance between Lawlor and the Maxima was approximately 130 to 150 feet. The parking lot sloped downward from the street and the back (easternmost) part of the lot was four feet lower than the front (westernmost) section of the lot adjacent to the street.

Immediately after Brandon Henry's apprehension, during questioning by Hartford Detective Andrew Weaver, Henry responded that he couldn't believe he had gotten shot over drugs. When questioned as to the whereabouts of the weapon, Henry said, "I didn't have a gun." Following the capture of Brandon Henry, police conducted a massive search of the area, shooting scene and Henry's direction of travel. No weapon was found. Two subsequent searches were conducted on May 8, 2005 during daylight hours, and again no weapon was found.

On May 7, 2005, while at Hartford Hospital, Officer Morrison and Officer Leger, advised Henry of his Miranda rights. Subsequent to that advisement, Henry was interviewed. Henry stated that there was no gun in the car. Henry stated that he and his boy were parked, that the cops were walking up on them that he knew they were cops in plainclothes when one of them flipped his badge out from under his shirt. Henry stated that there was a lot of yelling, then all of a sudden there was shooting. Henry stated that his boy fell back into the car and there was blood everywhere. Henry stated he was afraid so he just took off.

At approximately 2255 hours on May 7, 2005, Sergeant John Koch re-interviewed Henry at Hartford Hospital. After being advised of his rights, Henry agreed to be interviewed. Henry stated he and the deceased were both out of the Maxima when he saw the two males approaching, and he told the deceased to get in the car. That he saw one of the men pulled out a police badge from under his shirt, and he realized that the two males were police officers. Henry stated he had an eighth of an ounce of cocaine in the vehicle, and he did not want to go back to jail. One officer was on the driver's side while the other was on the passenger's side. Henry stated that he stepped on the gas to take off at which time he heard gunshots being fired. Henry looked at Bryant and said blood was coming out of his head like a "waterfall" and that one of his eyes was swollen like he had been shot through it. At this point Henry fled with the intention of taking Bryant to the hospital. After the collision with another car, Henry exited his vehicle and fled, subsequently hiding under a residence porch until taken into police custody. When asked where the "half an eight ball" was now, Henry said it was probably still in his car. When asked whether there was a firearm in the car Henry stated that he had "half an eight ball" but they didn't have a gun. The interview was stopped at 2330 hours. That the cocaine was later located in the vehicle, under the driver's seat, and submitted into evidence. Nothing was found under the passenger's seat where Bryant was seated.

On May 8, 2005 at approximately 2145 hours, Detectives Michael Sheldon and Patricia Beaudin conducted an interview with Brandon Henry at the Hartford Police Department. Henry was in custody for the narcotics charge. When questioned as to what happened before and after the shooting, Henry indicated that he went to 2374 Main Street Hartford with his friend Jashon Bryant. Henry admitted to having a half an eight ball of cocaine (an eighth of an ounce) in the car and noticed two plainclothes officers approaching his car with their guns drawn and pointed at him and Bryant. That when asked how he knew they were cops he stated he heard their police radios. Henry stated he didn't want to go back to jail and knew he was headed back if caught with the drugs. Henry stated he heard the officer on the passenger side of the car yelling "keep your hands where I can see them." Henry then blamed the shooting incident on himself stating "because I made the decision to drive off that's when the shots were fired." Henry stated he realized he and Jashon had been shot while fleeing the scene. Henry stated he decided to run because he still didn't want to go to jail for the cocaine that was in the car. When asked if he or Bryant had a gun in the car he stated "no there was no gun."

On December 6, 2005, Brandon Henry testified before the Grand Jury under a grant of immunity, to the following:

> Henry was driving the black Maxima on May 7, 2005 and drove to the Ideal Market on Main Street in Hartford. Henry parked on Main Street but told Jashon Bryant to move the car into the lot behind the Ideal Market while Henry went into the Ideal Market because Bryant wanted to look for his money. When Henry returned from the Ideal Market, the Maxima was in the lot and Jashon Bryant was outside the car. As Henry neared his car, he saw two men looking at him. One man was wearing a hoodie (Lawlor) and the other a hat (Prather). Henry and Bryant both entered the car and Henry began to back up. The cop with the hoodie pulled out a gun and ordered them to stop and put their hands up. Henry indicated both he and Bryant complied. Henry indicated that he realized they were police officers when he heard their police radios. Henry indicated that both officers were initially on the driver's side of the car but that the man with the gun moved in front of the car to the passenger side. The other man (Prather) remained on the driver's side of the car. The man with the gun ordered Henry to turn off the car and he did. Henry saw the man with the gun take out his cell phone and start dialing. Henry saw the other cop with the walkie-talkie turn his head, so Henry started the car "real quick

and pulled off, and like just started hearing shots." Henry heard the shots fired after he pulled off. Henry decided to try to get away because he was on probation, had drugs in the car, was scared and did not want to go back to jail. Henry did not tell Jashon Bryant that he was going to attempt to flee. Henry never saw Bryant reach under the seat or to the floor.

On May 9, 2005, Lieutenant Achilles Rethis contacted Robert Lawlor's attorney Michael Georgetti to schedule an interview of Officer Lawlor. Attorney Georgetti notified Lieutenant Rethis that his client had received information from one of his confidential informants that a junkie had picked up the gun thrown from the vehicle occupied by Mr. Henry and Mr. Bryant. Attorney Georgetti was advised to have Officer Lawlor transmit his information to the Major Crimes Division.

On May 10, 2005 at approximately 10 a.m., Detective William Rivera received a phone call from Robert Lawlor. In said phone call, Lawlor told Rivera that he (Lawlor) had received information from a confidential source that a "fiend" had picked up the gun and the "fiend" was from the Nelton Court housing project. According to Detective Rivera, *fiend* is a slang term for a drug addict. Detective Rivera indicated Lawlor was referring to a gun having been thrown from the Maxima. Detective Rivera told Lawlor to report that information to Sergeant Hawkins.

Robert Lawlor never notified Sergeant Hawkins or the Major Crimes Division of the Hartford Police Department of any information concerning a "fiend" finding a gun.

On May 13, 2005, Jaime Diaz telephoned Hartford Community Relations Officer Daniel Auciello and stated that he had the gun involved in the police shooting on May 7, 2005. Diaz subsequently dictated a detailed statement to Hartford Detectives Bruskey and Sheldon, in which he described how he came into possession of the gun. In response to questions from the police officers he denied knowing Officer Lawlor and Special Agent Prather.

A subsequent investigation revealed that Jaime Diaz had previously worked as an informant for Officer Lawlor in 1995. Diaz had been involved in a drug sting of a major drug dealer in Hartford in which he provided information to Lawlor that resulted in the arrest of Angel Garcia and the seizure of (600) bags of Heroin. Angel Garcia was arrested as a result of Jaime Diaz' cooperation with Officer Lawlor, but Diaz was not arrested.

On May 14, 2005, at 4:55 p.m. Detectives Beaudin and Shaw re-interviewed Diaz. Diaz was shown a picture of Officer Lawlor. Diaz denied ever having any contact with Lawlor. When asked about the 1995 incident,

Diaz still denied knowing Lawlor. Diaz left the police department at 5:15 p.m.

On May 16, 2005 at 11:15 p.m., Diaz again contacted Detective Shaw and said he was at the police station and needed to change his written statement. Diaz subsequently dictated a detailed statement to Hartford Detective Mike Sheldon in which he stated he had lied on his previous statement, and fabricated the information about the pellet gun to help Lawlor as a favor to Lawlor for not arresting Diaz in 1995.

An arrest warrant was subsequently issued for Jaime Diaz charging him with violation of Connecticut General Statutes Section 53a-155—Tampering with or Fabricating Physical Evidence, 53a-157b False Statement in The Second Degree, 53a-167a Interfering with Police. The Waterbury States Attorney's Office is handling the prosecution of Jaime Diaz.

On January 31, 2006, Officer Lawlor testified before the Grand Jury. He testified to the following:

> He has been a Hartford police officer for more than eighteen years. On May 7, 2005, he saw a black Maxima in the parking lot across the street from Olga's market at Main and Nelson Streets. The Maxima was "parked inconsistent with standard—with parking for the parking lot." Main Street runs north and south. The car was facing northwest. He saw a black male (Jashon Bryant) on the passenger's side of the Maxima, outside the vehicle. The male appeared to be clutching a small semiautomatic handgun with both hands, and fumbling with it. Lawlor crossed the street to approach the vehicle, and said to Prather "83" to signify a firearm. However, Prather did not realize what "83" meant because "he was never even familiarized with our Ten Codes."

This testimony was contradicted by Prather's, in that Prather testified he never heard Lawlor say "83," and Prather was aware that "83" signified a firearm in Hartford Police Code.

Lawlor also testified that

> Henry exited the Ideal market and returned to the car. Both Henry and Bryant entered the vehicle, Henry as driver and Bryant as passenger. Henry started the car, and began to slowly drive toward the exit, heading due west toward Lawlor and Prather. Lawlor drew his service weapon, and began ordering the two occupants of the Maxima to shut off the vehicle and put their hands up. The car stopped and then began to go backwards.

The car was again facing northwest. Lawlor moved from the driver's side to the passenger's side of the car while Prather remained on the driver's side, between the driver's door and the front tire. The passenger's window was partially down. Lawlor repeatedly commanded the occupants to show their hands. Lawlor indicated he could see Henry's hands and he did not have anything in them. Lawlor could not see Bryant's hands because "he would bring 'em up a little bit, and then he would bring 'em back down again." Lawlor told Prather to call for backup. Lawlor then took out his phone and attempted to call for backup but could not because it was so cumbersome. At some point the Maxima was shut off. Lawlor testified the driver and the passenger did communicate with one another and he felt they made the decision to flee. "... I saw that their mind was made up, and they both—one went for the keys, and whatever he did to get that car moving again. The passenger of that car made—his hands were not up. He made movement to go to the floor. He went down."

This testimony is contradicted by the physical evidence, in that Bryant's right thumb injury suggests that his hand was at or above the level of the front passenger window at the time he sustained the wound.

Lawlor testified that he jumped back and started shooting, first at the passenger and then at the operator.

This testimony is contradicted by the physical evidence and reconstruction conclusions of Dr. Henry C. Lee that the first shots were at the operator.

Lawlor testified he fired at the passenger because "in my heart that passenger was coming up with a handgun to shoot at me." Lawlor testified that at no time did he actually see a handgun in the vehicle.

Lawlor further testified that he never saw a gun while he was at the car, he never saw either the driver or the passenger pull a gun on him, did not see the passenger point a gun at Lawlor, did not see the passenger point a gun at Prather, and did not see the passenger point a gun at Lawlor as the car drove away.

When questioned as to what he meant when he said to Detective Rivera in the I-call shortly after the shooting that "fucking guy almost hit me and fucking pulled a gun on me," Lawlor testified that, "I would have been referring to the driver of the car. And I would have been referring to 'fucking pulled a gun on me' because that's exactly what I believe that the passenger was about to do to me."

Lawlor testified that he intended to fire into the "occupiable compartment of the vehicle."

Lawlor testified that he began firing because the car was moving forward, which is a violation of Hartford Police Department Order 1-20.

Hartford Police Officer Lewis Crabtree, a Hartford Police Department firearms instructor, testified on January 31, 2006 that all Hartford police officers are governed by General Order Policy and Procedures Number 1-20, effective 11/20/88. Order 1-20 pertains to firearms guidelines, and establishes the limits within which the use of firearms by members of the Hartford Police Department is permitted, as well as prohibited. Under Order 1-20, § III. B.3. The use of firearms is prohibited "to fire from or at a moving vehicle unless the occupants of the other vehicle are using deadly physical force against the officer or another person."

The evidence showed that neither occupant of the Maxima was using deadly physical force against Lawlor or Prather at the time Lawlor fired into their vehicle, and that neither occupant was armed.

Lawlor testified in response to whether he had ever told anyone that a junkie had picked up the gun that was thrown from the car, "I just don't believe I ever said that."

Lawlor's testimony was contradicted by Detective William Rivera's testimony regarding the phone call he received from Lawlor regarding a "fiend."

Determination of whether officer lawlor's use of deadly force was appropriate

Section 51-277a of the Connecticut General Statutes provides that "the Division of Criminal Justice shall cause an investigation to be made whenever a peace officer, in the performance of his duties, uses deadly physical force upon another person and such person dies as a result thereof ..." The State's Attorney must determine the circumstances of the incident, and whether the use of deadly physical force by the peace officer was appropriate under Connecticut General Statutes Section 53a-22. Connecticut General Statutes Section 53a-22 provides, in part, that

> A peace officer ... is justified in using deadly physical force upon another person ... only when he reasonably believes that such is necessary to (c) defend himself or a third person from the use or imminent use of deadly physical force.

Based upon the forensic investigation, autopsy and medical reports, statements of the witnesses, Officer Robert Lawlor's own sworn testimony and the applicable case law (*State v. Smith*, 73 Conn. App. 173, 807 A.2d 500, cert. denied 262 Conn. 923, 812 A.2d 865 (2002); *Graham v. Connor*, 490 U.S. 386, 396, 109 S. Ct. 1865, 104 L.Ed.2d

443 (1989)), the State's Attorney for the Judicial District of Waterbury determines that the use of deadly physical force by Officer Robert Lawlor was not appropriate under Connecticut General Statutes Section 53a-22,

Further action

As a result of the determination that the use of deadly physical force by Officer Robert Lawlor was not appropriate under Connecticut General Statutes Section 53a-22, and the Grand Juror's findings that a crime or crimes have been committed by Officer Lawlor resulting in the death of Jashon Bryant and physical injury to Brandon Henry, an arrest warrant should be applied for, charging him with Manslaughter in the first degree in violation of Connecticut General Statutes Section 53a-55(a)(3) for the homicide of Jashon Bryant and Assault in the first degree in violation of Connecticut General Statutes Section 53a-59 for the wounding of Brandon Henry.

Signed and Submitted this 15th day of May 2006.[11]

Assessment of deadly force in the Philadelphia Police Department

George Fachner and Steven Carter[12] conducted research on officer-involved shootings in Philadelphia during the years 2007–2013. During that period, there were 394 officer-involved shootings (OIS). OISs mostly involved three or fewer officers. The vast majority (94%) of officers involved in shootings were men. The majority (59%) of officers were white, whereas 34% were black, 7% were Hispanic, and less than 1% were Asian.

Officers were 33 years old, on average, and usually in a patrol function. Although patrol officers had the greatest number of OISs, when the size of different Philadelphia Police Department (PPD) units was controlled for, the highway patrol, major crimes unit, and narcotics strike force had the highest rates of OISs. The average age of suspects was 20 years old. The racial composition of suspects in OISs was 80% black, 10% Hispanic, 9% white, and 1% Asian. Suspects were unarmed in 15% of OISs.

Suspects were armed with firearms 56% of the time; used vehicles as weapons 9% of the time; were armed with a sharp object 8% of the time; were armed with a BB gun 3% of the time; and were armed with a blunt object 3% of the time. In 6% of cases, it has not been determined whether the suspect was armed.

Unarmed OIS incidents were mostly attributable to one of two factors: threat perception failures and physical altercations. Threat perception failures occur when the officer(s) perceives a suspect as being armed due to the misidentification of a nonthreatening object (e.g., a cell phone) or movement (e.g., tugging at the waistband).

This was the case in 49% of unarmed incidents. Physical altercations refer to incidents in which the suspect reached for the officer's firearm or overwhelmed the officer with physical force. This was the case in 35% of unarmed OISs. The remaining unarmed incidents involved toy guns (10%), unarmed accomplices (3%), and accidental discharge (2%).

White suspects were unarmed in 8 of 32 OISs (25%), black suspects were unarmed in 45 of 285 OISs (15.8%), Hispanic suspects were unarmed in 5 of 34 OISs (14.7%), and Asian suspects were unarmed in 1 of 5 OISs (20%). A closer look at OISs shows that black suspects in OISs were most likely to be the subject of a threat perception failure (8.8%) and white suspects in OISs were most likely (18.8%) to be involved in a physical altercation resulting in an OIS.

They also examined the race of officers involved in threat perception failure OISs to gain a greater understanding of how cross-race encounters may influence threat perception. They found that the threat perception failure rate for white officers and black suspects was 6.8%. Black officers had a threat perception failure rate of 11.4% when the suspect was black. The threat perception failure rate for Hispanic officers was 16.7% when involved in an OIS with a black suspect.

The report noted that officers

- Do not receive regular, consistent training on the department's deadly force policy.
- The PPD requires officers to complete crisis intervention training (CIT) in order to obtain an electronic control weapon (ECW). This requirement conflates both tactical approaches and limits the distribution of less-lethal tools throughout the department.
- The PPD's drafted ECW policy is not detailed enough regarding the circumstances in which use of the tool should be limited.
- PPD recruit training is not conducted in a systematic and modular fashion. As a result, some recruit classes receive firearms training close to the end of the academy, whereas others receive it early on.
- The PPD lacks a field-training program to help transition academy graduates into full-time work as officers.
- The PPD's annual in-service training requirements tend to be limited to municipal police officer education and training commission standards. As a result, officers do not regularly receive in-service training on threat perception, decision-making, and de-escalation.
- OIS investigations generally lack consistency.
- The PPD's current practice for recording interviews of witnesses and discharging officers is through typed notes.

- The IAD shooting team waits for the district attorney's office (DAO) to decline charges against an officer before it interviews discharging officers and closes its investigation. As a result, most officers involved in shootings are not interviewed until three or more months after the incident has occurred.
- The PPD has begun posting a significant amount of data and case information on its website. Still, more transparency is needed to keep the community properly informed.

The research report concluded that the PPD is a large, complex organization with a deeply rooted history and culture. The department's complexity reflects, in part, the growing complexity of the role of police in society, which has evolved from reactive to proactive in its fight against crime. They recommended that the department take the same evolutionary steps in its approach to public interactions, use of force, and use of deadly force.

Summary

- An article published by the *Economist* magazine, shortly after the Ferguson shooting, indicated that "last year, in total, British police officers actually fired their weapons three times."
- Between 2010 and 2014, the police force of Albuquerque, New Mexico, shot and killed 23 citizens. This was seven times more than the number of British citizens killed by all of England and Wales 43 police forces.
- In 2013, 30 American police officers were shot and killed in the line of duty compared with none among the England and Wales police forces.
- FBI special agents may use deadly force only when necessary—when the agent has a reasonable belief that the subject of such force poses an imminent danger of death or serious physical injury to the agent or another person. If feasible, a verbal warning to submit to the authority of the special agent is given prior to the use of deadly force.
- The leading case on when the police may use deadly force is the U.S. Supreme Court case of *Tennessee v. Garner*.
- The court stated that the use of deadly force to prevent the escape of all felony suspects, whatever the circumstances, was constitutionally unreasonable. The court stated that it was not better that all felony suspects die than that they escape.
- Native Americans get shot by cops at an astonishing rate, and the media rarely mentions it.

According to the center, the following groups are more likely to be killed by law enforcement:

- African Americans aged 20–24: 7.1 per million population per year
- Native Americans aged 24–35: 6.6 per million population per year
- Native Americans aged 35–44: 5.9 per million population per year
- African Americans aged 25–34: 5.6 per million population per year
- Native Americans aged 20–24: 4.6 per million population per year
- Latinos aged 20–24: 4.4 per million population per year
- Latinos aged 25–34: 3.2 per million population per year
- African Americans aged 35–44: 3.0 per million population per year
- African Americans aged 15–19: 2.9 per million population per year
- Average, all races and ages: 1.2 per million population per year

Practicums

Practicum one

Two FBI agents possess an arrest warrant for a man who is wanted for bank fraud and embezzlement. As they approach his residence to make the arrest, they observe a man matching the subject's description standing on the front porch. When the agents are within about 20 yards of the residence, the man looks in their direction and immediately jumps from the porch and runs down the sidewalk away from them.

One of the agents shouts, "FBI! Stop!" When the man ignores that command, the agent shouts a second time, "FBI! Stop or I'll shoot!" The suspect continues running, increasing the distance between himself and the pursuing agents. Realizing that they are not going to be able to overtake the fleeing suspect, the agent fires a shot, striking the suspect in the back.

Discussion: Does this use of force violate FBI policy?

This incident is discussed in John C. Hall (April, 1996) "FBI training on the new federal deadly force police," *The FBI Law Enforcement Bulletin*.

Practicum two

A defendant, police officer Scott Smith, is being tried for the death of a suspect that he was in the process of arresting. The fact is that the officer observed the victim standing with his back to him; he could not see the victim's hands. At that time, the victim looked back at the defendant with what the defendant termed a confrontational or thousand yard stare. Consistent with training that he had received as a police officer, the defendant perceived those looks, or cues, as indicative of a threat to his safety. The defendant drew his sidearm from the holster on his hip and pointed it at the victim, cradling the weapon with both hands. Immediately after drawing his weapon, the defendant began yelling to the victim, "Show me your hands, show me your hands," and he began to approach him. The defendant wanted to "get both of them out of the middle of the road." The last place the defendant wanted to take somebody into custody was in the middle of a busy street. The victim then raised his hands and surrendered.

On reaching the victim's location at the center of the road, the defendant took hold of the victim and attempted to move him to the side of the road to arrest and handcuff him. To move the victim, the defendant changed the position he used to hold his weapon. Consistent with his training, the defendant held his weapon in his right hand, which he held close to the center of his body, while holding his empty left hand out straight to take hold of the victim. The purpose of that change in position was to maximize the distance between the weapon and the victim.

The defendant led the victim back to the same grassy area next to the road. On arriving at the grassy area, the victim initially lay down on his back and elbows with his feet pointed toward the road, and then lay on his stomach with his hands pointed straight over his head. The defendant straddled the victim, standing over him with his gun pointed at his back. At some point, the defendant placed his left foot on the victim's back. The defendant used his left hand to take the victim's hands and secure them behind his back. None of the witnesses that testified at trial observed a struggle between the defendant and the victim. Moments later, the defendant fired his weapon once at the victim, killing him. After the defendant shot the victim, witnesses observed the victim lying on the ground with his hands out in front of him.

As a trial judge would you convict the defendant, a police officer, of murder?

See: State v. Smith, 73 Conn. App. 173 (2002)

Discussion questions

1. What guidelines should law enforcement officers follow regarding the use of deadly force?
2. Who is most likely to be killed by law enforcement officers?
3. Why are U.S. police more often involved in deadly force compared with U.K. police?
4. What actions should be taken to lessen the number of deaths resulting from deadly force?
5. What criminal actions does a police officer face if he or she uses deadly force without justification?

References

1. Armed police: Trigger happy. *The Economist*, August 15, 2014.
2. Al Vicens (July, 2015) Native Americans get shot by cops at an astonishing rate so why aren't you hearing about it? *Mother Jones*, p. 35.
3. Mike Males (August 26, 2014) Who are police killing? Center on juvenile justice and criminal justice website at http://www.cjcj.org/mobile/news/8113. Accessed on October 23, 2015.
4. Amy Brittain (October 25, 2015) On duty, under fire. *Washington Post*, p. A1.
5. Miller's article was posted on PoliceOne website at http://www.policeone.com/health-fitness/articles/8104031-When-cops-kill-The-psychology-of-deadly-force-encounters/ Accessed on October 29, 2015.
6. H. Lee and M.S. Vaughn (2010) Organizational factors that contribute to police deadly force Liability. *Journal of Criminal Justice*, 38, 193–206.
7. Michael Planty, Andrea Burch, Duren Banks, Lance Couzens, Caroline Blanton, and Devon Cribbs (March 2015) *Arrest-Related Deaths Program: Data Quality Profile*. NCJ 248544. Washington, DC: U.S. Department of Justice.
8. Shannon Bohrer and Robert Chaney (January 2010) Police investigations of the use of deadly force can influence perceptions and outcomes. *FBI Law Enforcement Bulletin*. vol. 79, no. 1, pp. 1–11.
9. Manny Fernandez (October 11, 2015) Relatives of black man shot by off-duty officer in Texas question police actions. *New York Times*, p. A-1.
10. Brian Roach, Kelsey Echols, and Aaron Burnett (July, 2014) Excited delirium and the dual response: Preventing in-custody deaths. *FBI Bulletin*. vol. 83, no. 7, pp. 13–20.
11. Report obtained from the State of Connecticut, Division of Criminal Justice website at http://www.ct.gov/Csao/cwp/view.asp?q=314666 Accessed on October 29, 2015.
12. George Fachner and Steven Carter (2015) *Collaborative Reform Initiative: An Assessment of Deadly Force in the Philadelphia Police Department*. Washington, DC: Office of Community Oriented Policing Services.

chapter five

Other types of misconduct

Learning objectives

After studying this chapter, the reader should understatnd the following concepts and issues:

- The treatment of minorities by the police
- Police contact during traffic stops
- The issue of profiling
- Gender profiling issues
- Illegal searches by police
- Police behavior during stops and frisks
- What actions the police should take when a suspect refuses to stop
- Whether police have a duty to break off a high-speed pursuit
- High-speed pursuits as excessive use of force
- Sexual misconduct by police officers

Introduction

> "There is no crueler tyranny than that which is exercised under cover of law, and with the colors of justice ..."

United States v. Jannotti, 673 F.2d 578, 614 (3d Cir. 1982)

In earlier chapters, we explored the excessive use of force and the use of deadly force by law enforcement officers. In this chapter, we will explore other forms of misconduct. While most of the examples used in this text pertain to U.S. law enforcement officers, that does not mean that the officers in the United States are the only ones involved in misconduct.

Police misconduct statistics gathered by the Cato Institute's National Police Misconduct Reporting Project state that around 1% of all police officers commit police misconduct in a given year. Keith Findley from the Wisconsin Innocence Project concluded that police misconduct was a factor in as many as 50% of wrongful convictions involving DNA evidence. As noted by the Cato Institute, in most police misconduct cases, the misconduct is more subtle than torture. Oftentimes, police simply push the envelope in order to obtain a witness statement.

One of the most controversial issues involves allegations of police abuse of minority groups. As noted by Robert Weitzer, race is one of the strongest predictors of

attitudes toward the police. Weitzer states that, regardless of class background, African Americans suffer substantial racial discrimination and this in turn influences their assessments of police misconduct.[1] He states that, because crime rates typically are higher in both poor black and white neighborhoods than in middle-class neighborhoods, the former are more likely to generate frequent police–citizen encounters. And, according to Weitzer, more contacts can go awry as a result, and the chances of conflict are greater. He also notes that poor neighborhoods generate more frequent involuntary contacts with police officers; these are associated with more negative evaluations of police than are voluntary contacts.

Much of the misconduct may be attributed to implicit racial bias. For example, in many jurisdictions it appears to be a crime to "drive while black." A researcher once commented that, rather than use the phrase "driving while black," we should use the phrase "patrolling while racially biased." The implicit racial bias is not solely a U.S. problem. For example, the September 2015 issue of the prestigious English journal *CJM* (*Criminal Justice Matters*) devoted the entire issue to implicit racial bias in the United Kingdom.[2]

Rebekah Delsol noted that "Police officers are racially profiling when they view people as suspicious because of who they are, what they look like, or where they pray, rather than what they have done." She states that race should be considered as a social construct; not knowable by sight. She concludes that racial profiling exacts a high price on individuals, groups, and communities that are singled out for disproportionate police attention.[3] She also points out that the damage that racial profiling can do is slowly being recognized in America and the United Kingdom.

Jules Holroyd, in her discussion on recent psychological findings, contends that there are robust findings that indicate that, in a contemporary society, implicit race bias is pervasive. He notes that the main strategies adopted to combat institutional racism in the United Kingdom have been to challenge "canteen culture" and the use of explicitly racist language, and to take steps to diversify the police force. He also notes that if biases are affecting practice then, as a matter of urgency, there should be an investigation into how police practices should be reformed to try to prevent racial bias from infecting conduct.[4] He concludes his article with the comment that implicit biases are not inevitable and that there are things that can be done to stop them from having an impact on actions.

Rebecca Roberts, in her article on "Racism and criminal justice," quotes a statement by the former U.K. prime minister Tony Blair. She reports that Blair, while discussing black-on-black crime in 2007, stated that

> What we are dealing with is not general social disorder; but specific groups or people who for one reason or another, are deciding not to abide by the same code of conduct as the rest of us…The black community-vast majority of whom in these communities are decent, law-abiding people horrified at what is happening—need to be mobilized in denunciation of this gang culture that is killing innocent young black kids. But we won't stop this by pretending it isn't young black kids doing it.

Many of those listening to Tony Blair came away with the opinion that he was declaring war on young black people in the United Kingdom. While there is no research on the issue, I am almost certain that his words had an effect on how the British police officers felt when engaging with a young black person.

The National Police Misconduct Statistics and Reporting Project's 2010 (NPMSRP) Police Misconduct Statistical Report indicates that, from January 2010 to December 2010, there were 4861 unique reports of police misconduct that involved 6613 sworn law enforcement officers and 6826 alleged victims (Box 5.1).

Traffic stops

According to Lynn Langton and Matthew Durose, statisticians with the Bureau of Justice Statistics (BJS), in 2011, over 62.9 million U.S. residents aged 16 or older—26% of the population—had one or more contacts with police during the prior 12 months. For about half (49%) of persons experiencing contact with police, the most recent contact was involuntary or police initiated. In 2011, 86% of persons involved in traffic stops during their most recent contact with police and 66% of persons involved in street stops (i.e., stopped in public but not in a moving vehicle) believed that the police both behaved properly and treated them with respect during the contact. A greater percentage of persons involved in street stops (25%) than those pulled over in traffic stops (10%) believed that the police had not behaved properly. Regardless of the reason for the stop, less than 5% of persons who believed that the police had not behaved properly filed a complaint.[5]

BOX 5.1   FORMER INDIANA LAW ENFORCEMENT OFFICIALS SENTENCED ON CONSPIRACY, TAX, AND MONEY LAUNDERING CHARGES

On June 27, 2013, in Hammond, Indiana, Ronald Slusser was sentenced to 70 months in prison and 1 year of supervised release, and ordered to pay $198,817 in restitution to the Internal Revenue Service (IRS) for the tax years 2005–2010. Slusser pleaded guilty to conspiring to provide false information to a federal firearms licensee, conspiracy to defraud the Food and Drug Administration (FDA), making false statements on a tax return, and laundering/structuring of monetary instruments. Joseph Kumstar was sentenced to 57 months in prison and 1 year of supervised release, and ordered to pay $22,612 in restitution to the IRS for tax years 2005–2009. Kumstar also pleaded guilty to conspiracy to provide false information to a federal firearms licensee, conspiracy to defraud the FDA, and making false statements on a tax return. According to documents filed by the government, Slusser, while a patrol officer with the Lake County Sheriff's Department, and Kumstar, while the Deputy Chief for the Lake County Sheriff's Department, conspired to obtain restricted firearms and defraud the FDA in order to retain restricted laser sights. The conspiracy involved the trafficking of between 25 and 99 firearms. According to the indictment, from about September 2008 until January 2010, Slusser, Kumstar, and a third defendant used the Lake County Sheriff's Department letterhead to create letters falsely indicating that the weapons were purchased and would be used by the sheriff's department, despite the fact that the defendants used their own funds to purchase the weapons. When the weapons arrived, Slusser illegally removed the upper receivers and other parts that could be removed from the lower receiver. These parts were then illegally sold over the Internet with Slusser, Kumstar, and the third defendant retaining the profits. In April 2007, Slusser filed his 2006 federal income tax return, understating his income by approximately $298,566, and around December 16, 2008, Slusser made a series of cash withdrawals from various banks, partly to avoid currency transaction reports and to hide the fact that the monies involved were derived from an unlawful activity. Court documents also show that, in May 2010, Kumstar filed a federal tax return understating his total income by about $30,102.

According the researchers, relatively more black drivers (13%) than white (10%) and Hispanic (10%) drivers were pulled over in a traffic stop during their most recent contact with police. There were no statistical differences in the race or Hispanic origin of persons involved in street stops. The highlights of their research included the following findings:

- Persons involved in street stops were less likely (71%) than drivers in traffic stops (88%) to believe that the police had behaved properly.
- Of those involved in traffic and street stops, a smaller percentage of black people than white people believed that the police had behaved properly during the stop.
- Drivers pulled over by an officer of the same race or ethnicity were more likely (83%) than drivers pulled over by an officer of a different race or ethnicity (74%) to believe that the reason for the traffic stop was legitimate.
- White drivers were both ticketed and searched at lower rates than black and Hispanic drivers.
- Across race and Hispanic origin, persons who were searched during traffic stops were less likely than persons who were not searched to believe that the police behaved properly during the stop.
- About 1% of drivers pulled over in traffic stops had physical force used against them by police. Of these drivers, 55% believed that the police had behaved properly during the stop.
- About 6 in 10 persons aged 16 or older involved in street stops believed that they were stopped for a legitimate reason.
- About 19% of persons involved in street stops were searched or frisked by police. The majority of persons who were searched or frisked did not believe that the police had a legitimate reason for the search (Box 5.2).

Profiling

Most incidents involving profiling take place during traffic and street stops. A special report on police behavior during traffic and street stops indicated that, in each calendar year, about 26% of the population had one or more contacts with police.[5] The report noted that

- Relatively more black drivers (13%) than white (10%) and Hispanic (10%) drivers were pulled over at a traffic stop during their most recent contact with police. There were no statistical differences in the race or Hispanic origin of persons involved in street stops.
- Persons involved in street stops were less likely (71%) than drivers at traffic stops (88%) to believe that the police had behaved properly.
- Of those involved in traffic and street stops, a smaller percentage of black people than white people believed that the police behaved properly during the stop.
- Drivers pulled over by an officer of the same race or ethnicity were more likely (83%) than drivers pulled over by an officer of a different race or ethnicity (74%) to believe that the reason for the traffic stop was legitimate.
- White drivers were both ticketed and searched at lower rates than black or Hispanic drivers.
- Across race and Hispanic origin, persons who were searched during traffic stops were less likely than persons who were not searched to believe that the police had behaved properly during the stop.
- About 1% of drivers pulled over in traffic stops had physical force used against them by police. Of these drivers, 55% believed the police behaved properly during the stop.
- About 6 in 10 persons age 16 or older involved in street stops believed that they were stopped for a legitimate reason.

BOX 5.2   FORMER TEXAS SHERIFF SENTENCED FOR MONEY LAUNDERING

On July 17, 2014, in McAllen, Texas, Guadalupe Trevino, aka Lupe Trevino, of McAllen, was sentenced to 60 months in prison and 2 years of supervised release, and ordered to pay a $60,000 fine. Trevino, the former sheriff of Hidalgo County, pleaded guilty on April 14, 2014, to conspiracy to commit money laundering. According to court documents, Trevino received cash contributions during 2011 and 2012 for his election campaign from an alleged drug trafficker. Trevino admitted that he had accepted the money, knowing it was from illegal activities. Trevino also admitted that he accepted the monies directly and through others as donations to assist with his 2012 election campaign. Some of the monies received were subsequently deposited into bank accounts that Trevino controlled and were comingled with other funds. During and after the transactions, Trevino and others acted to disguise and conceal the nature, location, source, ownership, and control of the currency by filing false candidate/officeholder campaign finance reports and by producing other documents.

Racial profiling

The President's Task Force on 21st Century Policing Report noted in their summary report that racial bias in the broader society, public concern about officer use of racial profiling, and the development of agency policies addressing racial profiling presented opportunities for departments to engage officers, line supervisors, leadership, and the broader community in proactive and constructive strategies to ensure fair and equitable treatment under the law.

The report recommended that all law enforcement agencies be required to have a written policy against the use of racial profiling and sanctions for any officer who violated the policy. Furthermore,

- Departments should engage the community in formulating their policies on racial profiling.
- Early warning tracking should be initiated for all law enforcement officers who enforce traffic and arrest laws on minorities at a rate greater than their population census rates.
- When police officers serve in the communities in which they live, violence and abuses go down, public safety goes up, and trust is built.
- Officer training, supervision, and performance review should address knowledge and skills related to critical race theory, implicit bias, and cultural competency.

Gender profiling

Professors Samuel Walker and Dawn Irlbeck, in a special report sponsored by the Police Professionalism Institute at the University of Nebraska, indicated that a national problem in police misconduct was "driving while female."[6] They related one case where a Suffolk County, New York police officer stopped a female driver for an alleged traffic violation and, instead of issuing her a citation, forced her to strip and walk home wearing only her underpants. Reports of this incident brought forth similar allegations—by 13 women and 1 man—of sexual abuse arising from traffic stops conducted by the police departments on Long Island. The professors concluded that "driving while female" is a nationwide problem and that many departments failed to implement a complaint system that allows the victims to come forward, and also failed to take their complaints seriously.

The professors recommended five remedies to curb this type of abuse. Those were

- Better data collection so that the departments can determine whether there is a problem and exactly how extensive it is

- Provide training and establish policies to prevent the abuse
- Provide better supervision of officers on the street
- Establish an open and accessible citizen complaint system
- Hire more female officers (Box 5.3)

Police searches

How often do police conduct illegal searches of citizens? According to researchers Jon Gould and Stephen Mastrofski, direct field observations suggest that official records vastly understate the extent of constitutional violations in this area. They cite studies indicating that police officers are "pushing the Fourth Amendment" to the verge of or beyond what is legally permissible.[7] The researchers noted that, for the past several decades, police researchers have tried to determine the extent and causes of police activities that fail to conform to the requirements of the law.

Gold and Mastrofski indicate that there is no well-developed theory that explains police conformance or nonconformance to the Constitution. They note that some persons may be more at risk than others to be targeted for punitive or intrusive police interventions. They contend that there are a variety of relevant social dimensions—wealth, race, gender, culture, and organization affiliation—but all are premised on a single point; those least able to wield social, political, or economic power may be at the greatest risk of improper police practices.

The researchers noted that wealthy suspects, because they command greater respect and are capable of retaining a competent and motivated attorney, are less likely to experience improper police practices than poor suspects. And suspects who show deference to police reduce the risk of punitive and intrusive police behavior. The authors reported that a small sample of 115 suspects were analyzed in one medium-sized city and estimated that about 30% of the searches were unconstitutional.[8]

The researchers noted that if the rates were extrapolated to cover a one-year period, based on typical staffing levels, it would equal to about 12,000–14,000 unconstitutional searches per year in that city, or roughly six unconstitutional searches per 100 citizens. The researchers also noted that a search was more likely to be unconstitutional when the suspects were released than when they were charged, and that 44% of released suspects were searched unconstitutionally whereas only 7% of the arrested/cited suspects were searched unconstitutionally. Because a high percentage of those who were released had been unconstitutionally searched, no records of their searches were made.

BOX 5.3 HIGHLIGHTS

Police Use of Nonfatal Force, 2002–2011
Special Report (Nov. 2015) NCJ 249216
U.S. Department of Justice
Office of Justice Programs
Bureau of Justice Statistics

This report examines the prevalence of police threat or use of nonfatal force and whether it varies across race and Hispanic origin. Data are from the 2002, 2005, 2008, and 2011 Police–Public Contact Survey (PPCS) supplement to the National Crime Victimization Survey (NCVS).

- Across the four PPCS data collections from 2002 to 2011, black people (3.5%) were more likely to experience nonfatal force during their most recent contact with police than white (1.4%) or Hispanic (2.1%) people.
- A greater percentage of persons who experienced the use of force (44%) had two or more contacts with police than those who did not experience force (28%).
- Black people (14%) were more likely than Hispanic (5.9%) people, and slightly more likely than white (6.9%) people, to experience nonfatal force during street stops.
- Of those who experienced force during their most recent contact, approximately three-quarters described the verbal (71%) or physical (75%) force as excessive.
- Of those who experienced force during their most recent contact, 87% did not believe that the police behaved properly.
- Traffic stops involving an officer and driver of different races were more likely to involve force (2.0%) than traffic stops involving an officer and driver of the same race (0.8%).
- Black people (1.4%) were twice as likely as white people (0.7%) to experience force during contacts involving a personal search.
- Persons who had three or more contacts with police were more likely to experience the use of force during the prior 12 months than persons with one or two contacts.
- The difference between white and Hispanic people in the prevalence of force during the 12-month period was statistically significant among persons with one or two contacts, but not among those with three or more contacts.
- Across all races and Hispanic origin, the perception that the force used was excessive varied with the type of police action taken.
- A lower percentage of persons who were shouted or cursed at by police believed that the force was excessive (49%) compared with those who were pushed or grabbed (79%), hit or kicked (97%), had pepper spray used against them (81%), or had a gun pointed at them (81%).

Of the 115 cases examined, only 16% of the individuals involved identified themselves as white. This fact, while from only a small sample, tends to indicate that race plays an important factor in an officer's decision to search an individual. Since most officers were observed for only one work shift, the researchers were unable to offer a rigorous test of any individual officer's proclivity to conduct illegal searches. The researchers did note, however, that one officer made nine illegal searches (Box 5.4).

Stop and frisks

Nicholas Peart testified in writing to the President's Task Force on 21st Century Policing regarding the New York Police Department's (NYPD) stop and frisk policy. He stated that the NYPD's purpose of stop and frisk is to remove guns from the streets. Under the law, the NYPD is supposed to have reasonable suspicion before stopping and frisking an individual. Yet, over the last decade, less than 0.1% of those stopped had a gun, and less than 5% of these were arrested. Nearly 4 million stops have occurred in New York City in the last decade, with nearly 700,000 stopped in 2012. Eighty-four percent of those stopped were black or Latino.

Peart testified that, in 2011, he was on the way to the store when two police officers jumped out of an unmarked car and told him to stop and put his hands up against the wall; he complied. Without his permission, they took his cell phone from his hand and one

BOX 5.4   CAN OFFICERS DETAIN AN OCCUPANT OF A HOUSE FOR THREE HOURS WHILE THEY SEARCH THE HOUSE WITH A SEARCH WARRANT?

In *Muehler v. Mena,** respondent Mena and others were detained in handcuffs during a search of the premises they occupied. The petitioners were lead members of a police detachment executing a search warrant of the premises for, *inter alia*, deadly weapons and evidence of gang membership. Mena sued the officers under 42 U.S.C. § 1983, and the district court found in her favor. The Ninth Circuit affirmed, holding that the use of handcuffs to detain Mena during the search violated the Fourth Amendment and that the officers' questioning of Mena about her immigration status during the detention constituted an independent Fourth Amendment violation.

The U.S. Supreme Court held that

- Mena's detention in handcuffs for the length of the search did not violate the Fourth Amendment. That detention was consistent with *Michigan v. Summers*, 452 U.S. 692, 705, in which the court held that officers executing a search warrant for contraband have the authority "to detain the occupants of the premises while a proper search is conducted."

The court noted there that minimizing the risk of harm to officers is a substantial justification for detaining an occupant during a search, and ruled that an officer's authority to detain incident to a search is categorical and does not depend on the "quantum of proof justifying detention or the extent of the intrusion to be imposed by the seizure." Because a warrant existed to search the premises, and Mena was an occupant of the premises at the time of the search, her detention for the duration of the search was reasonable under *Summers*. Inherent in *Summers'* authorization to detain is the authority to use reasonable force to effectuate the detention.

The use of force in the form of handcuffs to detain Mena was reasonable because the governmental interest in minimizing the risk of harm to both officers and occupants, at its maximum when a warrant authorizes a search for weapons and a wanted gang member resides on the premises, outweighs the marginal intrusion. Moreover, the need to detain multiple occupants made the use of handcuffs all the more reasonable. Although the duration of a detention can affect the balance of interests, the 2–3 hour detention in handcuffs in this case does not outweigh the government's continuing safety interests.

- The officers' questioning of Mena about her immigration status during her detention did not violate her Fourth Amendment rights. The Ninth Circuit's holding to the contrary appears premised on the assumption that the officers were required to have independent reasonable suspicion in order to so question Mena. However, this court has "held repeatedly that mere police questioning does not constitute a seizure." Because Mena's initial detention was lawful and the Ninth Circuit did not hold that the detention was prolonged by the questioning, there was no additional seizure within the meaning of the Fourth Amendment, and, therefore, no additional Fourth Amendment justification for inquiring about Mena's immigration status was required.

- Because the Ninth Circuit did not address Mena's alternative argument that her detention extended beyond the time for the police to complete the tasks incident to the search, this court declined to address it.

* Muehler v. Mena, 544 U.S. 93 (2005).

of the officers reached into his pocket and removed his wallet and keys. The officer looked through his wallet and then handcuffed him. The officer asked if he had just come out of a particular building. "No" he told them, he lived next door. They put him in a car, removed his shoes and went through his socks, and asked if he had any marijuana in his possession and, if so, that he should let them know. They then took his keys, went into his building, and tried to enter his apartment. His terrified younger siblings tried to call him as they heard strangers trying to get in. He couldn't answer because the police had confiscated his phone. The police tried to use his keys to get into his apartment; they banged on the door but his siblings replied that only children were in the house, so they left. The police came back downstairs; he was simply let go, and he felt helpless.

Police pursuits

How many persons are killed during high-speed car chases? According to an ABC news report, more bystanders are injured or killed during high-speed police chases than by stray bullets. In California, more than 10,000 people have been injured and over 300 people killed because of police chases in the last decade, according to newly released statistics from the California Highway Patrol. The report noted that, nationally, it is estimated that nearly 300 people die each year as a result of high-speed police chases. But a watchdog group reported that the figure is easily two or three times higher because there is no mandatory reporting system.[9]

Exactly what is reported is left to the discretion of local law enforcement agencies. One watch group stated that bystanders who die later at the hospital are often not counted in the police chase statistics. Also, babies and children trapped inside the suspect's vehicle are not counted as innocent victims.

Whether or not to engage in a high-speed vehicle pursuit depends on the police pursuit regulations of the law enforcement unit and a balancing test. If the officer's agency allows the pursuit, then the officer must balance the values of crime control and offender apprehension with ensuring the safety of all parties who potentially might be involved. This concern for safety should include police officers, suspects, victims, bystanders, and the community.

David Schultz, Ed Hudak, and Geoffery Alpert noted that police pursuit records provide some frightening statistics. First, the majority of police pursuits involve a stop for a traffic violation. Second, one person dies every day as a result of a police pursuit. On average, from 1994 to 1998, one law enforcement officer was killed every 11 weeks in a pursuit, and 1% of all U.S. law enforcement officers who died in the line of duty lost their lives in vehicle pursuits. Innocent third parties who just happened to be in the way constitute 42% of persons killed or injured in police pursuits. Furthermore, 1 out of every 100 high-speed pursuits results in a fatality.[10]

The authors state that officers must understand that when a suspect refuses to stop for the emergency lights and siren, a common encounter quickly turns into a high-risk and dangerous event where the "show of authority" may negatively affect the suspect's driving. And if the suspect continues his or her reckless operation of the vehicle, the officer, basing his or her reaction on policy and training, must respond to the potential benefit and risk of the pursuit and also understand the influence of the chase on the participants. The need to "win" and make that arrest can be influenced by the adrenaline rush felt by the officer who also must recognize that the fleeing suspect will have the same experience.

The authors note that research has demonstrated the impact of this on an officer's vision, hearing, motor skills, and decision-making, and therefore it would appear necessary to prepare for the same adverse effect it could have on fleeing suspects. While a pursuit is an exciting event and involves one person running to escape and another chasing to catch, one important challenge for the officer is that there are only limited ways to get the suspect to stop, including a tire deflation devise, a precision immobilization technique (PIT) maneuver at proper speeds and locations, or an application of deadly force.

As pointed out by the authors, the dynamics of most pursuits include the fleeing suspect raising risks to the welfare of the officer, the public, and himself or herself by not stopping and then driving recklessly. The authors contend that the fleeing suspect is attempting to escape the consequences of his or her actions and avoid being taken into custody. Most pursuits are for minor offenses, and whether those fleeing suspects have committed a serious crime is pure speculation.

The demographics of those who fled from the police are

- Average age of 26 years
- 94% were male
- 30% of the suspects crashed
- 30% stopped
- 25% outran the police

Why they fled:

- 32% were driving a stolen car
- 27% had a suspended driver's license
- 27% wanted to avoid arrest
- 21% were driving under the influence

One of the more interesting findings noted by the authors was that suspects who have fled from the police report that, once the officer terminates the pursuit, they will slow down within a reasonable period of time.

Do the police have a duty to break off the high-speed pursuit?

In the *McCain v. Florida Power Corp.* case, the Florida state court questioned whether or not the police have a duty to break off the chase when it becomes dangerous to the public.* In the case of *Brown v. City of Pinellas Park*,† the pursued vehicle hit another vehicle, killing two people. The facts are as follows: After running a

* McCain v. Florida Power Corp., 593 So.2d 500, 503 (Fla. 1992).
† Brown v. City of Pinellas Park, 557 So.2d 161, (Fla. App. 2 Dist., February 16, 1990).

red light in Pasadena, Florida, John Deady attempted to elude a sheriff's deputy in a high-speed chase. Before this chase ended on a stretch of U.S. 19, it would pass along a 25-mile course in Pinellas County through which normal urban traffic was also passing. Thirty-four separate traffic signals—at least some of which were ignored by this ill-fated caravan—were encountered along the way, thereby endangering everyone lawfully passing through those intersections. The route stretched from the suburbs of St. Petersburg, northward through the urban area surrounding Clearwater, and on beyond the fringes of Dunedin. This is part of the densely populated Tampa–St. Petersburg urban area.

As the chase continued, the sheriff's deputy was joined by at least 14 and as many as 20 separate police or sheriff's vehicles, each of which was pursuing Deady at speeds that varied between 80 and 120 mph. Although the chase was initiated by a Pinellas sheriff's deputy, officers from Kenneth City and the City of Pinellas Park also joined in. However, most of the officers involved were from the sheriff's department. At some point, the Pinellas County Sheriff's Department ordered its officers to discontinue the chase. For unknown or unstated reasons, this order was not obeyed.

By this time, the caravan was approaching the intersection of U.S. 19 and State Road 584 at very high speeds. At this intersection, Sheriff's Corporal Daniel Rusher was waiting in the turn lane, ready to move onto the highway that Deady and the caravan were traveling on. In the through-lane immediately next to Rusher was a vehicle occupied by two sisters, Susan and Judith Brown. Rusher made no attempt to block the intersection or to prevent the Browns from proceeding into the intersection. Rather, he was preparing to become part of the caravan.

When the light turned green, Rusher moved his vehicle onto U.S. 19 so that he could wait for Deady to pass and then join the chase. At the same time, the vehicle containing the Brown sisters moved forward into the intersection to pass through it. Deady's vehicle illegally entered the intersection at this precise moment and struck the Browns' vehicle at 90 mph. Deady and Susan Brown died instantly, and Judith Brown died 3 days later.

The state appellate court noted that:

> We think it manifest that a high-speed chase involving a large number of vehicles on a public thoroughfare is likely to result in injury to a foreseeable victim, and that the discontinuance of this chase by police is likely to diminish the risk. In other words, some substantial portion of the risk is being created by the police themselves, notwithstanding any

contributory negligence of the person being chased. Accordingly, we believe the law must recognize a duty in this context even though the accident did not involve a police vehicle.[*]

This case was appealed to the Florida Supreme Court, which held that

1. Police who engaged in 25-mile, caravan-type chases owed a duty to deceased motorists.
2. Sovereign immunity did not shield officers from liability.
3. Whether negligence of police officers was the proximate cause of the accident was a jury question.[†]

Not all state decisions have agreed with the *Brown* case. For example, in a Kansas Supreme Court case, the court stated:

> The proper definition for "reckless disregard," as applied in statute requiring drivers of emergency vehicles to drive with due regard for the safety of all persons, is driving a vehicle under circumstances that show a realization of the imminence of danger to another person or the property of another where there is a conscious and unjustifiable disregard of that danger.[‡]

Kansas therefore holds that the police are only liable to injured bystanders when the officer shows a reckless disregard for human life.

High-speed pursuit as excessive use of force

If the police pursuit results in the death of a person, is this an excessive use of force? This question was raised in the *Plumhoff v. Richard* case.[§] In that case, the U.S. Supreme Court unanimously found that Arkansas police officers did not use excessive force in violation of the Fourth Amendment when they shot and killed a fleeing motorist, ending a high-speed car chase which risked the lives of both the officers and numerous innocent bystanders.

In July 2004, driver Donald Rickard was stopped by a West Memphis, Arkansas police officer because his car had only one operating headlight. After Rickard refused to give up his driver's license when asked, and the officer noticed Rickard's nervous appearance and

---

[*] Brown v. City of Pinellas Park, at p. 177.
[†] City of Pinellas Prak v. Brown, 604 So.2d 1222 (Fla. Sup Ct. 1992).
[‡] Robbins v. City of Wichita, 172 P. 3rd 1187 (Ka. Sup. Ct. 2007).
[§] Plumhoff, et al., v. Rickard, et al. (2015) 572 U.S. ___.

damage to the car consistent with vehicle theft, the officer ordered Rickard to step out of the vehicle. Rather than comply, Rickard sped away.

The ensuing pursuit, ultimately involving six police cruisers, lasted some 5 minutes, exceeded speeds of 100 mph, and came within close proximity to other motorists on the road, including swerving through traffic at high speeds. It was estimated that the pursuit passed more than two dozen vehicles. Eventually, Rickard lost control of his vehicle, "spun out" into a parking lot, and collided with one of the pursuing officer's vehicles. Now cornered, Rickard put his car into reverse in an attempt to escape, but collided with another officer's vehicle. At that point, two officers got out of their cars and approached Rickard's car, with one of the officers drawing his pistol and ordering Rickard to stop and get out while knocking on his passenger window. Once again, instead of complying, Rickard slammed on the accelerator in an apparent attempt to push through the sitting police cruiser blocking his car's escape. At this point, one of the officers fired three shots into Rickard's car. Rickard then reversed in "a 180° arc," narrowly avoiding a diving officer, managed to maneuver onto a side street, and began to speed away. Other officers on the scene then fired 12 shots into the car. Rickard crashed shortly thereafter, and both he and his passenger died.

Rickard's daughter filed a federal lawsuit against the shooting officers, among other defendants, alleging "excessive force" in violation of the Fourth Amendment. The daughter made two central arguments considered by the court: first, the officers used excessive force by using deadly force to terminate the pursuit, and second, the officers used excessive force by firing 15 shots in total to end the pursuit.

The district court favored the daughter's arguments, ruling that the defending officers' conduct violated the Fourth Amendment and also that they were not entitled to "qualified immunity," as their conduct violated "clearly established" Fourth Amendment law. The Sixth Circuit Court of Appeal agreed on both points.

The Supreme Court reversed, rejecting both of the daughter's contentions and the lower courts' rulings. Specifically, the court made two rulings: first, none of the officers' conduct violated the Fourth Amendment, and second, even if it did, they were entitled to "qualified immunity." The court also engaged in an interesting discussion about Rickard's passenger's right to be free from unreasonable force under the Fourth Amendment.

Strongly affirming *Graham v. Connor*'s familiar Fourth Amendment analysis, the court reiterated the rule that allegations of unreasonable force must be analyzed "from the perspective of a reasonable officer on the scene, rather than with the 20/20 vision of hindsight... We thus allow for the fact that police officers are often forced to make split-second judgments—in

circumstances that are tense, uncertain, and rapidly evolving—about the amount of force that is necessary in a particular situation." Using this framework, the court referred to the prior case of *Scott v. Harris* (2007) 550 U.S. 372, for support of its position that the officers' use of deadly force here was reasonable. In *Scott*, the court noted that, where a suspect leads police on a car chase that poses "an actual and imminent threat" to bystanders, "a police officer's attempt to terminate a dangerous high-speed car chase that threatens the lives of innocent bystanders does not violate the Fourth Amendment, even when it places the fleeing motorist at risk of serious injury or death."

In this case, the court saw "no basis for reaching a different conclusion." It noted that "Rickard's outrageously reckless driving posed a grave public safety risk," as it "exceeded 100 mph," "lasted over five minutes," and "passed more than two dozen other vehicles." Furthermore, the court found that the chase was not "over" when Rickard was "cornered" in the parking lot, as he was still attempting to speed away, nearly hitting an officer: "[u]nder the circumstances at the moment when the shots were fired, all that a reasonable police officer could have concluded was that Rickard was intent on resuming his flight and that, if he was allowed to do so, he would once again pose a deadly threat for others on the road." Thus, "it [was] beyond serious dispute that Rickard's flight posed a grave public safety risk, and here, as in Scott, the police acted reasonably in using deadly force to end that risk."

Regarding the 15 shots fired, the court stated that it stands to reason that, if police officers are justified in firing at a suspect in order to end a severe threat to public safety, the officers need not stop shooting until the threat has ended. This is what occurred, as during the 10 second span, Rickard never abandoned his attempt to flee. The court did note that, had the officers initiated a second round of shots after an initial round had clearly incapacitated Rickard and had ended any threat of continued flight, or if Rickard had clearly given himself up, the results may have been different.

The court held that the passenger's presence in the car did not alter the analysis before it, because the passenger's presence in the car did not enhance Rickard's Fourth Amendment rights. It would be perverse if his disregard for the passenger's safety worked to his benefit.

The passenger's presence did not alter the analysis of any possible violation of Rickard's Fourth Amendment rights, because they are personal rights that may not be vicariously asserted. If a suit were brought on behalf of the passenger, under the Fourth Amendment or state tort law, the analysis would focus on the officer's actions in relation to his right to be free from unreasonable force.

Sexual misconduct

In the International Association of Chiefs of Police (IACP) Executive Guide on Addressing Sexual Offenses and Misconduct by Law Enforcement, sexual misconduct by law enforcement is defined as any behavior by an officer that takes advantage of the officer's position in law enforcement to misuse his authority and power (including force) in order to commit a sexual act, initiate sexual contact with another person, or respond to a perceived sexually motivated cue (from a subtle suggestion to an overt action) from another person. It also includes any communication or behavior by an officer that would likely be construed as lewd, lascivious, inappropriate, or conduct unbecoming of an officer and violates general principles of acceptable conduct common to law enforcement.[11]

In November 2015, the Associated Press (AP) stated that, in a yearlong investigation of sexual misconduct by U.S. law enforcement, about 1000 law enforcement officers lost their badges in a 6-year period for rape, sodomy, and other sexual assault; sex crimes that included possession of child pornography; or sexual misconduct such as propositioning citizens or having consensual but prohibited on-duty intercourse.[12]

The AP report stated that the number was unquestionably an undercount because it represented only those officers whose licenses to work in law enforcement were revoked, and not all states take such action. The report noted that California and New York—with several of the nation's largest law enforcement agencies—offered no records because they have no statewide system to decertify officers for misconduct. Even among states that provided records, some reported that no officers were removed for sexual misdeeds even though cases were identified via news stories or court records.

The AP report quoted the Sarasota, Florida, police chief as stating "It's happening probably in every law enforcement agency across the country." The chief who had helped study the problem for the IACP is reported to also have stated "It's so underreported and people are scared that if they call and complain about a police officer, they think every other police officer is going to be then out to get them."

The report noted that law enforcement officers frequently accused of sexual misconduct have jumped from job to job and sometimes faced fresh allegations, including the raping of women, because of a tattered network of laws and lax screening that allowed them to stay on the beat. The report also noted a broken system for policing bad officers, with significant flaws in how agencies deal with those suspected of sexual misconduct and with glaring warning signs that go unreported or are overlooked.

The AP investigation looked at court records and news reports during the period 2009–2014. The report noted that during that period, Alabama decertified 20 officers for sex-related misconduct. Arizona decertified 27 officers during that period, Florida decertified 162, and Georgia 161. The report excluded the states of California, Massachusetts, District of Columbia, New Jersey, and New York because those states did not have statewide records, provide the information, or decertify officers at the state level.

The Cato Institute's NPMSRP noted that sexual misconduct by the police is one form of police brutality that nobody talks about, but that officer-involved sexual misconduct consistently ranks first or second among the types of police misconduct that the NPMSRP tracks each month.[13] Some of the cases reported by the NPMSRP included

- A Louisiana deputy who was fired after he was charged with sexual battery and forcible rape of a juvenile; no other details were released pending an ongoing investigation.
- A Massachusetts police officer who was arrested for viewing child pornography on a government computer in the department's evidence room.
- An Alabama State trooper who had been indicted for allegedly sexually abusing the female passenger of a car belonging to the person driving her home who was arrested on outstanding warrants. The officer drove her down a dirt road and began to molest her, though he claims it was consensual.
- A Florida police officer with an apparent penchant for spanking women, who was recently sentenced to probation for pulling the pants off of an unwilling victim and spanking her a dozen times, is now seeking to cut that probation short.
- A Louisiana deputy who was arrested on rape charges for allegedly forcing a woman to perform an unspecified sexual act on him under threat of being jailed after a traffic stop arrest.
- A Tuskegee University, Alabama, police officer who was indicted for conspiracy to commit rape and a count of conspiracy to commit sodomy of a 15-year-old girl who was allegedly raped by a second officer who was arrested a few weeks previously.
- A California police officer who was arrested at work on charges of lewd acts with a child, for allegedly molesting a 14- or 15-year-old child.

Many of the victims reported that the coerced sex was not based on the threat of arrest and jail but that the officer was armed and made suggestive moves toward his gun while discussing sex. The Cato project also noted that cultural issues within police departments contribute to climates where sexual predators feel emboldened or accepted since officers can tend toward chauvinistic attitudes as part of the "macho cop" image many try to project. These can be tempered by proper management, training, and policies prohibiting sexually discriminatory behaviors and harassment and strict enforcement of those policies. The report also indicated that a lax disciplinary response to sexual misconduct reports was a massive contributing factor to repeat sexual misconduct by officers because it reinforces an attitude that the authority to sexually assault the people they are sworn to protect comes as a fringe benefit of the authority of a badge.[13] The report concludes with the statement that victims of sexual assault often feel safe because they believe that the police will help them, but soon realize that victims of officer-involved sexual misconduct can't even trust the police.

In 2003, the federal government enacted the Prison Rape Elimination Act (PREA) to protect prison inmates. Many advocates believe that a similar act should be enacted to help those who are sexually abused while in police custody, detained on the street, or in patrol vehicles. One advocate was reported to have stated that the PREA had established some requirements for the independent investigation of prisoners' accusations of rape and sexual assault, which could benefit those who come forward to report sexual assault by a police officer.[14]

The Rape, Abuse, and Incest National Network website contends that sexual assault is one of the most unreported crimes and that only 32 out of every 100 rapes are even reported to the police.[15] It is estimated that victims of officer-involved sexual assault are even less likely to report the crime than the victims of sexual assaults not involving officers. There appears to be a natural reluctance to report to the police when a police officer is the offender. From a review of some of the cases, it appears that officers tend to choose victims that would lack so-called credibility in the eyes of other law enforcement officers, whether it was somebody who was engaged in sex work or somebody who was intoxicated or using drugs, and then they often use that justification for why the victim cannot be believed.

In reviewing victims of officer-involved sexual conduct reports, a common complaint is that the department, after receiving the complaint, failed to investigate it. For example, in May 2011, a 22-year-old woman claimed that she was raped by two on-duty Chicago police officers. In her section 1983 federal lawsuit, she alleged a widespread practice of abuse within the department that goes largely unpunished. In her lawsuit, she alleged that "Chicago police officers accused of sexual misconduct against citizens can be confident that the city will not investigate those accusations in earnest." The lawsuit also alleged that "This ... victim reported the rape, yet the Chicago Police Department allowed (officers) to retain their employment as patrol officers, thus enabling them to commit a similar crime ... less than 1 month later."[16]

Abusive interrogation

Consider the facts of the situation set forth in the case of *Dahlia v. Rodriguez.* Following an armed robbery on December 28, 2007, at a cafe in Burbank, California, Dahlia was assigned to assist in the robbery investigation, which was supervised by defendant Lieutenant Jon Murphy. The day after the robbery, Dahlia observed defendant Lieutenant Omar Rodriguez grab a suspect by the throat with his left hand, retrieve his handgun from its holster with his right hand, and place the barrel of the gun under the suspect's eye, saying, "How does it feel to have a gun in your face m------f---." Rodriguez noticed Dahlia looking on in disbelief. Later that same evening, Dahlia heard yelling and the sound of someone being hit and slapped from inside a room where defendant Sergeant Edgar Penaranda was interviewing another suspect.

Dahlia was subsequently excluded from participating in suspect interviews, and high-ranking officers within the department essentially took control of the investigation. Witnesses and suspects continued to be physically assaulted and beaten in the interview rooms, while officers prevented anyone from walking past the rooms or into the audio room. Dahlia met with Murphy to disclose the abuse that he had witnessed. Dahlia told Murphy that the interviews were getting too physical and that he was having difficulty maintaining order in the investigation. Murphy responded by telling Dahlia to "stop his sniveling."

The physical beatings continued in interview rooms and in the field, evidenced by the booking photos of various suspects. At one point, Chief of Police Stehr appeared at a briefing and, on learning that not all of the robbery suspects were in custody, said, "Well then beat another one until they are all in custody."

After witnessing the misconduct and abuse, Dahlia approached Murphy a second time and pleaded that he did not have control over the case. Murphy became upset and told Dahlia that he "didn't want to hear this shit again" and that he was "tired of all the B.S." In January 2008, Dahlia and another detective met with Murphy a third time, telling him that "the beatings have to stop" and "the madness ha[s] to stop." Murphy did nothing to respond to these complaints and the abusive tactics continued.

* Dahlia v. Rodriguez, 735 F.3rd 1060 (9th Cir. 2013).

On May 11, 2009, the Los Angeles County Sheriff's Department (LASD) interviewed Dahlia about the a robbery investigation. During the interview, Dahlia disclosed the defendants' misconduct, threats, intimidation, and harassment. Four days later, Dahlia was placed on administrative leave pending discipline.

Dahlia alleges that he was subjected to adverse employment actions as a result of his protected speech activities and that there was no legitimate justification for the adverse actions. In alleging a § 1983 violation, Dahlia claims that defendants' retaliatory acts included, *inter alia*, threats, ostracism, denial of employment opportunities, undue scrutiny of work performance, denial of continued employment, and malicious statements calculated to destroy his reputation.

The appellate court ruled that malfeasance by officers of the Burbank Police Department, which Dahlia witnessed, and the threats and intimidation he endured—if true—were shocking and intolerable. "Yet, we must stay our collective hand, ever mindful that the Constitution does not provide a cure for every social ill", nor does it vest judges with a mandate to try to remedy every social problem. Alongside his First Amendment cause, Dahlia brought claims under the provisions of California law that (1) protect public employees from retaliation for disclosing an abuse of authority or a danger to the public safety, California Government Code § 53298; and (2) that shield employees who complain to a government agency, California Labor Code § 6310. These are the kinds of remedies that the Supreme Court has explained that whistleblowers should pursue in the absence of a constitutional claim. However righteous the aims, when the court stretches the Constitution to match its sense of justice, the courts exceed "the judicial power" vested to the courts in Article III and, by rendering state law nugatory, disserve our federal union.

In earlier chapters, we explored the excessive use of force and the use of deadly force by law enforcement officers. In this chapter, we will explore other forms of misconduct. While most of the examples used in this text pertain to U.S. law enforcement officers, that does not mean that the officers in the United States are the only ones involved in misconduct.

One of the most controversial issues involves allegations of police abuse of minority groups. As noted by Robert Weitzer, race is one of the strongest predictors of attitudes toward police. Weitzer states that, regardless of class background, African Americans suffer substantial racial discrimination and that this in turn influences their assessments of police misconduct. He states that, because crime rates typically are higher in both poor black and white neighborhoods than in middle-class neighborhoods, the former are more likely to generate frequent police–citizen encounters. And, according to

Weitzer, as a result, there are more contacts to go awry as a result, and the chances of conflict are greater. He also notes that poor neighborhoods generate more frequent involuntary contacts with police officers; these are associated with more negative evaluations of police than are voluntary contacts.

Much of the misconduct may be attributed to implicit racial bias. For example, in many jurisdictions, it appears to be a crime to "drive while black." One researcher once commented that rather than use the phrase "driving while black" we should use the phrase "patrolling while racially biased." The implicit racial bias is not solely a U.S. problem. For example the September 2015 issue of the prestigious English journal *CJM* (*Criminal Justice Matters*) devoted the entire issue to implicit racial bias in the United Kingdom.

Rebekah Delsol noted that "Police officers are racially profiling when they view people as suspicious because of who they are, what they look like, or where they pray, rather than what they have done". She states that race should be considered as a social construct; not knowable by sight. She concludes that racial profiling exacts a high price on individuals, groups, and communities that are singled out for disproportionate police attention. She also points out that the damage that racial profiling can do is slowly being recognized in both America and the United Kingdom.

Jules Holroyd, in her discussion on recent psychological findings, contends that there are robust findings that indicate that, in a contemporary society, implicit race bias is pervasive. He notes that the main strategies adopted to combat institutional racism in the United Kingdom have been to challenge "canteen culture" and the use of explicitly racist language, and to take steps to diversity the police force. He also notes that, if biases are affecting practice, then as a matter of urgency there should be investigation into how police practices should be reformed to try to prevent racial bias from infecting conduct. He concludes his article with the comment that implicit biases are not inevitable and there are things that can be done to stop them from having an impact on actions.

Rebecca Roberts, in her article "Racism and criminal justice," quotes a statement by the former United Kingdom prime minister Tony Blair. She reports that Blair, while discussing black-on-black crime in 2007, stated that

> What we are dealing with is not general social disorder; but specific groups or people who for one reason or another, are deciding not to abide by the same code of conduct as the rest of us…The black community-vast majority of whom in these communities

are decent, law-abiding people horrified at what is happening—need to be mobilized in denunciation of this gang culture that is killing innocent young black kids. But we won't stop this by pretending it isn't young black kids doing it.

Many of those listening to Tony Blair came away with the opinion that he was declaring war on young black people in the United Kingdom. While there is no research on the issue, his comments undoubtedly had an effect on how British police officers felt when engaging with a young black person.

Other police misconduct

The types of misconduct that police have been involved are probably too varied to list. In this section, a few of those types are discussed. The types of misconduct are frequently grouped by type of corruption. These include

- Demanding free or discounted meals or services
- Demanding and receiving kickbacks
- Thefts of opportunity such as stealing money from a dead victim or a suspect
- Shakedowns
- Bribery
- Internal payoffs
- Protection payments
- Abuse of authority
- Street justice
- Lying and false testimony

Stealing money from a suspect

In the New Jersey case of *In Re Furlow*,* the appellant was a police officer with the City of Newark Police Department (NPD). On December 3, 2002, the appellant arrested a suspect for possession of a handgun, knowing that the charge was false; took money from the suspect for his personal gain; failed to submit the money as property/evidence; and falsified the police report. On April 18, 2003, the appellant took money from another suspect for his personal gain, and failed to submit the money into property/evidence. The appellant admitted both thefts to the NPD internal affairs department in August 2004, and signed a plea agreement promising to cooperate in an investigation of police corruption. However, in 2009 and 2012, the appellant falsely testified in court that he was coerced into making his 2004 confession. The appellate court denied his claim.

Retaliation

In *Abella v. Simon*,† Officers Juan Rodriguez, Benjamin Rivera, and Richard Baez, and their supervising officer, Major Frank Bocanegra, appealed the denial of their motion to dismiss Gustavo Abella's third amended complaint based on qualified immunity. Abella complained about retaliation by each of the officers. The appellate court affirmed.

Abella complained that Rodriguez, Rivera, Baez, and their superior officer, Bocanegra, retaliated against Abella for engaging in conduct protected by the First Amendment. Abella alleged that his conduct included displaying a political sign in his truck, reporting police misconduct, and photographing officers.

Abella complained that Rodriguez had retaliated against Abella and his family for displaying a political sign, voicing their opinion about the ordinance at town meetings, and filing grievances against Rodriguez. Abella alleged that Rodriguez ordered Abella to remove the sign from his truck; threatened to issue a citation to Abella if he failed to remove the sign; appeared outside Abella's home and his daughter's school; and "made signs" at Abella while following him around town. Abella also alleged that, after he photographed Rodriguez outside the school, Rodriguez issued a citation to Abella for a parking violation and told Abella that "the complaints he had filed with the Commission on Ethics would not do anything."

Abella's complaint alleged that Rivera had retaliated for Abella's complaints about police misconduct. Abella alleged that Rivera had issued Abella with a parking citation, followed him home, and then yelled out, asking Abella's wife if she wanted his badge number or the phone number for the Miami–Dade internal affairs office. Later, during a hearing about the citation, Rivera grumbled about being assigned to the school because of the grievances filed by Abella.

Abella also complained that Baez interfered with his being photographed and retaliated for the photos and having a grievance filed against him. Abella alleged that his wife photographed Baez standing outside her house and Baez approached the house to question her about the photos. Because the encounter frightened Abella's wife, she reported Baez's conduct to his supervisor. Two days later, Baez noticed that he was being photographed outside the school, walked to Abella's vehicle, and pushed the camera into Abella's face.

Abella's complaint also alleged that Bocanegra deliberately ignored the grievances against his subordinate officers and failed to discipline them for their alleged misconduct. Abella alleged that his attorney

---

* 2014 WL 9966171 (NJ app. Div. 2014).

† 522 Fed. Appx. 872 (11th Cir. 2013).

complained to Bocanegra about Rodriguez, but Abella did not witness a change in Rodriguez's conduct. Abella also alleged that he and his wife filed grievances and sent letters and e-mails to Bocanegra about his officers' misconduct.

To survive a motion to dismiss, based on retaliation for exercising rights under the First Amendment, Abella had to allege facts establishing, "first, that his speech or act was constitutionally protected; second, that the officers' retaliatory conduct adversely affected the protected speech; and third, that there is a causal connection between the retaliatory actions and the adverse effect on speech." The First Amendment affords the broadest protection to political expression, and protects the rights of speech and to petition for redress, and to photograph police activities. To establish a causal connection, Abella had to allege that his protected conduct was a "motivating factor behind" the officers' alleged misconduct, and that the history of widespread abuse put their responsible supervisor on notice of the need to correct the alleged deprivation, and that he failed to do so.

The district court did not err by denying the officers' motion to dismiss based on qualified immunity. Abella alleged facts sufficient to establish that Rodriguez, Rivera, and Baez had retaliated because Abella had exhibited a political sign, reported police misconduct, and photographed the officers. Abella also alleged facts sufficient to establish that Bocanegra knew about, and failed to correct, his subordinate officers' unlawful conduct. Although Abella was not deterred by being followed, stopped, ticketed, and intimated by the officers, those actions would likely deter a person of ordinary firmness from the exercise of First Amendment rights. The appellate court denied the officers' motion to dismiss.

In *Golodner v. Berliner*,* the plaintiffs Golodner and his company brought suit under 42 U.S.C. 1983, alleging that that the City of New London and two city officials retaliated against Golodner for exercising his rights under the First Amendment when he filed an earlier lawsuit against the city and several of its officers. The claims in the first lawsuit arose from a dispute that Golodner had had with his neighbors, and that he was arrested multiple times as a result of those disputes. Golodner asserted two factors that motivated the arresting officers: a constitutionally impermissible policy promulgated by the city, and malice directed toward him personally. He claimed that the city's policy of arresting both the complaining witness and person complained about in the context of a neighborhood dispute resulted in a denial of equal protection of the law.

* 770 F.3d. 196 (2nd Cir. 2014).

Golodner's theory based on the second alleged motivating factor was the fact that he had previously "made complaints about police misconduct to the New London Police Department." Golodner claimed that, because the officers "harbored actual malice against" him and did not "want to have anything to do with him," they disregarded his complaints concerning disputes he had with his neighbors, and further because the officers "knew that he had previously complained about police misconduct to their Superiors at the New London Police Department, they were inspired by a malicious intent to retaliate against him for having complained against a brother officer." He asserted that his arrests based on this motive were unsupported by probable cause. The appellate court held that Golodner had alleged that the individual defendants' conduct violated a clearly established right.

False testimony

A Philadelphia police officer was charged with perjury in 2014 after a complaint was made to the internal affairs unit about testimony he gave in 2011. The indictment indicated that the officer gave false testimony during a hearing about the circumstances surrounding the arrest of a suspect. The officer testified that, when the suspect was arrested, the car's windows were tinted. Three other witnesses testified in court that the windows were not tinted. When the officer and his partner stopped the vehicle in question and searched it, they found narcotics. The officer testified that, after stopping the car, he and his partner waited for a search warrant before conducting the search. That statement was determined to be false.

Why would the officer commit perjury? Probably because after he and his partner discovered the narcotics as the result of their illegal search, they concluded that it was noble to lie to make sure that the criminals would be prosecuted.

Corruption

A Philadelphia police officer was promoted in 2015 after he was acquitted of corruption charges after being implicated in a wide-ranging federal investigation. The police commissioner had described the officer's involvement as one of the worst cases of corruption he had seen. The commissioner's decision to dismiss the officer and the others involved was overturned by an arbitrator and the officers were reinstated.

The officer and the others were charged in a sweeping racketeering conspiracy case in which prosecutors alleged that the officers beat drug suspects, stole money from them, and then filed false police reports to cover up their actions. One witness testified that the officers held him over the balcony of his high-rise apartment and threatened to let him fall to his death if he did not provide information on his drug business.

Since 2012, the District Attorney's Office has refused to accept testimony in cases stemming from arrests by any of the officers implicated in the criminal case. Now that the officers have been reinstated, prosecutors announced that they will decide on a case-by-case basis whether to allow their testimony in future cases. To date, 393 convictions in criminal cases that relied on arrests or testimony by the six officers have been reversed. An additional 89 are scheduled to be reversed.

According to a *New York Post* story, the top reason people are falsely imprisoned is because of official misconduct. The article states that 47% of cases of people falsely imprisoned are the result of misconduct by authorities. Prosecutorial misconduct includes withholding exculpatory evidence from the defense, destroying evidence, and allowing unreliable witnesses or fraudulent experts to testify. Police misconduct includes coercing false confessions, lying on the witness stand, or failing to turn over evidence to prosecutors.[17]

Executing search warrants in an unreasonable manner

In *Basilio v. City of Philadelphia*,[*] Mercedes Basil asserted a claim for damages from the City. Specifically, the amended complaint alleged that it is the pattern and practice of the City, through its police officers, "to execute search warrants in an unreasonable manner, which includes destroying personal property, ruining personal belongings, and disrupting the homes and businesses of citizens in violation of the Fourth and Fourteenth Amendments of the United States Constitution." Plaintiffs claimed that the City "routinely executes search warrants in an unreasonable manner that causes unnecessary destruction of property." They asserted that, as a direct and proximate result of this policy, the individual defendants executed the search of Basilio's home in an allegedly unreasonable and violent manner, used excessive force, and caused unnecessary damage to Basilio's property.

The appellate court in the Basilio case found no evidence suggesting that the City should have had notice about any history or pattern of these individual officers, or of the narcotics officers in general, executing search warrants in the unreasonable manner alleged in this case. Therefore, summary judgment for the City was appropriate on this claim. The decision, however, indicated that had the city known, it probably would have been liable for failure to train. Note: The plaintiff's case against the individual officers was not dismissed.

Malicious prosecution

In *Groark v. Timek*,[†] plaintiff Matthew Groark alleged that Atlantic City police officers Frank Timek and Sterling Wheaten beat him up without provocation and then filed false criminal charges. The plaintiff learned, in discovery, that from May 2001 to November, 2013. Timek and Wheaten had collectively been the subject of approximately 78 complaints similar to those asserted here—excessive force, assault, threats, improper search and arrest, and malicious prosecution. Atlantic City's Police Department ("Atlantic City") did not sustain any of the complaints and Timek and Wheaten were never disciplined. The plaintiff's Motion to Compel Discovery asked the court to order Atlantic City to produce Timek and Wheaten's complete internal affairs (IA) files so that the plaintiff could determine if Atlantic City's IA unit and investigations were a sham.

The plaintiff argued that Atlantic City was deliberately indifferent to its police officers' misconduct and condones the obvious consequences of its failure to properly train, supervise, and discipline its officers. The plaintiff also argued that he wanted to get to the bottom of why it appeared that Timek and Wheaten had repeatedly used excessive force with impunity. The plaintiff's motion had been fully briefed and argued. The court granted the motion. The court also noted that complaints made against Timek and Wheaten by senior police department personnel fared no better than citizen complaints. The charges made by Chief Snellbaker, Captain Wm. Burke, Captain Dooley, and Acting Chief Jubilee were also "not sustained." The same was true for Chief Mooney's complaint against Wheaten of "simple assault and standard of conduct."

Summary

- The NPMSRP states that around 1% of all police officers commit police misconduct in a given year.
- As noted by the Cato Institute, in most police misconduct cases, the misconduct is more subtle than torture. Oftentimes, police simply push the envelope in order to obtain a witness statement.
- One of the most controversial issues involves allegations of police abuse of minority groups. As noted by Robert Weitzer, race is one of the strongest predictors of attitudes toward police.
- The NPMSRP Police Misconduct Statistical Report indicates that, from January 2010 to December 2010, there were 4861 unique reports of police misconduct that involved 6613 sworn law enforcement officers and 6826 alleged victims.

---

[*] Basilio v. City of Philadelphia, 2013 WL 4823146 (ED, Pen. 2013).

[†] 989 F.Supp 2d. 378 (NJ DC, 2013).

POLICE PERFORMANCE MANAGEMENT AND CRIME REPORT MANIPULATION

By John A. Eterno, PhD and Eli B. Silverman, PhD

Police crime reports are a staple of research, crime analysis, police strategies, real estate values, politics, and much more. They are significant because they determine and provide the public face of the crime rate. Often mayors and other politicians will talk about their cities, towns, and villages being the safest, based on these crime numbers. These numbers will influence real estate values, tourism, obtaining money for grants, police tactics, and many other things. Subsequently, there are enormous pressures on the police to make sure these numbers are "going in the right direction."

Police agencies throughout the United States are now using a performance management system known as Compstat (to compare statistics). Under this system, commanders of local areas such as precincts are held strictly accountable for the crimes that occur in their commands. The commanders are constantly compared to what happened last year with respect to these crime numbers. The focus of Compstat is not simply on any crime numbers, but more specifically on the 7 major felonies that are used to determine the crime rate (murder/nonnegligent manslaughter, robbery, burglary, aggravated assault, grand larceny, grand larceny auto, forcible rape (arson is also included but not included Compstat meetings).

Commanders are grilled quite extensively about these index crimes. If the numbers are going up, commanders may be in trouble. At times, commanders are yelled at and berated in front of their peers. The informal message is: if crime goes up you may lose your command and have a terrible career—pigeon-holed as a failure. However, if crime decreases, you may be rewarded with promotion and an excellent career. Based on a survey of 1770 retired New York City officers, we know that the pressures on commanders to ensure that crime goes down as well as the pressures to downgrade crime have skyrocketed in recent years.[18] Additionally, this model of policing in New York City has been emulated throughout the United States and the world.

Police are tasked with taking crime reports from the public. With pressure so high, there is strong temptation to manipulate the crime reports. We have found that police will succumb to this temptation and manipulate the reports. How is this done? In short, it is "creative accounting." Based on research[19] conducted in New York City, there are many ways to change the classification of reports—often very nefariously. Some examples:

- A police captain racing with lights and sirens will go to the scene of an obvious homicide. The captain then orders the lieutenant to take the report as "investigate a dead human body" rather than the homicide it actually clearly is. This buys time to try to find any way possible to keep the crime away from the 7 majors such as: the District Attorney does not charge homicide, the lack of clarity in the case allows it to be classified as something else, the medical examiner leaves room for another interpretation. It is ambiguity that is the key. Any little bit will be used to keep the report out of the 7 majors.
- Officers in crime analysis units reviewing websites to find lower prices for stolen property so that the crime could be lowered to petty larceny (downgraded).
- Taking reports for lost property, even though the property was obviously stolen.
- Leaving a few key words out of a report to lower a crime classification. This was especially a problem in New York City with sex crimes victims, who had to approach the police commissioner because the problem became so severe. One victim advised how she was groped and attacked in an attempted rape (which is counted as a full rape in the crime reporting system that counts index crime). The officers responding to the scene took the report but left out key words that reduced the crime to a minor misdemeanor crime forcible touching. The victim, however, knew the right people and the report was changed to reflect the rape. However, what happens to the vast majority of victims who do not know anyone?

Creative accounting involves changing words, calling victims back to change stories, scrubbing reports by numerous officers to find another crime to classify the acts (often parsing the crime into its constituent parts such as criminal trespass and petit larceny (rather than burglary). Officers might take one big report for numerous burglaries in apartment buildings rather than the correct way of recording each apartment as a burglary—one burglary for each apartment.

Officers today will look for any ambiguity at all to classify a report as a non-seven majors offense. There are numerous officers dedicated to this task at the lower level. One commander even took an officer off patrol to try to find cars that were reported stolen but were not. Such accounting practices are a completely different way of counting, compared with the past and with the rules required by the Federal Bureau of Investigation, who collects and collate these reports.

The pressures on commanders ultimately lead to these unethical behaviors. These pressures are inherent in the police performance management system known as Compstat. With most departments now using some form of Compstat, how much crime report manipulation is taking place? Just a short list of jurisdictions where crime report manipulation has been reported includes Atlanta, Baltimore, Broward County (Florida), Dallas, Los Angeles, Milwaukee, Mobile (Alabama), New Orleans, New York City, and Philadelphia. Clearly this is not a localized problem. It influences the official crime report numbers that are used for numerous purposes. It appears that the eminent social psychologist[20] is correct when he writes, "The more any quantitative social indicator is used for social decision-making, the more subject it will be to corruption pressures and the more apt it will be to distort and corrupt the social processes it is intended to monitor."

- In 2011, over 62.9 million U.S. residents age 16 or older, or 26% of the population, had one or more contacts with police during the prior 12 months. For about half (49%) of persons experiencing contact with police, the most recent contact was involuntary or police initiated.
- In 2011, 86% of persons involved in traffic stops during their most recent contact with police and 66% of persons involved in street stops (i.e., stopped in public but not in a moving vehicle) believed that the police both behaved properly and treated them with respect during the contact.
- Most incidents involving profiling take place during traffic and street stops. A special report on police behavior during traffic and street stops indicated that in each calendar year, about 26% of the population had one or more contacts with police.
- The President's Task Force on 21st Century Policing Report noted, in their summary report, that racial bias in the broader society, public concern about officer use of racial profiling, and the development of agency policies addressing racial profiling presented opportunities for departments to engage officers, line supervisors, leadership, and the broader community in proactive and constructive strategies to ensure fair and equitable treatment under the law.
- How often do police conduct illegal searches of citizens? According to researchers Jon Gould and Stephen Mastrofski, direct field observations suggest that official records vastly understate the extent of constitutional violations in this area.
- Under the law, the NYPD is supposed to have reasonable suspicion before stopping and frisking an individual. Yet, over the last decade, less than 0.1% of those stopped had a gun and less than 5% of these were arrested. Nearly 4 million stops have occurred in New York City in the last decade, with nearly 700,000 people stopped in 2012. Eighty-four percent were black or Latino.
- How many people are killed during high-speed car chases? According to an ABC news report, more bystanders are injured or killed during high-speed police chases than by stray bullets.
- *Plumhoff v. Richard* case: The U.S. Supreme Court unanimously found that Arkansas police officers did not use excessive force in violation of the Fourth Amendment when they shot and killed a fleeing motorist, ending a high-speed car chase that risked the lives of both the officers and numerous innocent bystanders.
- In November 2015, the AP stated that, in a year-long investigation of sexual misconduct by U.S. law enforcement, about 1000 law enforcement officers lost their badges in a 6-year period for rape, sodomy, and other sexual assault; sex crimes that included possession of child pornography; or sexual misconduct such as propositioning citizens or having consensual but prohibited on-duty intercourse.
- The types of misconduct that police have been involved are probably too varied to list.

Practicums

Practicum one

In 2015, a U.S. border agent in South Texas was arrested in connection with the decapitation of a Honduran national earlier in the year. Cameron County sheriff's deputies arrested a 30-year-old U.S. border patrol agent for possession of a controlled substance. The officer now faces charges of capital murder and engaging in organized criminal activity charges, local authorities said.

The officer was arrested at his home in Hebbronville after local authorities seized around a kilo of cocaine, three handguns, and nearly $90,000 hidden in a safe at his mother-in-law's home in San Juan. It is believed that the officer was dealing with the Mexican organized crime gangs.

What can a supervisor do to ensure that none of his or her officers are involved with organized crime units?

Practicum two

Consider that you are serving as the police commissioner of a major U.S. city. An officer is charged with giving false testimony in several cases. She is acquitted. The officer now demands to be reinstated as a police officer.

What action would you take?

Discussion questions

1. What is the best way to identify officers who are corrupt?
2. Why do officers give false testimony?
3. What steps can be taken to eliminate racial profiling by police?
4. Explain why officers use abusive interrogation.
5. Should there be a national register of police officers who have been fired for cause?

References

1. Ronald Weitzer (December, 1999) Citizen's perceptions of police misconduct: Race and neighborhood context. _Justice Quarterly_, 16(4), 819–846.
2. Centre for Crime and Justice Studies (September, 2015) Black lives matter. _CJM_ (_Criminal Justice Matters_), 101, 1–12.
3. Rebekah Delsol (September, 2015) Racial profiling. _CJM_, 101, 34–35.
4. Jules Holroyd (September, 2015) Implicit racial bias and the anatomy of institutional racism. _CJM_, 101, 30–31.
5. Lynn Langton and Matthew Durose (September, 2013) BJS Special Report, NCJ 242937 Police behavior during traffic and street stops, 2011. Washington, DC: U.S. Department of Justice.
6. Samuel Walker and Dawn Irlbeck (March, 2002) Driving while female, a Special Report by the Police Professionalism Institute available on line at http://samuelwalker.net/wp-content/uploads/2010/06/dwf2002.pdf. Accessed on November 2, 2015.
7. Jon Gold and Stephen Mastrofski (July, 2004) Suspect searches: Assessing police behavior under the U.S. Constitution. _Criminology and Public Policy_, 3(3), 315–361.
8. Jon Gold and Stephen Mastrofski (July, 2004) Suspect searches: Assessing police behavior under the U.S. Constitution. _Criminology and Public Policy_, 3(3), 331.
9. David Wright (June 19, 2012) Police pursuits in California have injured more than 10,000. _ABC News_. website http://abcnews.go.com/US/police-chases-california-injured-10000/story?id=16605443. Accessed on November 3, 2015.
10. David Schultz, Ed Hudak, and Geoffery Alpert (March, 2010) Evidence-based decisions on police pursuit: The officer's perspective. _FBI Law Enforcement Bulletin_, 79(3), 12–18.
11. International Association of Chiefs of Police's Executive Guide on Addressing Sexual Offenses and Misconduct by Law Enforcement (2011) Washington, DC, IACP, p. 3.
12. As reported in the Orlando Sentinel article by Jonathan Banks (November 2, 2015) Hundreds of officers lose licenses over sex misconduct: AP investigation. p. A-1.
13. David Packman (November 5, 2009) The police brutality nobody talks about—Officer-involved sexual misconduct, Cato website at http://www.policemisconduct.net/the-police-brutality-nobody-talks-about-officer-involved-sexual-misconduct/. Accessed on November 2, 2015.
14. Candice Bernd (July 2, 2014) Police departments ignore Rampart sexual assault by officers. Truth-Out Organization website at http://www.truth-out.org/news/item/24677-police-departments-ignore-rampant-sexual-assault-by-officers. Accessed on November 2, 2015.
15. Rape, Abuse, and Incest National Network website at https://www.rainn.org/get-information/statistics/reporting-rates. Accessed on November 2, 2015.
16. Jason Meisner (May 25, 2011) Lawsuit: Sex misconduct by Chicago cops not instigated by city. _Chicago Tribune_, p. A-1.
17. Reuvion Fenton (November 15, 2015) Top reasons people are falsely imprisoned. _New York Post_, p. A-1.
18. Eterno, J. A., Verma, A., and Silverman, E. B. (2014). Police manipulations of crime reporting: Insiders' revelations. _Justice Quarterly_, doi:10.1080/07418825.2014.980838 31(3), 1–27.
19. Eterno, J., and Silverman, E. B. (2012). _The Crime Numbers Game: Management by Manipulation_. Boca Raton, FL: CRC Press.
20. Campbell, D. T. (1976). Assessing the impact of planned social change. _Evaluation and Program Planning_, 2, 67–90. https://www.globalhivmeinfo.org/CapacityBuilding/Occasional%20Papers/08%20Assessing%20the%20Impact%20of%20Planned%20Social%20Change.pdf

chapter six

Police corruption in international and transnational situations

Learning objectives

After studying this chapter, the reader should understand the following concepts and issues:

- Police corruption is both an international and a transnational problem
- There are forms of police corruption in all nations
- The issues involved in organizing an international police force
- The problems with police corruption in Liberia
- Police corruption in nation building
- Police misconduct in Canada

Introduction

Police corruption is both an international and a transnational problem, as noted by Asfaw Kumssa in his article on police corruption.[1] Kumssa notes that police corruption is a global phenomenon that is widespread in both developed and developing nations. He argues that police officers in New York City were involved not only in the usual shakedown and protection activities, but also in trafficking cocaine and other illicit drugs. Similarly, police officers in the United Kingdom were involved in corrupt activities, including concealment of serious crimes, bribery, and the fabrication and planting of evidence. Kumssa comments on a study on corruption within a South African police force that noted that police corruption is one of the biggest challenges the government is faced with, hitting rock bottom when South Africa's former National Commissioner of police was relieved of his duties in 2010 because of corruption charges.

According to Kumssa, police corruption is a reflection of the weakness in a country's legal and political institutions. Kumssa states that police corruption will undermine good governance and adversely affect the fight against crime, violence, and effective protection of property. In this kind of environment, citizens live in fear, and are compelled to hire private security guards, install alarms, grills, and so on, thus increasing their personal costs and reducing their disposable incomes. The people who suffer most from these types of corrupt practices are the poor, refugees, and those who live in slum areas as they do not have the economic or political power to protect themselves against crime or corrupt police officers who extort money from them through all manner of threats.

Kumssa concludes that police corruption is a vice that must be addressed for peace and tranquility to prevail in a society, and to maintain public order and the rule of law. This will restore public trust in the democratic processes and public institutions. Although police corruption is a universal problem, it is chronic and rampant in developing countries due to weak institutions, poverty, and poor enforcement of laws. A prime example of police corruption is set forth in Box 6.1.

Police corruption involving international and transnational commerce

Bribery on the international level

According to Transparency International's "Global Corruption Barometer 2013 Report," bribery is one of the most frequent forms of police corruption in international and transnational commerce.[3] Citizens in 36 of the 107 countries surveyed perceived that the police were among the most corrupt organizations. Worldwide, 31% of citizens concluded that police were one of the most corrupt organizations in their county. Only political parties were considered more corrupt. The judiciary took third place, with 24% of the citizens concluding that the judiciary was among the most corrupt.

The low opinion of police organizations was comparable with reports from the years 2010–2012. Most citizens opined that police corruption had increased rather than declined in the previous 10 years. While only 5% of citizens in Australia, Belgium, Canada, and Denmark reported having paid a bribe to the police, 75% of citizens in Liberia and Sierra Leone claimed to have paid at least one bribe to the police. About 10% of U.S. citizens reported having paid a bribe to the police.

Arbitrary arrests in Argentina

A 2005 report on Argentina by the U.S. Department of State stated that arbitrary arrests or detentions were frequent in Argentina.[4] The Argentina Federal Code

BOX 6.1   MEXICO FEDERAL POLICE AND THE DISAPPEARANCE OF 43 STUDENTS

Many researchers in Mexico believe that Mexico's federal police collaborated with local criminals in the September 26, 2014, attack on 43 students. The disappearance and presumed murder of the 43 students has led to mass protests in the country. One reporter stated that "We have information that proves the federal government knew what was happening in the moment it was happening, and participated in it." The reporter also stated that the government has tried to hide this information.

In 2015, it was announced that investigators are now certain that the 43 college students missing since September 2014 are dead. According to one report by the Mexican attorney general, the students were killed and incinerated after they were seized by police in the southern Guerrero state.[2] According to the news article, the attorney general cited confessions and forensic evidence from an area near a garbage dump where the crime occurred, showing that the fuel and temperature of the fire were sufficient to turn 43 bodies into ashes. Note that an independent group of investigators has disputed the fact that the method used to burn the bodies was sufficient to create the necessary heat to completely destroy all traces of DNA.

Mexican authorities announced that the students' incinerated remains were found in garbage bags dumped in a nearby river. An independent commission studying the crime concluded that the government's account of the incident was not correct. By 2015, 99 individuals had been detained in connection with the crime, including a former mayor.

The case has sparked protests both inside and outside Mexico and has forced the Mexican government to refocus its attention from touting economic and education reforms to dealing with the country's crime and insecurity issues. A movie, *The Documentary 43*, has been developed based on the crime.

of Criminal Procedure limits arrests and detention without warrants to certain restricted situations, for example, criminals caught in the act, fleeing suspects, or overwhelming evidence of a crime being committed and, while the government generally observed these prohibitions, provincial police sometimes ignored these restrictions and arbitrarily arrested and detained citizens. In the past, human rights groups reported difficulties in documenting such incidents because victims were reluctant to file complaints for fear of police retaliation or inaction.

In addition to the Argentine Federal Police (PFA) and border police, each province has its own police force. These generally come under a provincial police hierarchy, which in turn responds to a provincial security ministry or secretariat. The effectiveness of and respect for human rights among different forces varies considerably. Corruption is systemic in some forces, and impunity for police abuse is common.

Some of the most common abuses included contract abuses, extortion of and protection for those involved in illegal gambling, prostitution, and auto-theft rings, as well as detention and extortion of citizens under the threat of planting evidence to charge them with crimes. Some police were also involved in drug trafficking and kidnapping. Addressing police corruption was difficult, in part because the suspects intimidated whistleblowing colleagues, judicial officials, and civilian witnesses. Threats and beatings allegedly aimed to intimidate witnesses were common and, in some cases,

occurred in connection with killings believed to be committed by members of the security forces or their criminal allies.

Police may detain suspects for up to 10 hours without an arrest warrant if the authorities have a well-founded belief that the suspects have committed, or are about to commit, a crime, or if they are unable to determine the identity of a suspect. Human rights groups have argued that this provision of law has been disregarded to extort money from persons by threatening to charge them with illegal weapon or drug possession.

The law provides for the right of prompt determination of legality, but this right has often not been respected in practice. The law provides for investigative detention of persons charged with a crime but awaiting or undergoing trial for up to 2 years. This term can be extended to 3 years under certain situations: A particularly complex or serious crime; intentional delays by the defense, or where investigations could be hampered by release of the detainee; or if there is a serious risk of flight. The slow pace of the justice system has often resulted in lengthy detentions beyond the period stipulated by law. If convicted, a prisoner usually receives credit for time already served. According to the Federal Bureau for Criminal Policies, approximately 62% of inmates in federal prisons have been charged but are awaiting trial or completion of their trials. The effectiveness of and respect for human rights by different forces varies considerably. Corruption is systemic in some forces, and impunity for police abuses are common.

Arbitrary police actions in Brazil

According to a 2013 report by the U.S. Department of State, human rights problems in Brazil include excessive force and unlawful killings by state police; excessive force, beatings, abuse, and torture of detainees and inmates by police and prison security forces; prolonged pretrial detention and inordinate delays of trials; judicial censorship of media; government corruption; violence and discrimination against women; violence against children, including sexual abuse; social conflict between indigenous communities and private landowners that occasionally led to violence; discrimination against indigenous persons and minorities; violence and social discrimination against lesbian, gay, bisexual, and transgender (LGBT) persons; insufficient enforcement of labor laws; and child labor in the informal sector.[5]

In Rio de Janeiro, there were reports that both on- and off-duty police employed indiscriminate use of force. These acts often occurred in the city's approximately 763 favelas, where an estimated 1.4 million persons lived, according to the 2010 census by the Brazilian Institute of Geography and Statistics (IBGE). The Rio de Janeiro Public Security Institute, a state government entity, reported in 2013 that from January to July, police killed 197 civilians in "acts of resistance" (similar to resisting arrest) in Rio de Janeiro state, compared with 263 during the same period in 2012. Most of these deaths occurred while police were conducting operations against drug-trafficking gangs operating in Rio's poor communities. A disproportionate number of the victims were Afro-Brazilian and under 25 years of age. Nongovernmental organizations (NGOs) in Rio de Janeiro questioned whether all of the 197 victims had truly resisted arrest, contending that police continued to depend on repressive methods.

On June 24, 2014, the Special Police Operations Battalion entered the New Holland favela in Rio de Janeiro in pursuit of criminals. The operation resulted in a gunfight that left 10 dead, including at least two residents who were not implicated in criminal activity. In another case, Rio de Janeiro resident Amarildo de Souza went missing after officers from the Police Pacification Unit (UPP) operating in the Rocinha favela brought him in for questioning on July 14, 2014. Family members claimed that the police were responsible for his disappearance; other Rocinha residents alleged that the police offered them money in exchange for false testimony casting suspicion on drug traffickers. In September, the Public Ministry charged 10 UPP police officers, including commanding officer Major Edson Santos, with torture, murder, and hiding the body of de Souza.

The Sao Paulo State Secretariat for Public Security reported that state military police killed 239 civilians from January to June 2014, compared with 251 in the same period in 2012. In April 2014, a court sentenced police officer Carlos Adilio Maciel Santos from the Seventh Military Police Battalion in Rio de Janeiro to 19 years and 6 months in prison for the 2011 killing of Judge Patricia Lourival Acioli. Four other military police officers had already been tried, convicted, and sentenced, while the six remaining defendants continued to await trial dates.

The federal police, operating under the Ministry of Justice, is a small, primarily investigative entity that plays a minor role in routine law enforcement. Most police forces fall under the control of the states, where they are divided into two distinct units: the civil police, performing an investigative role, and the military police, charged with maintaining law and order.

Despite its name, the military police does not report to the Ministry of Defense. The law mandates that special police courts exercise jurisdiction over state military police except those charged with "willful crimes against life," primarily homicide. The police are often responsible for investigating charges of torture and excessive force carried out by fellow officers, although independent investigations have increased. Delays in the special military police courts have allowed many cases to expire due to statutes of limitations.

The Brazilian Association of Investigative Journalism has reported that police tactics, including excessive force, rubber bullets, and tear gas, have resulted in injuries to hundreds of individuals, including at least 15 journalists, during the 2014 June 13 protests in Sao Paulo.

According to the Rio de Janeiro State Secretariat for Public Security, human rights courses are a mandatory component of training for entry-level military police officers. UPP officers for the favela pacification program have received additional human rights training. Under the pacification program, the Rio de Janeiro State Secretariat for Public Security inaugurated six new UPPs during the year, for a total of 34. As of September 2014, 8592 UPP officers are responsible for patrolling approximately 226 favela areas in Rio de Janeiro state.

In Rio de Janeiro's favelas, so-called militia groups, composed of off-duty and former law enforcement officers, often took policing into their own hands. Many militia groups intimidated residents and conducted illegal activities such as extorting protection money and providing pirated utility services. Human rights observers believed that militia groups controlled up to half of Rio's favelas.

Former Alagoas police officer Edgelson Ribeiro Guimaraes and 10 other members of an illegal militia group, arrested in mid-2011 for committing murders in the states of Pernambuco and Alagoas, were freed on bail awaiting trial, but Ribeiro Guimaraes was arrested again on August 22 for alleged involvement in a robbery in Pernambuco. He was later cleared of the robbery charges but remains in prison awaiting trial for homicide.

With the exception of arrests of suspects caught in the act of committing a crime, arrests must be made with a warrant issued by a judicial official. Officials must advise suspects of their rights at the time of arrest or before taking them into custody for interrogation. The law prohibits use of force during an arrest unless the suspect attempts to escape or resists arrest. According to human rights observers, some detainees have complained of physical abuse by police officers while being taken into custody.

Authorities generally respect the constitutional right to a prompt judicial determination of the legality of detention. Detainees are informed promptly of the charges against them. The law permits provisional detention for up to 5 days under specified conditions during an investigation, but a judge may extend this period. A judge may also order temporary detention for an additional 5 days for processing. Preventive detention for an initial period of 15 days is permitted if police suspect that a detainee may leave the area.

The law does not specify a maximum period for pretrial detention, which is decided on a case-by-case basis. Time in detention before trial is subtracted from the sentence.

Defendants arrested in the act of committing a crime must be charged within 30 days of arrest. Other defendants must be charged within 45 days, although this period may be extended. The backlog in the courts has often resulted in an extension of the period for charging defendants.

International obligations

Human Rights Watch (HRW) has noted that police brutality is one of the most serious, enduring, and divisive human rights violations in the United States. The problem is nationwide, and its nature is institutionalized. For these reasons, the U.S. government—as well as state and city governments, which have an obligation to respect the international human rights standards by which the United States is bound—deserve to be held accountable by international human rights bodies and international public opinion.[6]

United Nations Convention against Corruption (UNCAC)

The United Nations Convention against Corruption (UNCAC) was adopted by the UN General Assembly Resolution 58/4 of October 31, 2003. The concern of the UN General Assembly when the resolution was passed was about the seriousness of the problems and threats posed by corruption to the stability and security of societies, undermining the institutions and values of democracy, ethical values, and justice, and jeopardizing sustainable development and the rule of law.[7]

While the UNCAC was directed at corruption in general, several portions of the resolution concerned police misconduct. For example, Article 25 Obstruction of Justice provides:

> Each State Party shall adopt such legislative and other measures as may be necessary to establish as criminal offences, when committed intentionally:
>
> (a) The use of physical force, threats or intimidation or the promise, offering or giving of an undue advantage to induce false testimony or to interfere in the giving of testimony or the production of evidence in a proceeding in relation to the commission of offences established in accordance with this Convention;
>
> (b) The use of physical force, threats or intimidation to interfere with the exercise of official duties by a justice or law enforcement official in relation to the commission of offences established in accordance with this Convention. Nothing in this subparagraph shall prejudice the right of States Parties to have legislation that protects other categories of public official.

The resolution (convention) requires countries to establish criminal and other offenses to cover a wide range of acts of corruption, if these are not already crimes under domestic law. In some cases, states are legally obliged to establish offenses; in other cases, in order to take into account differences in domestic law, they are required to consider doing so. The convention goes beyond previous instruments of this kind, criminalizing not only basic forms of corruption such as bribery and the embezzlement of public funds, but also trading in influence and the concealment and laundering of the proceeds of corruption. Offenses committed in support of corruption, including money-laundering and obstructing justice, are also dealt with. Convention offenses also deal with the problematic areas of private-sector corruption.

Since the passage of the resolution, nations worldwide have been observing the International Anti-Corruption Day (IAC) of December 9 each year. UNCAC was the first multilateral convention negotiated by the member countries of the UN aimed at preventing corruption worldwide.

World corruption police

In a column in the *New York Times*, Alexander Lebedev proposed the creation of a "world corruption police."[8] Lebedev, a businessman and former senior officer in the KGB, is an owner of the Moscow newspaper *Novaya Gazeta* and publisher of the *London Evening Standard* and the *Independent*. Lebedev notes that, whenever government representatives from around the world meet, they're often able to make progress in many areas of common interest: combating climate change, poverty, the drug trade, Islamic extremism, human trafficking and modern-day slavery, and even cybercrime—the list is long. What these officials often fail to dwell on is corruption. All of their nations suffer from it; they agree it's a cancer of our age and should be stamped out.

Lebedev notes that in China, nearly $4 trillion is thought to have disappeared between 2000 and 2011, much of it the profits of corruption, channeled into secret offshore financial havens. In Russia, the figure is close to $1 trillion. In the European Union, the total is estimated at $1.2 trillion. Various nations have launched initiatives to tackle corruption, but these moves ignore the international, cross-border nature of the problem: Recovering stolen assets inevitably involves some degree of cooperation with another jurisdiction. Countering this, however, is an entire industry devoted to helping people hide their wealth overseas, far from the prying eyes of the authorities. Lebedev opines that if governments want to have any chance of recovering what has been lost, they must join together to create an international anticorruption force, along the lines of Interpol, to defeat these financial oligarchs.

Police corruption in nation building

According to a special report of the U.S. Institute of Peace, police corruption is a universal challenge to nation building. In emerging nations, it appears that police corruption wastes resources, undermines security, makes a mockery of justice, slows economic development, and alienates citizens from their governments.[9] According to Bayley and Perito, general surveys reveal that police corruption is a fundamental obstacle to fulfilling the basic objectives of most interventions, namely establishing the rule of law.

Bayley and Perito consider that corruption in the administration of law means that equal access is denied, and it undermines fair trials, fair elections, economic and social opportunities, cultural expression, and access to the necessities of food, housing, health, education, and water. Because the police are the primary institution for implementing law in any society, police corruption stops the implementation of the rule of law.

The authors noted that, when police sell their services for private profit, the rule of law ceases to exist. Eliminating police corruption is required for any country that has establishing the rule of law as a national objective. They see that ignoring this imperative means that international efforts at nation building proceed at their own peril. The lesson has been powerfully demonstrated in Afghanistan, where one of the fundamental objectives of the U.S. assistance effort has been to establish the rule of law. Illicit revenue from opium production has fueled widespread corruption, affecting all levels of the Afghan government from ministers and members of parliament to local officials and the Afghan national police (ANP).

Afghans believe that officials of the Ministry of Interior (MOI), provincial police chiefs, and members of the ANP are involved in the drug trade, based on reports of senior MOI officials accepting large bribes for protecting drug traffickers and for selling senior provincial and district police positions to people engaged in drug trafficking. The authors see how drug money combined with local loyalties, links to criminal networks, low or often no pay, and a residual culture of impunity have contributed to endemic corruption in the ANP.

In most of the communities, the ANP is considered as predatory and a greater threat to the citizens than the Taliban. To many Afghans, the police are identified with corruption that includes bribery, illegal taxes, and various types of human rights violations. Apparently, the corrupt police activities are felt most directly by the poorest Afghan citizens.

The authors noted that the reports of the 32 police commissions on the police identified 35 forms of corruption, which can be grouped into four categories: scale and organization, predatory forms, subversion of justice, and gifts and discounts. They saw the most common forms of corruption as making false reports and committing perjury, protecting illegal gambling, theft of drugs on the street, theft of seized property, receiving discounts on purchases, and selling information about police operations. According to the authors, these forms accounted for slightly less than 40% of the 117 times that the reports noted specific incidents of corruption. The nature of the corruption varied considerably from report to report; only a third of the commissions reported the most common form (false reports and perjury). According to Bayley and Perito, this implies that even blue-ribbon panels have not found a strong standard model of police corruption.

In addition, the reports noted another category of corruption that was not a focus of investigation, namely, corrupt manipulation of internal administrative processes such as corruption of promotions and assignments and the diversion of police property to personal use. Police frequently reported this type of internal corruption as a major irritant, and were much less forgiving of it compared with the public forms.

The authors noted that there were two trends in the reporting about the forms of police corruption. First, drug involvement is not mentioned at all before 1970. In the category of vice, drugs became the major driver of corruption after 1970, replacing gambling, prostitution, and alcohol. An interesting exception is the 2000 Uganda report, which reported corruption to be endemic but did not mention drugs as a corruptor at all. The authors wondered if this meant that drug-related police corruption was a problem only in the developed West. Given what is known from other sources about police corruption in supplier and transshipping countries, they opined that this was unlikely.

The second trend was described by the authors as being systemic in police departments only since 1970, and rarely before then. This is curious, since the impression from general histories of the police in Western countries is that internal discipline was characteristically lax in earlier periods and that newly recruited officers had to "go along" in order to be accepted. Corruption before 1970 seems to have been part of a general lack of discipline, meaning the failure of police officers to do what they were assigned to do. In effect, the systemic character of corruption seems to have been so pervasive earlier that it was not considered remarkable.

Research on foreign aid policies

According to a Sweden research report, corruption has become a major issue in foreign aid policies. However, it has always been there behind the scene, referred to as the "c word." The major concern for international aid policy over the last five decades was to improve the living conditions for the poor in the poorest countries of the world.[10] According to the report, the phenomenon of corruption ranges from the single act of a payment contradicted by law to an endemic malfunction of a political and economic system. The problem of corruption has been seen either as a structural problem of politics or economics, or as a cultural and individual moral problem. The definition of corruption consequently ranges from the broad terms of *misuse of public power* and *moral decay* to strict legal definitions of corruption as an act of bribery involving a public servant and a transfer of tangible resources.

Corruption Perception Index

Police corruption is a dangerous phenomenon in any society. Approximately one-third of the countries surveyed in the Corruption Perception Index (CPI) perceived the police as the institution most affected by corruption. The CPI is the most comprehensive quantitative indicator of cross-country corruption available, where each single country is recognizable. It is compiled by a team of researchers at Göttingen University, headed by Johann Lambsdorff. The CPI assesses the degree to which public officials and politicians are believed to accept bribes, take illicit payment in public procurement, embezzle public funds, or commit similar offenses. The index ranks countries on a scale from zero to 100, according to the perceived level of corruption. A score of 100 represents a reputedly totally honest country, while zero indicates that the country is perceived as completely corrupt.[11]

The CPI has ranked 175 countries. The 2014 rank of countries includes the following:

1. Denmark (92)
2. New Zealand (92)
3. Finland (89)
10. Canada (81)
14. United Kingdom (78)
17. United States (74)
136. Russia (27)

Organizing an international police force

The information in this section was taken from the U.S. Marine Corps Warfighting Publication, No. 3.33.5 and the U.S. Army Field Manual No. 3-24.[12] This section addresses aspects of developing host nation (HN) security forces. It begins with a discussion of the challenges involved and the resources required, and provides a framework for organizing the development effort. It concludes with a discussion of the role of police in counterinsurgency operations.

6-49. Effective security forces can help improve HN social and economic development through the benefits each member receives. Every recruit should receive a basic education, job training, and morals and values inculcation.

Leader recruiting and selection

6-50. Officer candidate standards should be high. Candidates should be in good health and pass an academic test with a higher standard than the test for enlisted recruits. Officer candidates should be carefully vetted to ensure that they do not have close ties to any radical or insurgent organization.

6-51. Non-commission officers (NCOs) should be selected from the best enlisted security force members. Objective standards, including proficiency tests, should be established and enforced to ensure that promotion to the NCO ranks comes from merit, not through influence or family ties. Many armies lack a professional NCO corps; establishing one for a host nation may be difficult. In the meantime, adjustments will have to be made, placing more responsibility on commissioned officers.

Personnel accountability

6-52. HN leaders must carefully track and account for security force personnel. Proper personnel accountability reduces corruption, particularly in countries with manual banking systems where security force personnel are paid in cash. In addition, large numbers of personnel failing to report for duty can indicate possible attacks, low unit morale, or insurgent and militia influences on the security forces.

6-92. Police often consist of several independent but mutually supporting forces. These may include

- Criminal and traffic police
- Border police
- Transport police for security of rail lines and public transport
- Specialized paramilitary strike forces
- In addition, a host nation may establish various reserve police units or home guards to provide local security

The force may include paramilitary units. Police might be organized on a national or local basis. Whatever police organization is established, soldiers and marines must understand it and help the host nation effectively organize and use it. This often means dealing with several police organizations and developing plans for training and advising each one.

6-93. A formal link or liaison channel must exist between the HN police and military forces. This channel for coordination, deconfliction, and information sharing enables successful Counterinsurgency (COIN) operations.

6-94. Military forces might have to perform police duties at the start of an insurgency; however, it is best to establish police forces to assume these duties as soon as possible. U.S., multinational, and HN partners should institute a comprehensive program of police training. Moreover, plans for police training need to envision a several-year program to systematically build institutions and leadership.

6-95. Although roles of the police and military forces in COIN operations may blur, important distinctions between the two forces exist. If security forces treat insurgents as criminals, the police may retain the primary responsibility for their arrest, detention, and prosecution.

6-96. Countering an insurgency requires a police force that is visible day and night. The host nation will not gain legitimacy if the populace believes that insurgents and criminals control the streets. Well-sited and protected police stations can establish a presence in communities as long as the police do not hide in those stations. Police presence provides security to communities and builds support for the HN government. When police have daily contact with the local populace, they can collect information for counterinsurgents.

6-97. Good pay and attractive benefits must be combined with a strict code of conduct that follows the rule of law and allows for the immediate dismissal of police officers for gross corruption. Good planning ensures that police pay, housing, benefits, and work conditions attract a high quality of police recruit as well as discourage petty corruption. Such corruption undermines the populace's confidence in the police and government. An important step in organizing a police force involves setting up an independent review board composed of experts, government officials, or nongovernmental organization members. It should not be under the direct command of the police force. This board should have the authority to investigate charges of police abuse and corruption, oversee the complaints process, and dismiss and fine police found guilty of misconduct (Box 6.2).

Police corruption in Liberia

It would be easy to write a chapter on police corruption in every country. There is not a single country in the world that does not have some form of police corruption. But, for this section, I will focus on Liberia primarily because its level of corruption is documented. It is not necessarily the most corrupt police force.

A common description used when referring to police corruption in Liberia is "no money, no justice."[13] For example one individual complained about his arrest in 2012. Apparently, he was arrested and jailed for 5 days. He was told that he would be released when he paid some money.

During the period 1989–2003, Liberia was involved in two deadly civil wars that resulted in over 200,000 deaths. Since 2013, with the removal of peacekeeping forces, the Liberian police has been solely under the stewardship of the Liberian government. But the HRW noted that the country's ability to enforce the law and investigate crimes was severely compromised by the lawlessness and abuse that was being inflicted by the Liberian police.

During this period, the HRW concluded that the Liberian police acted like predators, violating the law rather than protecting the citizens of Liberia, and that the police often hustled on the street for money, compelling citizens to pay bribes.

BOX 6.2   DEVELOPING A POLICE FORCE IN MALAYA

In 1948, the Malayan Communist Party, whose members were primarily ethnic Chinese, began an insurgency against the British colonial government. The British first responded by dramatically expanding the Malayan security forces. The police, not the army, served as the lead counterinsurgency force. Between 1948 and 1950, the number of Malayan police expanded fivefold to 50,000, while the British army garrison expanded to 40,000. However, there was only time to provide a few weeks of rudimentary training to the new police officers before throwing them into operation. Police with little training and little competent leadership were ineffective in conducting operations. They also abused the civilian population and fell into corrupt practices. The population largely regarded the police as hostile; they were reluctant to give them information on the insurgents.

By 1952, the insurgency had reached a stalemate. The British then established a new strategy. The strategy included reforming and retraining the entire Malaya police force. First, 10,000 corrupt or incompetent police officers were removed from the force. Then, police officers who had proved the most competent in operations were made instructors in new police schools. During 1952 and 1953, every police officer attended a 4-month basic training course. Commissioned and noncommissioned police officers were sent on 3–4 month advanced courses. All senior Malayan police officers were required to attend the police intelligence school, where they learned the latest criminal investigation techniques. Teams of Britain's top police officers also taught them intelligence collection and analysis methods. Dozens of the most promising Malayan officers attended the full year-long course in advanced police operations in Britain.

To win the ethnic Chinese away from the insurgents, the British worked closely with ethnic Chinese organizations to recruit Chinese for the Malaya police force. In 1952, the number of ethnic Chinese in the force more than doubled. Although the percentage of ethnic Chinese in the police force did not equal their percentage in the population, the ethnic Chinese saw this reaching out as a sign that the government was addressing their interests. At the same time, some Chinese and Malay political groups were building a coalition to establish an independent Malaya in which all the major ethnic groups would participate. The two efforts complemented each other.

Better trained police officers and soldiers led by fully trained commissioned and noncommissioned officers dramatically improved discipline in the Malayan security forces. Better relations between the population and security forces resulted, and the people began to provide information on the insurgents. Thanks to their intelligence training, the security forces could develop intelligence from that information and act on it. They began to break the insurgent organization. In 1953, the government gained the initiative. After that, the insurgent forces and support structure declined rapidly. In late 1953, the British began withdrawing forces. They progressively turned the war over to the Malayans, who were fully prepared to conduct counterinsurgency operations without a drop in efficiency.

The Malaya insurgency provides lessons applicable to combating any insurgency. Manpower is not enough; well-trained and well-disciplined forces are required. The Malayan example also illustrates the central role that police play in counterinsurgency operations. British leaders concentrated on training the Malayan leadership. The British insisted that chosen personnel receive the full British Army and police officer courses. These actions built the Malayan security forces on a sound foundation. By taking a comprehensive approach to security force training and reform, the British commanders transformed a demoralized organization into a winning force. This transformation required only 15 months.

People smuggling

People smuggling is an international problem. It is also a complex issue. While many of the criminals involved in people smuggling are not police officers, unfortunately many of the criminals are also police officers. The modus operandi of criminal organizations involved in people smuggling is becoming increasing sophisticated. Crimes that are necessarily included in people smuggling include human trafficking, identity-related crimes, corruption, money laundering, and violence. In many cases, people-smuggling organizations are operating under the protection of local police agencies.

Summary

- Police corruption is both an international and a transnational problem.
- According to Kumssa, police corruption is a reflection of the weaknesses in a country's legal and political institutions.

POLICE MISCONDUCT IN CANADA: INTERNAL AND EXTERNAL OVERSIGHT

Figure 6.1 Professor Rick Parent.

[Dr. Rick Parent is Associate Professor and Associate Director, Police Studies Centre, School of Criminology, Simon Fraser University, Vancouver, Canada (Figure 6.1). Dr. Parent completed 30 years of service as a police officer with the Delta Police and is the coauthor of the book *Community-based Strategic Policing in Canada*. His research interests include comparative policing, the police use of deadly force, and police ethics and account-ability. Dr. Parent can be contacted at rparent@sfu.ca www.rickparent.ca]

Canada, with a population of roughly 36 million, employs just under 70,000 full-time police officers. Within the 10 provinces and 3 territories that make up this northern nation, there are 238 police agencies, and of those, 117 have fewer than 25 staff. Five Canadian police agencies—the Royal Canadian Mounted Police (RCMP), the Toronto Police Service, the Ontario Provincial Police (OPP), the Sûreté du Québec (SQ), and the City of Montreal Police Service (Service de police de la Ville de Montréal, or SPVM)—account for just over 60% of all full-time police officers in Canada. In most areas of this large nation (the second largest geographi-cal area in the world), police officers work alone. With a police-to-population ratio of only 193 per 100,000 population (lower than the United States and England/Wales), back-up in rural areas may be more than an hour away.[14] In most jurisdictions across Canada, police activities are overseen both internally and externally. Police commissions, boards, and bodies established under provisions of various legislated police acts exist as a measure of external oversight of policing. Boards and commissions, typically governed by elected officials, ensure accountability at both the municipal and provincial level. Within police agencies, there are sections often titled "Professional Standards" or "Internal Affairs" that investigate allegations of professional mis-conduct on the part of officers and, in rare instances, police corruption. Police officers may be held liable for violating the policies and procedures of the police agency in which they work. They can also be held liable administratively, civilly, and criminally for their conduct. Over the last 15 years, police officers and police departments have been found civilly liable for negligently supervising employees, conducting deficient inves-tigations, and failing to warn the community about dangerous persons.

Canadian police officers can be held accountable for conduct that occurs both on and off duty. Off-duty conduct may include involvement in domestic violence, impaired driving, and assault. While these issues impact all individuals, regardless of their occupation, police officers additionally face the real possibility of being disciplined in the workplace for their off-duty behavior. Disciplinary measures may include manda-tory counseling, suspension from work without pay, reduction in rank (pay), and termination of employment.

Transparent and accountable policing

The police are responsible for the services they provide to the community as well as for their conduct within the community. There are both legislative and administrative frameworks for holding Canadian police offi-cers accountable for their actions and for dealing with police misconduct. The Canadian Charter of Rights and Freedoms has had a significant impact on police work; since its enactment, there have been a number of major decisions by the Supreme Court of Canada that have defined the role and powers of the police. One of the most significant developments is the Supreme Court of Canada's decision in *R. v. McNeil,** that requires police agencies to release a police officer's disciplinary records to defense counsel prior to criminal prosecutions.[15]

Police agencies and their employees are also held externally accountable by coroner's inquests or fatality inquiries and by human rights boards, commissions, and civil litigation. In addition, freedom of information legislation has also established a heightened level of accountability in relation to police records and their management. These legislative provisions, combined with public recording and posting of policing activities on social media sources, have placed Canadian police personnel under increased scrutiny and often criticism.

While misconduct in policing has generally been considered an individual officer phenomenon, the investigation of serious misconduct and criminal acts by police officers has required police departments to reorganize their resources to better respond to these emerging challenges. The RCMP, for example, has established internal anticorruption units in major urban centers. The Toronto Police Service has also enhanced their internal investigative capacity following a serious investigation into the misappropriation of money and property in their drug unit.

To maintain public confidence in policing, investigations must be transparent and open to the public. Police officers who work in internal investigation units have a difficult and challenging mandate. They must investigate fellow police officers as objectively and neutrally as possible. Critics of this system argue that it is virtually impossible for the police to objectively investigate their own personnel, while those who favor this approach argue that investigations are conducted thoroughly by insiders who know and understand policing. In certain situations, police agencies will request that officers from another police agency conduct the internal investigation. For example, in the eastern province of Quebec, it is common practice for the Montreal Police Service to call on the Quebec provincial police (and vice versa) to conduct investigations into serious matters such as police shootings and police conduct resulting in death. In recent years, there has also been a trend toward external oversight in order to achieve transparent and accountable policing. All Canadian provinces have external agencies that are mandated with receiving and reviewing complaints against police officers (excluding RCMP officers policing under contract). These include the province of Alberta Law Enforcement Review Board, the province of Manitoba's Law Enforcement Review Agency, the province of Nova Scotia Police Review Board, and the Office of the Police Complaint Commissioner in British Columbia. Oversight of the federal RCMP occurs through the Commission for Public Complaints against the RCMP and the External Review Committee (ERC).

In the province of Ontario, the Special Investigations Unit (SIU) and the Ontario Civilian Commission on Police Services (OCCPS) perform these tasks. Of note, the role of each oversight body varies, ranging from reviewing complaint investigations and making recommendations to conducting the investigation itself. Models of police oversight that have the mandate to conduct actual independent investigations of police officers have been established in the western Canadian provinces of Alberta, through the creation of the Alberta Serious Incident Response Team (ASIRT),[16] and in British Columbia, through the creation of the Independent Investigations Office (IIO).[17]

The province of Ontario and the Special Investigation Unit

Canada's most populous province of Ontario employs roughly 26,148 police officers. These officers are responsible for policing roughly 14 million individuals, representing nearly 40% of all Canadians in the second largest province in total area.[18] Ontario employs their own provincial police agency to enforce the majority of laws, typically in rural and sparsely populated areas. Regional, municipal, or city police agencies such as the Toronto Police Service provide the bulk of policing to large urban centers or townships. Notably, Canada's internationally famous federal police agency, the RCMP, plays a very minor role in Ontario, enforcing only a few federal laws.

Within Ontario, the SIU is perhaps the best example of a Canadian civilian review of police activities. Created in 1990, the SIU came about due to controversial police shootings and racially charged interactions involving police officers and youth from visible minority groups. Established under provisions of the Police Services Act, the SIU investigates cases involving serious injury, sexual assault, or death that may have been the result of criminal offenses committed by police officers. A serious injury inflicted by a police officer is initially presumed when the complainant:

---

* *R. v. McNeil* [2009] Supreme Court of Canada, 3.

is admitted to the hospital; suffers a fracture to a limb, rib or vertebrae or to the skull; suffers burns to a major portion of the body or loses any portion of the body; suffers loss of vision or hearing, or alleges sexual assault.[19]

The SIU is independent of any police agency; operates directly under the provincial attorney general; and has the authority to investigate municipal, regional, and provincial police officers. An attempt is made to complete case investigations within 30 days, although in more complex cases this is typically not possible. The SIU's primary purpose is to enhance police accountability and maintain public confidence by assuring the Ontario public that police actions resulting in serious injury, death, or allegations of sexual assault are subjected to rigorous and independent investigations.

If a preliminary investigation determines that a police officer was involved in a serious injury or death of a civilian, a full investigation is conducted. SIU investigators are required to go to the scene of the incident, collect and secure evidence, interview police and civilian witnesses, and provide evidence to forensic specialists for examination.

Following a comprehensive and independent (of police) investigation, a detailed report is referred to the director of the SIU to review. The director's job is to determine if, based on the investigation, there are reasonable and probable grounds to believe that the suspected police officer(s) committed a criminal offense. If there is evidence of a criminal wrongdoing on the part of the officer(s) involved, the director will make a decision on whether or not there are reasonable grounds to lay a criminal charge. These charges can include manslaughter, criminal negligence causing death, assault causing bodily harm, and sexual assault.[19] After a charge is laid, the director then forwards his report to the Justice Prosecutions branch of the Crown Law Office, thus ensuring that the process is carried out.[19] See Table 6.1 regarding the yearly number of SIU occurrences and investigations.

Police use of deadly force: Canada and the United States

In both Canada and the United States, police shootings and the use of deadly force tend to generate the most media attention, public interest, and controversy in regard to police misconduct. However, the police use of deadly force is far more of a concern in the United States than in Canada. In absolute numbers, as well as proportionately, far more people die by legal intervention in the United States than in Canada. One explanation for this difference is the availability of handguns in the United States and the U.S. constitutional provision to bear arms. In contrast, the possession of a handgun is highly regulated and restricted in Canada and there is no provision within the Canadian Charter of Rights enshrining the right to possess firearms.

It is within this setting that approximately 500 individuals are shot and killed by U.S. law enforcement personnel each year.[20] It has been speculated that this number is far higher due to a lack of accurate reporting in the United States. In contrast, there have been 139 fatal police shootings in Canada between January 1, 1999 and December 31, 2009, reflecting a rate of approximately 12 fatal police shootings per year.[21] On adjusting for population figures, the number of deaths by legal intervention within the United States is almost three times greater than the corresponding number of legal intervention deaths within neighboring Canada.[22]

Table 6.1 Ontario special investigations unit—Occurrences

Types of occurrences	2005	2006	2007	2008	2009	2010	2011	2012	2013	2014
Firearm injuries	10	12	14	10	5	12	12	8	8	3
Firearm deaths	7	6	7	4	7	10	8	5	9	6
Custody injuries	98	128	124	182	172	165	172	214	200	154
Custody deaths	32	35	21	27	15	30	17	34	20	12
Vehicular injuries	25	28	29	33	51	26	33	48	33	38
Vehicular deaths	9	5	9	7	9	4	6	7	11	6
Sexual assault complaints	23	24	41	34	24	44	55	49	34	41
Other injuries/deaths	0	0	1	2	4	1	1	3	3	6
Totals	204	238	246	299	287	292	304	372	318	266

Interestingly, research has revealed that there are relatively few differences overall in relation to the dynamics and circumstances of police use of deadly force in the United States and Canada. The issues pertaining to police use of deadly force are, for the most part, very similar. The major difference that was noted between these two nations was in relation to the frequencies of incidents and not the individual characteristics of a police shooting.[23]

Discussion

The expectations placed on police officers have been shaped largely by Canadian society, ensuring that officers are held accountable for their actions. Police agencies have responded to this trend by developing organizational policies and procedures that are reinforced by internal processes and mechanisms. Several external factors, such as evolving case law and designated police oversight agencies, provide additional checks to ensure police transparency and accountability. However, the Canadian public continues to have the greatest impact on reducing police misconduct by demanding high standards and expectations of police agencies and their personnel within a supportive and constructive framework.

- Kumssa states that police corruption will undermine good governance and adversely affect the fight against crime, violence, and effective protection of property.
- According to Transparency International's report "Global Corruption Barometer 2013 Report," bribery is one of the most frequent forms of police corruption in international and transnational commerce.
- Worldwide, 31% of citizens concluded that police were one of the most corrupt organizations in their county.
- Only political parties were considered more corrupt worldwide.
- The judiciary took third place, with 24% of citizens concluding that the judiciary was among the most corrupt.
- A 2005 report by the U.S. Department of State on Argentina stated that arbitrary arrests or detentions were frequent in Argentina.
- According to a 2013 report by the U.S. Department of State, human rights problems in Brazil include excessive force and unlawful killings by state police; excessive force, beatings, abuse, and torture of detainees and inmates by police and prison security forces; prolonged pretrial detention and inordinate delays of trials; judicial censorship of media; government corruption; violence and discrimination against women; violence against children, including sexual abuse; social conflict between indigenous communities and private landowners that occasionally led to violence; discrimination against indigenous persons and minorities; violence and social discrimination against lesbian, gay, bisexual, and transgender (LGBT) persons; insufficient enforcement of labor laws; and child labor in the informal sector.
- The HRW noted that police brutality is one of the most serious, enduring, and divisive human rights violations in the United States.
- The problem is nationwide, and its nature is institutionalized. For these reasons, the U.S. government—as well as state and city governments, which have an obligation to respect the international human rights standards by which the United States is bound—deserve to be held accountable by international human rights bodies and international public opinion.
- The UNCAC was adopted by the UN General Assembly Resolution 58/4 of October 31, 2003.
- The concern of the General Assembly, when the resolution was passed, was about the seriousness of the problems and threats posed by corruption to the stability and security of societies, undermining the institutions and values of democracy, ethical values and justice, jeopardizing sustainable development, and the rule of law.
- According to a special report of the U.S. Institute of Peace, police corruption is a universal challenge to nation building.
- In emerging nations, it appears that police corruption wastes resources, undermines security, makes a mockery of justice, slows economic development, and alienates citizens from their government.
- According to a Sweden research report, corruption has become a major issue in foreign aid policies. However, behind the scenes it has always been there, referred to as the "c word."
- The major concern for international aid policy through the last five decades is to improve the living conditions for the poor in the poorest countries of the world.
- Police corruption is a dangerous phenomenon in any society. Approximately one-third of the countries surveyed in the CPI perceived the police as the institution most affected by corruption.

- The CPI is the most comprehensive quantitative indicator of cross-country corruption available, where each single country is recognizable.
- It is compiled by a team of researchers at Göttingen University, headed by Johann Lambsdorff.
- The CPI assesses the degree to which public officials and politicians are believed to accept bribes, take illicit payment in public procurement, embezzle public funds, and commit similar offenses.

Practicum

According to the Tax Justice Network, an independent group promoting efforts to curb tax avoidance, crooked business people, working with corrupt officials, have embezzled $30 trillion over the last 15 years—or half of the world's annual gross domestic product.

From China, nearly $4 trillion is thought to have disappeared between 2000 and 2011, much of it the profits of corruption, channeled into secret offshore financial havens. From Russia, the figure is close to $1 trillion. In the European Union, the total is put at $1.2 trillion.[24]

What steps can nations take to reduce or stop illegal tax avoidance?

Discussion questions

1. Why is transnational police corruption difficult to control?
2. Explain the rationale behind the UNCAC.
3. Explain the oversight control over Canadian police as described by Professor Parent.
4. Do we need a world police force?
5. What are the issues in trying to prevent people smuggling?

References

1. Asfaw Kumssa (March, 2015) Police corruption: A perspective on its nature and control. *Donnish Journal of Political Science and International Relations*, 1(1), 1–8.
2. Alberto Arce and Maria Verza (January 27, 2015) Mexico: All 43 missing students are dead. *The World Post* web site at http://www.huffingtonpost.com/2015/01/27/mexico-missing-students-dead_n_6559812.html. Accessed on November 25, 2015.
3. Transparency International (2014) Global corruption barometer 2013 report, available on line at http://www.transparency.org/research/gcb/overview. Accessed on November 25, 2015.
4. U.S. Department of State (2005) Report on Argentina, available online at http://www.state.gov/j/drl/rls/hrrpt/2004/41746.htm. Accessed on November 25, 2015.
5. U.S. Department of State (2014) 2013 Human Rights reports: Brazil, available online at http://www.state.gov/j/drl/rls/hrrpt/2004/41746.htm. Accessed on November 25, 2015.
6. Allyson Collins (1998) *Shielded from Justice: Police Brutality and Accountability in the United States*. New York: Human Rights Watch.
7. United Nations (October 31, 2013) *United Nations Convention against Corruption Resolution 58/4*. Geneva: UN.
8. Alexander Lebedev (February 26, 2014) A world corruption police. *New York Times*, Opinion page.
9. David Bayley and Robert Perito (November, 2011) "Police corruption: What past scandals teach about current challenges," posted on the U.S. Institute of Peace website at www.usip.com. Accessed on November 16, 2015.
10. Jens Chr. Andvig and Odd-Helge Fjeldstad (December, 2000) "Research on corruption: A policy oriented survey," posted on NORAD website at www.icgg.org accessed on November 16, 2015.
11. Posted on Transparency International website at https://www.transparency.de/. Accessed on November 16, 2015.
12. Marine Corps Warfighting Publication, No. 3-33.5 (2006) Headquarters, Marine Corps Combat Development Command, Department of the Navy, Headquarters, U.S. Marine Corps, Washington, DC.
13. An excellent description of Liberia's police corruption is contained in The Human Rights Watch (August, 2013) "No Money, No Justice" on the Human Rights Watch website at hrw.org. Accessed on November 17, 2015.
14. Statistics Canada (2015) Police officers, by province and territory (Police Officers). Retrieved from http://www.statcan.gc.ca/tables-tableaux/sum-som/l01/cst01/legal05a-eng.htm. Accessed on December 22, 2015.
15. Brian Whitelaw and Richard Parent (2013) *Community-Based Strategic Policing in Canada*. 4th edition. Nelson, Toronto.
16. Alberta Serious Incident Response Team (2012) A year in review. Retrieved from https://solgps.alberta.ca/asirt/publications/Documents/ASIRT%202012%20Annual%20Report.pdf. Accessed on December 22, 2015.
17. Brian Whitelaw and Richard Parent (2013) *Community-Based Strategic Policing in Canada*. 4th edition. Nelson, Toronto. pp. 25–28.
18. Statistics Canada (2015) Police officers, by province and territory (Police Officers). Retrieved from http://www.statcan.gc.ca/tables-tableaux/sum-som/l01/cst01/legal05a-eng.htm. Accessed on December 22, 2015.
19. Special Investigations Office (2015) Special investigations unit stats report 2014–2015. Retrieved from http://www.siu.on.ca/en/report.php?reportid=6. Accessed on December 22, 2015.
20. Uniform Crime Reports (2013) *Crime in the United States*. Washington, DC: Federal Bureau of Investigation. U. S. Department of Justice.
21. Richard Parent (2011) The police use of deadly force in British Columbia: Mental illness and crisis negotiation. *Journal of Police Crisis Negotiations*, 11(1), 57–71.
22. Uniform Crime Reports. (2013) *Crime in the United States*. Washington, DC: Federal Bureau of Investigation. U. S. Department of Justice.
23. Richard Parent (2004) *Aspects of Police Use of Deadly Force in North America: The Phenomenon of Victim-Precipitated Homicide*. Burnaby, BC: Simon Fraser University. (Doctoral Thesis).
24. Alexander Lebedev (February 26, 2014) A world corruption police *New York Times*, p. 1.

chapter seven

Preventing police misconduct

Learning objectives

After studying this chapter, the reader should understand the following concepts and issues:

- The mechanism in place to detect and prevent police misconduct
- The role of the U.S. Department of Justice (DOJ)'s Civil Rights Division
- The use of psychologists to control police misconduct
- The profiles of violence-prone officers
- How to request an investigation

Introduction

Remember that the police force is the most visible arm of the government, and its members often are the recipients of the public's dissatisfaction with the government. There are plenty of people out there who will use police missteps to paint all police officers as the enemy. When officers perform their duties with professionalism and compassion, not only do they show that they are not the enemy, they also strengthen the confidence and trust that the citizens have in their police.

Captain Michael Doyle (Ret.)
Cleveland, Ohio, Police Department (2015)

As noted by Captain Doyle in this statement, the police are the most visible arm of the government. Accordingly, any misconduct by the police is immediately scrutinized by both the public and the media. The misconduct makes first page news; whereas, when the officer does his or her job it does not make the news. In this chapter, we will discuss the methods currently used to police the police.

The police are subject to the same criminal laws to which all other citizens are subject. In addition, there are other statutes and regulations that are designed to help police the police. Probably the most frequently used are the civil rights actions, whereby an officer may be liable in a civil action for the violation of a citizen's rights. Civil actions are discussed in Chapter 8.

Criminal convictions

Law officers, like other citizens, are liable in criminal courts for violations of criminal law. For example, a federal jury in Huntsville, Alabama, convicted a Huntsville police officer in 2015 of deprivation of rights under the color of law (42 U.S. Code 1983) and obstruction of justice. The officer was found guilty after he injured a detainee and filed a false police report on the incident.[1]

A police car video showed police officer Brett Russell pulling a domestic violence suspect out the back of a squad car in 2011, then hitting and kicking him as he was held down by other officers. The suspect had kicked out the squad car's window and allegedly called Russell a racial slur.

After his conviction, the officer faced a statutory maximum sentence of 10 years in prison for the civil rights charge and a statutory maximum sentence of 20 years for the obstruction of justice charge. The Deputy Assistant Attorney stated that the U.S. Justice Department was committed to holding officers who engage in such criminal acts accountable. She noted that, "Today's verdict reflects that abusing the authority of a police badge is a serious crime and it will be punished accordingly …. Most police officers honor their oaths, day in and day out, to uphold the law and protect the public, but this defendant disgraced his badge."[1] On December 2, 2015, a federal judge sentenced the former Huntsville police officer Brett Russell to 18 months in prison for a violation of civil rights charge. Court records indicated that prosecutors sought a 33 month sentence for Russell followed by two years of supervised release.

Civil rights investigations by the U.S. Department of Justice

One effective method of combating police misconduct is the opening of an investigation by the U.S. DOJ. In the following focus box, Attorney General Lynch speaks on the opening of an investigation of the Chicago Police Department in 2015. Her statement is informative, in that it indicates what the DOJ considers in determining whether to open an investigation of a city police department (Box 7.1).

The Civil Rights Division is the primary institution within the U.S. DOJ responsible for enforcing federal statutes prohibiting discrimination on the basis of race,

BOX 7.1   EXCERPTS OF ATTORNEY GENERAL LORETTA E. LYNCH DELIVERS REMARKS AT PRESS CONFERENCE ANNOUNCING INVESTIGATION INTO CHICAGO POLICE DEPARTMENT ON DECEMBER 7, 2015

Good morning and thank you all for being here. I am joined today by Vanita Gupta, head of the department's Civil Rights Division, and Zachary Fardon, U.S. Attorney for the Northern District of Illinois.

The Department of Justice is committed to upholding the highest standards of law enforcement throughout the United States. Every American expects and deserves the protection of law enforcement that is effective, responsive, respectful and most importantly, constitutional—and each day, thanks to the tireless dedication of men and women who wear the badge, citizens from coast to coast receive just that. But when community members feel they are not receiving that kind of policing—when they feel ignored, let down or mistreated by public safety officials—there are profound consequences for the well-being of their communities, for the rule of law and for the countless law enforcement officers who strive to fulfill their duties with professionalism and integrity.

Today, I am announcing that the Department of Justice has opened an investigation into whether the Chicago Police Department has engaged in a pattern or practice of violations of the Constitution or federal law. Specifically, we will examine a number of issues related to the CPD's use of force, including its use of deadly force; racial, ethnic and other disparities in its use of force; and its accountability mechanisms, such as its disciplinary actions and its handling of allegations of misconduct. This investigation has been requested by a number of state and local officials and community leaders and has been opened only after a preliminary review and careful consideration of how the Justice Department can best use our tools and resources to meet Chicago's needs.

In the coming months, the investigation will be conducted by experienced career attorneys from the Civil Rights Division with the assistance of the U.S. Attorney's Office for the Northern District of Illinois. They will conduct a thorough, impartial and independent review of the allegations. The team will meet with a broad cross-section of community members, city officials and law enforcement command staff and officers to explain our process and to hear from anyone who wishes to share information relevant to the investigation. We will examine, with our experts, policies, practices and data. And at the end of our investigation, we will issue a report of our findings. If we discover unconstitutional patterns or practices, the Department of Justice will announce them publicly, seek a court-enforceable agreement with the Chicago Police Department and work with the city to implement appropriate reforms.

Our goal in this investigation – as in all of our pattern-or-practice investigations – is not to focus on individuals, but to improve systems; to ensure that officers are being provided with the tools they need – including training, policy guidance and equipment – to be more effective, to partner with civilians and to strengthen public safety. We understand that the same systems that fail community members also fail conscientious officers by creating mistrust between law enforcement and the citizens they are sworn to serve and protect. This mistrust from members of the community makes it more difficult to gain help with investigations, to encourage victims and witnesses of crimes to speak up, and to fulfill the most basic responsibilities of public safety officials. And when suspicion and hostility is allowed to fester, it can erupt into unrest.

Building trust between law enforcement officers and the communities they serve is one of my highest priorities as Attorney General. The Department of Justice intends to do everything we can to foster those bonds and create safer and fairer communities across the country. And regardless of the findings in this investigation, we will seek to work with local officials, residents and law enforcement officers alike to ensure that the people of Chicago have the world-class police department they deserve.

sex, disability, religion, and national origin. The Civil Rights Division was created in 1957 by the enactment of the Civil Rights Act of 1957; it works to uphold the civil and constitutional rights of all Americans, particularly some of the most vulnerable members of our society. Its jurisdiction to investigate police agencies is based on the due process clause of the Fourteenth Amendment to the U.S. Constitution.

As noted on its website, since its establishment, the division has grown dramatically in both size and scope, and has played a role in many of the nation's pivotal civil rights battles. Division attorneys prosecuted the defendants accused of murdering three civil rights workers in Mississippi in 1964, and were involved in the investigations of the assassinations of Dr. Martin Luther King, Jr., and Medgar Evers. The division enforces a wide array of laws that protect the civil rights of all individuals.

One of the more popular cases the division has prosecuted was *U.S. v. Watson, et al.* The indictment secured by the division alleged that on September 2, 2005, in the wake of Hurricane Katrina, Officer David Warren of the New Orleans Police Department (NOPD) shot Henry Glover in the back, as Officer Warren stood on a second-story balcony, and Glover stood in a parking lot below. Immediately after the shooting, as Glover lay wounded in the street, Glover's brother and a friend flagged down a passing motorist and asked the motorist to help them get medical attention for Glover. The motorist drove the three men to a nearby makeshift NOPD station, where other NOPD officers surrounded the vehicle at gunpoint, ordered the passengers out, and handcuffed them. As the police harassed the three men, they left Glover to die in the back seat of the car. Officer Gregory McRae then drove the car to a nearby levee and burned the car, with Mr. Glover's body still on the back seat.

In June 2010, Officers Warren and McRae were indicted by a federal grand jury for civil rights violations. Also indicted on civil rights charges was Lieutenant Dwayne Scheuermann, who was accused of helping McRae burn the car. NOPD Lieutenants Robert Italiano and Travis McCabe were charged with obstructing justice by authoring and submitting false reports to cover the illegal shooting and burning of Mr. Glover's body, and with other charges for lying to the FBI about the reports.

On December 9, 2010, a federal jury convicted Warren, McRae, and McCabe on civil rights and obstruction of justice counts. The jury acquitted Scheuermann and Italiano. On March 31, 2011, Warren was sentenced to serve 25 years and 9 months in prison, and was ordered to pay Glover's family $7642 for funeral expenses. That same day, McRae was sentenced to serve 17 years and 3 months in prison, and to pay restitution in the amount of $6000. Warren and McRae have appealed their convictions, and McCabe has been granted a new trial based on newly discovered evidence.*

United Kingdom restricts resignations or dismissal

In January 2015, the United Kingdom's Home Office issued new regulations to stop U.K. police officers from resigning or retiring when they are subject to gross misconduct investigations. A chief officer or police and crime commissioner will only be able to consent to an officer's resignation or retirement if they are deemed medically unfit or in other exceptional circumstances; for example where a covert criminal investigation could be prejudiced.

According to the press announcement, these regulations are aimed to ensure that officers are held to account for their actions, that the truth can be established, that victims of police misconduct and their families are provided justice, and that the police learn the full lessons of each incidence of serious misconduct.

It was reported that Home Secretary Theresa May stated:

- Direct damage has been done to public confidence by cases in which officers escaped justice by resigning or retiring where they might have been dismissed.
- The public rightly expects police officers to act with the highest standards of integrity and for those suspected of misconduct to be subject to formal disciplinary proceedings.
- The ability of officers to avoid potential dismissal by resigning or retiring is an unacceptable situation. That is why I have introduced these reforms to ensure victims and their families are not denied the truth of police misconduct.[2]

Police psychologists

According to police researcher Ellen Scrivner, police departments have been using psychologists since the 1980s to help control police use of force. The psychologists are involved in a broad range of activities, including screening job applicants and counseling, to help officers cope with the stress that is inherent in police work.[3]

In Scrivner's research on the use of police psychologists, she noted that some of the psychologists interviewed in the study had developed training models that take into account how people function under adverse conditions and in highly charged situations.

Components of these models include:

- Cultural sensitivity and diversity
- Intervention by fellow officers to stop the use of excessive force
- The interaction of human perception and threat assessment
- Decision-making under highly charged conditions
- Psychological methods of situation control
- Patrol de-escalation and defusing techniques that not only teach a tactical response but also respond to the fear stimulated by confrontations
- Anger management programs that use self-assessment and self-management techniques to provide

---

* Cases involved include *U.S. v. McRae*, 795 F. 3rd. 471 (5th Cir, 2015) and *U.S. v. Howard* 2015 WL 6669162 (E.D. La. 2015).

individual feedback to officers on how variable levels of legitimate anger influence judgment
- Training in verbal control and communication, including conflict resolution

Profiles of violence-prone officers

Psychologists interviewed in her survey were asked about the characteristics of officers who had been referred to them because of the use of excessive force. Their answers did not support the conventional view that a few "bad apples" are responsible for most excessive force complaints. Rather, their answers were used to construct five distinct profiles of different types of officers, only one of which resembled the "bad apple" characterization.

The data used to create the five profiles constitute human resource information that can be used to shape policy. Not only do the profiles offer an etiology of excessive force and provide insight into its complexity, but they also support the notion that excessive force is not just a problem of individuals but may also reflect organizational deficiencies. The profiles are presented in the following profiles in ascending order of frequency:

- Officers with personality disorders that place them at chronic risk
- Officers whose previous job-related experience places them at risk
- Officers who have problems at early stages in their police careers
- Officers who develop inappropriate patrol styles
- Officers with personal problems[4]

Steps in prevention

Scrivner contends that because the profiles reveal different reasons for the use of excessive force, police departments need to develop a system of interventions targeted to different groups of officers and at different phases of their careers. The types of profiles also reveal that individual personality characteristics are only one aspect of excessive force and that risk for this behavior is intensified by other experiences. Some of those experiences implicate the organizational practices of the police departments in which the officers work. To the extent that this is true, it indicates the need for remedial intervention at the departmental level as well as the individual level (Box 7.2).

Petitions for investigations

Civil rights organizations frequently pressure governmental units to investigate specific issues in law enforcement. For example, the American Civil Liberties Union of Nevada (ACLU-NV) and the National Association of the Advancement of Colored People (Las Vegas Chapter) (NACP-LV) filed a petition to the U.S. DOJ, Civil Rights Division, Special Litigation Section requesting an investigation into the Las Vegas Metropolitan Police Department (LVMPD). The petition alleged that the LVMPD had engaged in a pattern or practice of conduct by law enforcement officers that deprived persons of their rights, privileges, or immunities secured or protected by the U.S. Constitution or laws of the United States. The petition alleged that this pattern is manifest through the allegations of police misconduct and the excessive use of force, contrary to the Fourth

---

BOX 7.2   THE NEED FOR BODY CAMERAS

The use of body cameras by police became very popular in 2014 and 2015. Organizations including the Police Executive Research Forum and the American Civil Liberties Union argue that body cameras can increase transparency and accountability in police departments, ensuring that officers act within the letter of law and that, when they don't, there's documented evidence available to help try and punish them.

A video of an incident between Cleveland police officers and a citizen shows that body cameras may help both the police and the public understand what happened during the incident. The video probably saved four Cleveland policers' jobs. This incident establishes that body cameras are not just a tool to expose police wrongdoing it also protects the innocent officer.

According to media reports, on March 11, 2015 the Cleveland police officers were climbing stairs to a citizen's apartment. When one officer turned the corner, the citizen opened fire on the officers. One video recorded the officers pleading with the citizen to put his gun down. Another camera shows one officer telling the citizen to "put the gun down and we'll get you all the help you need." Another camera indicates that the wounded officer stating: "I know you shot me, but I'm not going to shoot you." A few seconds later the citizen raises his gun and the officers open fire killing him.

A grand jury determined that the four officers were justified in using lethal force against the citizen. The jury concluded that the officers had gone to the citizen's home that night after his wife went to a police station and reported that her husband had threatened to kill both her and their landlady.[5]

Amendment right against unreasonable searches and seizure and the right to due process of law under the Fourteenth Amendment.[6,7]

> **Note:** The author has no knowledge of and has not investigated the allegations contained in the petition, but for the purposes of demonstrating the nature of this complaint, is using those facts as if they are correct. The petition serves as an example of how an organization may request action from the DOJ.

The petition, with accompanying documents, alleges that the LVMPD is beset with serious systemic and training problems that include:

- Recurring, documented instances of violent and often fatal treatment of people who come in contact with the police, through both the intentional use of deadly force, excessive force and/or through negligent actions.
- False arrests and stops made without reasonable suspicion of criminal activity, much less probable cause, along with improper searches, malicious prosecutions, and other corrupt practices.
- An ineffective process for identifying and deterring such conduct.
- Insufficient processes for receiving, handling, adjudicating, and announcing the disposition of complaints alleging misconduct or violation of rules, or the excessive use of force.
- The failure to have a complete set of modem and meaningful policies, practices, or training procedures that effectively prevent the excessive use of force.
- Deliberate indifference to the constitutional rights of persons with whom the police come into contact.
- Costly litigation expenses, including verdicts, arbitrations, and settlements, together with the expenses of defending those cases: since 1991, the Las Vegas police have paid $18 million to settle various property damage, excessive force, and wrongful arrest claims (LVMPD fiscal affairs committee). At the same time, lawsuits and citizen complaints reveal continuing patterns of misbehavior, as if nothing has been corrected in response to prior lawsuits or complaints.

The petition requested: "On behalf of the people who reside, work and visit the city of Las Vegas and its surrounding areas, we implore the Civil Rights Division to investigate the LVMPD. The conduct described herein has left citizens dead, permanently injured and otherwise damaged. Further, this abuse has created an atmosphere of distrust with the local police department."

The petition contained a list of lawsuits filed by the people against the LVMPD alleging excessive use of force, wrongful death, unlawful seizures, false arrests, and wrongful incarceration. The petition claimed that the most egregious cases of police misconduct in recent Las Vegas history highlight the systemic and ongoing nature of LVMPD's excessive use of force, including deadly force, against Nevada citizens. These instances stimulate public dismay and lead the public to question LVMPD's dedication to the protections enshrined in the laws and the Constitution of the United States.

The petition noted that, currently, two primary civil mechanisms exist to review an officer's use of deadly force in the line of duty: the LVMPD's Use of Force Review Board and the Clark County coroner's inquest process. If the shooting results in death, homicide detectives investigate the case and present it to the coroner's inquest. Citizen jurors then determine if the officer's actions were justified, excusable, or criminal. The Use of Force Review Board also looks at fatal shooting cases to see if the officer violated department policy, but it has never disagreed with an inquest jury. The petition contended: "In essence, then, these amount to puppet institutions, and are incapable of providing meaningful review of an officer's misuse of deadly force."

The petition noted that the DOJ is well equipped to investigate the cause of these repeated incidents. The investigation should determine why the LVMPD initiated or escalated the confrontations; whether and why the officers perceived a threat from certain individuals; whether officers view the use of force differently when they are confronting a person of color; why the officers chose not to use de-escalation tactics in responding to perceived law violations to avoid the use of violence; whether LVMPD employees who witness excessive force report it promptly; whether the LVMPD supervisors promptly and properly gathered the evidence and fully investigated the allegations of excessive use of force.

About eight months after the petition was filed, the DOJ completed its review of LVMPD and the department's use of force policies. The DOJ report contained 75 findings and recommendations. Among the findings was the need for significant changes to the Use of Force Review Board, new tactical practices when multiple officers respond to a crime scene, and the implementation of new technologies, such as body cameras. The report also found that while the department's new use of force policy is comprehensive, the format of the policy is cumbersome and not structured in a clear and concise manner that would allow for quick guidance when needed. The report recommends that the new policy be separated into smaller, specific policies that quickly address issues such as the use of firearms and less-lethal weapons (Box 7.3).

**BOX 7.3   MANAGING POLICE MISCONDUCT AND APPLYING
DISCIPLINE: A CASE STUDY BY KEN PEAK**

[Dr. Ken Peak is Professor Emeritus and former Chairman, Department of Criminal Justice, University of Nevada, Reno. Ken has authored or coauthored 32 books and more than 60 monographs, journal articles, and invited chapters on a variety of policing topics. During 45 years in the criminal justice field, Ken devoted 37 years to academia (instructing policing, justice administration, victimology, planned change, and comparative justice systems courses), and eight years serving (twice) as a university police chief, criminal justice planner, director of a four-state Technical Assistance Institute, and municipal police officer. He received teaching awards and two gubernatorial appointments to statewide criminal justice committees, and held a number of national and regional offices.]

THE CASE STUDY

Clearly the public's trust and respect are precious commodities, quickly lost through improper behavior by police employees and the improper handling of an allegation of misconduct. Serving communities with professionalism and integrity should be the goal of every police agency and its employees in order to ensure that trust and respect are maintained. The public expects that police agencies will make every effort to identify and correct problems and respond to citizens' complaints in a judicious, consistent, fair, and equitable manner.

Employee misconduct and violations of departmental policy are the two principal areas in which discipline is applied. Employee misconduct includes acts that harm the public, such as corruption, harassment, brutality, and violations of civil rights. Violations of policy may involve a broad range of issues, from substance abuse and insubordination to tardiness or minor violations of dress.[9]

There are well-established minimum due process requirements for discharging public employees, including the right to:

- a public hearing.
- be present during the presentation of evidence against them
- cross-examine their superiors, and to present their own witnesses and other evidence concerning their side of the controversy.
- be represented by counsel.
- have an impartial referee or hearing officer presiding.
- have a decision based on the weight of the evidence introduced at the hearing.

Such protections apply to any disciplinary action that can significantly affect a police employee's employment, reputation, or future chances for special assignment or promotion.

With this in mind, and given the current close public scrutiny today in the aftermath of police shootings of unarmed people (primarily minorities), read the following case study and consider if and how you might have handled the matter differently. Also reflect on whether or not the current system of disciplining personnel who are part of a state civil service system affords such employees too many, not enough, or the proper amount of due process rights.

As a bit of background, the author has been a university police chief at two institutions of higher education. The following disciplinary matter occurred at one of them. I have often used this case study in my upper-division justice administration courses, dividing the classes into groups and giving them the basic facts, then soliciting their views as to how they would attempt to handle the matter and attempt to arrive at a proper outcome. This case study demonstrates for students the fortitude, types of knowledge, time and effort, and even personal threats and discomfort that can be involved in undergoing what is typically a multifaceted endeavor – involving several agencies and parties – as you attempt to administer disciplinary action for employee misconduct. It is almost an article of faith that administrators in medium- and large-sized agencies devote the majority of their time dealing with employee problems. As one former police manager once told the author, "I can't tell you how to make a DUI arrest, but I can tell you how to discipline an employee."

"Jones, Jurisdiction, and the Injudicious Report"

The agency was seeking to promote an employee to the position of detective. The process was not going to be particularly involved; the process to be used, and one that is used by many agencies, was what is termed a "T&E" (for training and education) exam, and examining each applicant's "KSAs" – or knowledge, skills, and abilities. Taken together, we hope to identify which individual might be the most qualified for this role (looking at the individual's productivity, quality of arrests, demonstration of investigative prowess, formal education and training, and so on). Certainly an assessment center or some other similarly rigorous process would have been preferred, but given the quality of personnel of the time, we felt this T&E/KSA approach would work well. As is often the case – due to the status accorded the detective position and the ability to wear civilian clothes, have weekends off, work largely in an unsupervised capacity, and so on - we anticipated that a number of quality personnel would aspire to become a detective.

One of the patrol officers wishing to obtain the detective grade was a nine-year veteran who had a reputation for being a tough cop who enjoyed displaying "swagger"; of course, he could outshoot anyone in the agency on the pistol qualification range as well. Tall, lean, and with a heavily pock-marked face, he did indeed present a threatening aspect and could cower lesser experienced officers with little difficulty.

It is important to note that I had heard rumors of this officer's heavy-handed behavior from his peers; one recent incident involved him forcibly shoving a high school student over the hood of his vehicle in the campus arena's parking lot for not being deferential enough. A former police chief in this agency informed me that this officer was also the kind of person who seemingly "had a screw in the back of his head, holding everything together, but if the screw ever came loose, he might be one of those crackpots who shoots at people from atop a campus building." Such was the type of officer I inherited and who wanted to become a detective – and who also had nine years of satisfactory and above personnel evaluations.

There had been some thefts of electronic equipment from a building on campus, and so on one particular weekend our officer ("Jones") was walking through the building and performing a visual check. He happened to encounter a graduate student who was working in a lab and began to question him. Apparently believing that the student might know more about the thefts that he was revealing, Jones decided to take the student to the campus police station for further questioning. Upon entering the station's interviewing room, witnesses said Jones slammed the door loudly and slammed his baton down on the desk (maneuvers that were apparently intended to show the student he meant business and to frighten the "suspect" into confessing to the crimes. Failing to obtain a confession from the student, Jones released him a short while later. The following Monday morning I was met at my office by the student, then quite incensed about the manner in which he had been treated and wishing to file a complaint against Jones.

While that complaint's investigation was in process, Jones had another opportunity to bring attention to himself. One day around noon a shooting was reported to have occurred inside a residence located a few blocks off-campus (outside of campus officers' jurisdiction). Jones, apparently bored but curious, drove his patrol vehicle to the home. Upon arrival he entered the home, where a number of fire and emergency medical personnel were working on an injured (shot) man who was lying prone on the kitchen floor. Jones happened to see a large handgun resting on a room divider; he picked it up and - apparently struck by the size and type of weapon (it being of some foreign brand) - waved it around in the air in awe and examined it from various angles. A fire department captain, observing this activity, yelled at Jones "Hey, put that pistol down, it might be evidence." Jones put the handgun back and left the scene.

Upon being contacted by the fire captain and informed of Jones's behavior, I requested that Jones draft a report for me setting forth his actions at the home, and why he had left his jurisdiction. He provided a report, but denied ever touching the handgun.

[At this point in my justice administration courses, I pose to students the following questions:

1. What are the primary issues that are involved in this situation?
2. Do you believe sufficient grounds exist for bringing disciplinary action against Jones? If so, what charges? Punishment?
3. Do his supervisors' past standard and above annual performance ratings have any bearing on this matter or its outcome? If so, how?]

Given our belief that Jones had lied in his report (knowing Jones' affinity with firearms, his report conflicting with credible information provided by the fire captain and other witnesses at scene) as well as our determination that he had violated a number of university and departmental codes and policies (as well as Jones' previous involvement with the graduate student), it was felt that some formal disciplinary action was required. Several meetings and discussions were held involving university human resources personnel, university counsel, and other police employees; together they consumed dozens if not hundreds of hours. In the final analysis, it was believed that we had enough justification for terminating Jones. A "statement of charges" was prepared, approximately fifty pages in length, setting forth all of the various state statutes, university code, and department policy violations that had been perpetrated by Jones.

Jones was then called into my office, where I (with a police sergeant as witness) presented Jones with his copy of the charges. I notified him that we fully intended to terminate him. As a card-carrying member of a state employees association, he immediately made a phone call and was quickly assigned legal counsel; of course, in their view, we were acting in unconscionable fashion in trying to separate a fine officer from his job and destroy his career.

The university had a hearing officer (an attorney) on retainer to conduct public hearings in such matters, so both sides were informed of the date and location the hearing would take place, at which time we would present our case setting forth reasons why we felt Jones should be compelled to forfeit his civil-service position; conversely, his attorneys would take the opposing position.

The day before the hearing was to be held, my family (wife and two small children) was stalked by someone following them in a vehicle as they were both going to and returning from the grocery running other errands. They were naturally quite frightened upon returning home and while relating the experience to me. Furthermore, that evening, several hang-up phone calls were made to our residence.

On the day of the hearing, all was in readiness and both sides prepared to present their arguments to the hearing officer. However, as can occur in actual criminal or civil trials, there was first an attempt on the part of the hearing officer to bring the attorneys together (representing the university and the employees' union) to see if an agreement might be reached beforehand. That was accomplished, and I was informed of the outcome minutes prior to the appointed start time of the hearing: Jones had agreed to accept a disciplinary action in the form of 7 days off without pay in exchange for all other charges being dropped.

It goes without saying that I (and many other campus police and HR personnel) were quite disappointed upon learning of this turn of events; we felt that neither did the punishment fit the offenses, nor all of our (to that point) hundreds of hours of preparation justified. The head of the campus HR office, a very learned and experience individual, came to me at once and simply said "You can't terminate someone, for these reasons, who has received nine years of satisfactory and above performance evaluations."

But we had in fact "won" something after all. Now, with Jones' having a formal record of misconduct and disciplinary action against him, both parties knew that he would be treading on thin ice in the future if he should engage in any misconduct. Indeed, after working one more year, he resigned his position and left the state. I might add that before resigning and shortly after the above matter concluded, he came by my office a few times; on such occasions our visits were amicable in nature. I interpreted his visits to mean that he knew he deserved to be terminated, and at least respected me for trying to do so.

Good to great

What does this case study have to say to aspiring criminal justice administrators, middle managers, and first-line supervisors about how to approach the problem of employee misconduct? First and foremost, it speaks to the need to be very honest and forthright in preparing and explaining employees' performance evaluations. In the above case, former chiefs had chosen to overlook Jones' misconduct, preferring instead to take the easier path and assign a satisfactory or above rating for Jones during a nine-year period, even in the face of heavy-handed behavior over the course of his agency tenure.

In a widely-read book entitled *Good to Great and the Social Sectors*, concerning how to take a good organization and convert it into a superb one, Jim Collins coined the term Level 5 leader to describe the highest level of executive capabilities; he said such leaders are ambitious, but their ambition is directed first and foremost to the organization and its success, not to personal renown. Level 5 leaders, Collins stressed, are "fanatically driven, infected with an incurable need to produce results." Collins used a bus metaphor when talking about igniting the transformation of an organization from good to great: they first got the right people on the bus (and the wrong people off the bus) and then figured out where to drive it. In fact, Collins wrote, good-to-great organizations, have a "culture of discipline" in which employees show extreme diligence and intensity in their thoughts and actions. Collins stated that picking the right people and getting the wrong people off the bus are critical: "By whatever means possible, personnel problems have to be confronted in an organization that aspires to greatness."[10, 11] Hence, the extremely important matter of being tough enough to tell people what they're doing wrong, where improvement is needed, and the consequences of not doing so. Second, we owe it to the other good employees to weed out the incompetent problem employees; it is in the best interest of the agency morale to do so.

Positive discipline

Which brings us to the topic of a positive discipline program (also known as positive counseling), which attempts to change employee behavior without invoking punishment. It is always preferable to salvage employees in lieu of termination whenever possible to do so; we have a lot of time and resources invested in recruiting, training, and equipping criminal justice employees, so, again, whenever possible, we want to try to re-direct ("save") the work habits of those employees who might be slipping in their performance.

Here's how it works: assume an employee ("John") has been nonproductive and non-punctual, has developed interpersonal problems with his co-workers, and/or has other problems on the job. To this point, *John* has been in control of the situation—he has been on the offensive, one might say—whereas the supervisor ("Jane") and his co-workers have been on the *defensive*. John is jeopardizing the morale and productivity of the workplace.

Jane calls John into her office. She might begin with a compliment to him (if indeed she can find one) and then proceeds to outline all of his workplace shortcomings; this demonstrates to John that Jane "has his number" and is aware of his various problems. Jane explains to him why it is important that he improve (for reasons related to accomplishing agency mission and values, interpersonal relations, morale, and so on) and the benefits he might realize from his improvement (promotions, pay raises, bonuses). She also outlines what can happen if he does *not* show adequate improvement (demotion, transfer, termination). Now having gained John's attention, she gives him a certain time period (e.g., 30, 60, or 90 days) in which to improve; she emphasizes, however, that she will be constantly monitoring his progress. She might even ask John to sign a counseling statement form that sets forth all they have discussed, indicating that John has received counseling and understands the situation.

Note that Jane is now on the offensive, thereby putting John on the defensive and in control of his destiny; if he fails to perform, Jane would probably give him a warning, and if the situation continues, he will be terminated. If he sues or files a grievance, Jane has proof that every effort was made to allow John to salvage his position. This is an effective means of giving subordinates an incentive to improve their behavior while at the same time making the department less vulnerable to successful lawsuits. It must be emphasized that adequate documentation of John's behavior is necessarily developed prior to making an attempt to terminate him. I have used this program to good success (including once with a parking employee who most definitely should not have been put in that position!); it can work well.

An important caveat: as with all of the information provided above relating to dealing with employee misconduct, your ability and approaches to discipline with your employees will depend on your local and state laws, agency and jurisdictional policies, and agency culture.

When the report was issued, the LVMPD had already made progress on implementing a number of the report's recommendations, addressing nearly half of the calls for action prior to the release of the report from the COPS office. "One of the most important issues facing law enforcement is the public perception of the legitimate use of force," said Community Oriented Policing Services (COPS) office director Bernard Melekian. "And far too often, the public perception of police use of force is different from those who are in law enforcement. We've now developed a tool to help assist agencies address community concerns, effectively revamp policies and practices, and enhance both community engagement and community support."[8]

Summary

- One effective method of combating police misconduct is the opening of an investigation by the U.S. DOJ.
- The Civil Rights Division is the primary institution within the U.S. DOJ responsible for enforcing federal statutes prohibiting discrimination on the basis of race, sex, disability, religion, and national origin.
- The Civil Rights Division was created in 1957 by the enactment of the Civil Rights Act of 1957; it works to uphold the civil and constitutional rights of all Americans, particularly some of the most vulnerable members of our society.
- In January 2015, the United Kingdom's Home Office issued new regulations to stop U.K. police officers from resigning or retiring when they are subject to gross misconduct investigations.
- A chief officer or police and crime commissioner will only be able to consent to an officer's resignation or retirement if they are deemed medically unfit or in other exceptional circumstances, for example where a covert criminal investigation could be prejudiced.
- According to police researcher Ellen Scrivner, police departments have been using psychologists since the 1980s to help control police use of force.
- The psychologists are involved in a broad range of activities including screening job applicants and counseling.
- The profiles are presented in the following profiles in ascending order of frequency: officers with personality disorders that place them at chronic risk; officers whose previous job-related experience places them at risk; officers who have problems at early stages in their police careers; officers who develop inappropriate patrol styles; and officers with personal problems.

- Civil rights organizations frequently pressure governmental units to investigate specific issues in law enforcement.

Practicum

TULSA, Okla.— An Oklahoma suspect accused of robbing another man at knifepoint has been arrested after the victim described his attacker's distinctive facial tattoos, including a pair of horns and an antipolice obscenity. If you were to stop a man with antipolice obscenities tattooed on his face, how would you handle him as a police officer?

Discussion questions

1. Explain how the FBI investigates police misconduct.
2. Explain what types of police officers are more likely to be violent.
3. What are the two principal reasons public employees are fired?
4. Are there well-established minimum due process requirements for discharging public employees?
5. How have video cameras helped the police?

References

1. Press announcement on Brett Russell by the Office of Public Affairs, U.S. Department of Justice on July 31, 2015.
2. Announcement by United Kingdom Home Office on 12 January 2015. Posted at https://www.gov.uk/government/news/new-regulations-prevent-police-officers-retiring-or-resigning-to-avoid-dismissal. Accessed on December 6, 2015.
3. Ellen Scrivner (October, 1994) *Controlling Police Use of Excessive Force: The Role of the Police Psychologist*. National Institute of Justice, Research in Brief, Washington, DC: Department of Justice.
4. Ellen Scrivner (October, 1994) *Controlling Police Use of Excessive Force: The Role of the Police Psychologist*, p. 3. National Institute of Justice, Research in Brief, Washington, DC: Department of Justice.
5. Henry Gass (October 13, 2015) Cleveland case shows how body cameras can help police. *Christian Science Monitor*, p. A4.
6. The material for this section as taken from the original petition filed with the DOJ on January 10, 2012 (copy available online at http://www.cops.usdoj.gov/pdf/01-14-12-ACLU-NAACP-DOJ-petition-LVMPD. Accessed on October 13, 2015).
7. Brian Haynes (January 12, 2012) Las Vegas police shoot and kill. *Las Vegas Review-Journal*, p. 1.
8. Justice News press release posted on the DOJ website at http://www.justice.gov/opa/pr/department-justice-completes-review-las-vegas-metropolitan-police-department-s-use-force. Accessed on October 19, 2015.

9. V. McLaughlin and R. Bing (1987) Law enforcement personnel selection. *Journal of Police Science and Administration*, 15, 271–276.

10. Jim Collins (2005) *Good to Great and the Social Sectors: A Monograph to Accompany Good to Great.* New York: HarperCollins.

11. Chuck Wexler, Mary Ann Wycoff, and Craig Fischer (2007) *Good to Great: Application of Business Management Principles in the Public Sector.* Washington, DC: Office of Community Oriented Policing Services and the Police Executive Research Forum, p. 5.

chapter eight

Civil liability for police misconduct

Learning objectives

After studying this chapter, the reader should understand the following concepts and issues:

- The civil statutes that may be used to combat police misconduct
- The meaning of the concept of color of law
- How summary judgments work
- How qualified immunity protects officers
- What areas qualified immunity does not protect
- The liability of cities and police departments

Civil rights actions

In the majority of cases where the police, city, and so on are sued for violation of civil rights in federal court, the suit is filed pursuant to Civil Rights Act, 42 U.S. Code 1983. The leading case on this issue is *Bivens v. Six Unknown Named Agents of the Federal Bureau of Narcotics.** As a side note, I have always wondered how the agents could be unknown but named.

In *Bivens*, the Supreme Court, with Mr. Justice Brennan writing the opinion, held that complaint alleging that agents of the Federal Bureau of Narcotics, acting under color of federal authority, made warrantless entry of petitioner's apartment, searched the apartment, and arrested him on narcotics charges, all without probable cause, stated federal cause of action under the Fourth Amendment for damages recoverable on proof of injuries resulting from agents' violation of that Amendment.

This case has its origin in an arrest and search carried out on the morning of November 26, 1965. Petitioner's complaint alleged that, on that day, respondents, agents of the Federal Bureau of Narcotics, acting under claim of federal authority, entered his apartment and arrested him for alleged narcotics violations. The agents manacled petitioner in front of his wife and children, and threatened to arrest the entire family. They searched the apartment from stem to stern. Thereafter, petitioner was taken to the federal courthouse in Brooklyn, where he was interrogated, booked, and subjected to a visual strip search.

On July 7, 1967, petitioner brought suit in federal district court. In addition to the allegations mentioned,

his complaint asserted that the arrest and search were effected without a warrant, and that unreasonable force was employed in making the arrest; fairly read, it alleged, as well, that the arrest was made without probable cause. Petitioner claimed to have suffered great humiliation, embarrassment, and mental suffering as a result of the agents' unlawful conduct, and sought $15,000 damages from each of them. The district court, on respondents' summary judgment motion, dismissed the complaint on the ground that it failed to state a cause of action. The U.S. Court of Appeals affirmed on that basis. The U.S. Supreme Court granted review and reversed the decision.

The Supreme Court noted that the respondents (agents) did not argue that petitioner should be entirely without remedy for an unconstitutional invasion of his rights by federal agents. In respondents' view, however, the rights that petitioner asserted—primarily rights of privacy—were creations of state and not of federal law. Accordingly, they argued, petitioner might obtain money damages to redress invasion of these rights only by an action in tort, under state law, in the state courts. In this scheme, the Fourth Amendment would serve merely to limit the extent to which the agents could defend the state law tort suit by asserting that their actions were a valid exercise of federal power: if the agents were shown to have violated the Fourth Amendment, such a defense would be lost to them and they would stand before the state law merely as private individuals. Candidly admitting that it was the policy of the Department of Justice to remove all such suits from the state to the federal courts for decision, respondents nevertheless urged that the court uphold dismissal of petitioner's complaint in federal court, and remit him to filing an action in the state courts so that the case might properly be removed to the federal court for decision on the basis of state law.

The Supreme Court held that respondents' thesis rested on an unduly restrictive view of the Fourth Amendment's protection against unreasonable searches and seizures by federal agents, a view that has consistently been rejected by the court. Respondents sought to treat the relationship between a citizen and a federal agent unconstitutionally exercising his authority as no different from the relationship between two private citizens. In so doing, they ignore the fact that power, once granted, does not disappear as if it were a magic gift

---

* *Bivens v. Six Unknown Named Agents of the Federal Bureau of Narcotics,* 403 U.S. 388 (1971).

when it is wrongfully used. An agent acting—albeit unconstitutionally—in the name of the United States possesses a far greater capacity for harm than an individual trespasser exercising no authority other than his or her own.

The court noted that its cases make clear that the Fourth Amendment operates as a limitation on the exercise of federal power, regardless of whether the state in whose jurisdiction that power is exercised would prohibit or penalize the identical act if engaged in by a private citizen. It guarantees to citizens of the United States the absolute right to be free from unreasonable searches and seizures carried out by virtue of federal authority. Where federally protected rights have been invaded, it has been the rule from the beginning that courts will be alert to adjust their remedies so as to grant the necessary relief.

The court noted that its cases have long since rejected the notion that the Fourth Amendment proscribes only such conduct as would, if engaged in by private persons, be condemned by state law. At the invitation of state law enforcement officers, a federal prohibition agent participated in the search. The court pointed out that its recent decisions regarding electronic surveillance have made it clear beyond peradventure that the Fourth Amendment is not tied to the niceties of local trespass laws. Respondents' argument that the Fourth Amendment serves only as a limitation on federal defenses to a state law claim, and not as an independent limitation on the exercise of federal power, was rejected.

The court pointed out that interests protected by state laws regulating trespass and the invasion of privacy, and those protected by the Fourth Amendment's guarantee against unreasonable searches and seizures, may be inconsistent or even hostile. Thus, citizens may bar the door against an unwelcome private intruder, or call the police if he or she persists in seeking entrance. The availability of such alternative means for the protection of privacy may lead the state to restrict imposition of liability for any consequent trespass. A private citizen, asserting no authority other than his or her own, will not normally be liable in trespass if he or she demands, and is granted, admission to another's house. But one who demands admission under a claim of federal authority stands in a far different position. The mere invocation of federal power by a federal law enforcement official will normally render futile any attempt to resist an unlawful entry or arrest by resort to the local police; and a claim of authority to enter is likely to unlock the door as well. In such cases, there is no safety for the citizen, except in the protection of the judicial tribunals, for rights which have been invaded by the officers of the government, professing to act in its name. Nor is it adequate to answer that state law

may take into account the different status of one clothed with the authority of the federal government. For, just as state law may not authorize federal agents to violate the Fourth Amendment, neither may state law undertake to limit the extent to which federal authority can be exercised. The inevitable consequence of this dual limitation on state power is that the federal question becomes not merely a possible defense to the state law action, but an independent claim, both necessary and sufficient to make out the plaintiff's cause of action.

The court's opinion, that damages may be obtained for injuries consequent on a violation of the Fourth Amendment by federal officials, should hardly seem a surprising proposition. Historically, damages have been regarded as the ordinary remedy for an invasion of personal interests in liberty. Of course, the Fourth Amendment does not, in so many words, provide for its enforcement by an award of money damages for the consequences of its violation. But, it is well settled that where legal rights have been invaded, and a federal statute provides for a general right to sue for such invasion, federal courts may use any available remedy to make good the wrong done. The present case involves no special factors counseling hesitation in the absence of affirmative action by Congress. The court noted that they were not dealing with a question of federal fiscal policy. Noting that Congress was normally quite solicitous where the federal purse was involved, the court pointed out that the United States was the party plaintiff to the suit, and the United States has power at any time to create the liability. Finally, the court noted that they could not accept respondents' formulation of the question as to whether the availability of money damages is necessary to enforce the Fourth Amendment; for there is no explicit congressional declaration that persons injured by a federal officer's violation of the Fourth Amendment may not recover money damages from the agents, but must instead be remitted to another remedy, equally effective in the view of Congress. The question is merely whether petitioner, if he can demonstrate an injury consequent on the violation by federal agents of his Fourth Amendment rights, is entitled to redress his injury through a particular remedial mechanism normally available in the federal courts. The very essence of civil liberty certainly consists in the right of every individual to claim the protection of the laws, whenever he receives an injury. Having concluded that petitioner's complaint states a cause of action under the Fourth Amendment, the court held that petitioner was entitled to recover money damages for any injuries he had suffered as a result of the agents' violation of the Amendment.

The judgment of the Court of Appeals was reversed and the case was remanded for further proceedings consistent with this opinion (Box 8.1).

BOX 8.1   42 U.S.C.A. § 1983

CIVIL ACTION FOR DEPRIVATION OF RIGHTS

Every person who, under color of any statute, ordinance, regulation, custom, or usage, of any State or Territory or the District of Columbia, subjects, or causes to be subjected, any citizen of the United States or other person within the jurisdiction thereof to the deprivation of any rights, privileges, or immunities secured by the Constitution and laws, shall be liable to the party injured in an action at law, suit in equity, or other proper proceeding for redress, except that in any action brought against a judicial officer for an act or omission taken in such officer's judicial capacity, injunctive relief shall not be granted unless a declaratory decree was violated or declaratory relief was unavailable. For the purposes of this section, any Act of Congress applicable exclusively to the District of Columbia shall be considered to be a statute of the District of Columbia.

State law torts

Frequently, state officers may be sued under §1983 in federal court for violations of state tort laws. Generally, the actions are based on allegations of negligence. The requirements necessary for a negligence action are summarized as follows:

- A duty or obligation, recognized by the law, requiring the person to conform to a certain standard of conduct, for the protection of others against unreasonable risks.
- A failure on the person's part to conform to the standard required; a breach of duty.
- A reasonably close causal connection between the conduct and the resulting injury. This connection is commonly known as "legal cause" or "proximate cause" and includes the notion of cause in fact.
- Actual loss or damage resulting to the interests of another.

Color of law

Police officers and other governmental officials have been given power over citizens by local, state, and federal government agencies. This is necessary to enforce to laws and ensure justice. The powers include the authority to detain, arrest, search persons and property, and to seize property or persons. To prevent abuse of this authority, it is a federal crime for anyone acting under "color of law" to abuse that authority.

U.S. Code 42 §1983 is not an appropriate cause of action for an injured party where a federal law enforcement officer is alleged to have caused the injury, because it is limited in application to those persons who are acting under apparent "authority of state law."

On the federal level, it is the FBI that is the lead authority to investigate possible color-of-law abuses. In a normal year, about 42% of the FBI's total civil rights caseload involves the issue of abuse of authority under color of law. Most of these cases can be grouped into five broad areas:

- Excessive use of force
- Sexual misconduct
- False arrest and fabrication of evidence
- Deprivation of property
- Failure to keep from harm

Filing a complaint

To file a color-of-law complaint, one should contact one's local FBI office by telephone, in writing, or in person. The following information should be provided:

- All identifying information for the victim(s)
- As much identifying information as possible for the subject(s), including position, rank, and agency employed
- Date and time of incident
- Location of incident
- Names, addresses, and telephone numbers of any witness(es)
- A complete chronology of events
- Any report numbers and charges with respect to the incident

One may also contact the United States Attorney's office in one's district or send a written complaint to:

Assistant Attorney General
Civil Rights Division
Criminal Section
950 Pennsylvania Avenue, Northwest
Washington, DC 20530

FBI investigations vary in length. Once their investigation is complete, the FBI should forward the findings to the U.S. Attorney's office within the local jurisdiction and to the U.S. Department of Justice in Washington, D.C., which will decide whether or not to proceed toward prosecution and handle any prosecutions that follow (Box 8.2).

BOX 8.2   FEDERAL CIVIL RIGHTS STATUTES

TITLE 18, U.S.C., SECTION 249 - MATTHEW SHEPARD AND JAMES BYRD, JR., HATE CRIMES PREVENTION ACT

This statute makes it unlawful to willfully cause bodily injury—or attempting to do so with fire, firearm, or other dangerous weapon—when (1) the crime was committed because of the actual or perceived race, color, religion, national origin of any person, or (2) the crime was committed because of the actual or perceived religion, national origin, gender, sexual orientation, gender identity, or disability of any person and the crime affected interstate or foreign commerce or occurred within federal special maritime and territorial jurisdiction.

TITLE 18, U.S.C., SECTION 241 - CONSPIRACY AGAINST RIGHTS

This statute makes it unlawful for two or more persons to conspire to injure, oppress, threaten, or intimidate any person of any state, territory or district in the free exercise or enjoyment of any right or privilege secured to him/her by the Constitution or the laws of the United States, (or because of his/her having exercised the same).

It further makes it unlawful for two or more persons to go in disguise on the highway or on the premises of another with the intent to prevent or hinder his/her free exercise or enjoyment of any rights so secured.

TITLE 18, U.S.C., SECTION 242 - DEPRIVATION OF RIGHTS UNDER COLOR OF LAW

This statute makes it a crime for any person acting under color of law, statute, ordinance, regulation, or custom to willfully deprive or cause to be deprived from any person those rights, privileges, or immunities secured or protected by the Constitution and laws of the U.S.

This law further prohibits a person acting under color of law, statute, ordinance, regulation or custom to willfully subject or cause to be subjected any person to different punishments, pains, or penalties, than those prescribed for punishment of citizens on account of such person being an alien or by reason of his/her color or race.

Acts under "color of any law" include acts not only done by federal, state, or local officials within the bounds or limits of their lawful authority, but also acts done without and beyond the bounds of their lawful authority; provided that, in order for unlawful acts of any official to be done under "color of any law," the unlawful acts must be done while such official is purporting or pretending to act in the performance of his/her official duties. This definition includes, in addition to law enforcement officials, individuals such as Mayors, Council persons, Judges, Nursing Home Proprietors, Security Guards, etc., persons who are bound by laws, statutes ordinances, or customs.

TITLE 18, U.S.C., SECTION 245 - FEDERALLY PROTECTED ACTIVITIES

This statute prohibits willful injury, intimidation, or interference, or attempt to do so, by force or threat of force of any person or class of persons because of their activity as:

(a) A voter, or person qualifying to vote...;
(b) a participant in any benefit, service, privilege, program, facility, or activity provided or administered by the United States;
(c) an applicant for federal employment or an employee by the federal government;
(d) a juror or prospective juror in federal court; and
(e) a participant in any program or activity receiving Federal financial assistance.

Prohibits willful injury, intimidation, or interference or attempt to do so, by force or threat of force of any person because of race, color, religion, or national origin and because of his/her activity as:

(a) A student or applicant for admission to any public school or public college;
(b) a participant in any benefit, service, privilege, program, facility, or activity provided or administered by a state or local government;

   (c) an applicant for private or state employment, private or state employee; a member or applicant for membership in any labor organization or hiring hall; or an applicant for employment through any employment agency, labor organization or hiring hall;

   (d) a juror or prospective juror in state court;

   (e) a traveler or user of any facility of interstate commerce or common carrier; or

   (f) a patron of any public accommodation, including hotels, motels, restaurants, lunchrooms, bars, gas stations, theaters...or any other establishment which serves the public and which is principally engaged in selling food or beverages for consumption on the premises.

Prohibits interference by force or threat of force against any person because he/she is or has been, or in order to intimidate such person or any other person or class of persons from participating or affording others the opportunity or protection to so participate, or lawfully aiding or encouraging other persons to participate in any of the benefits or activities listed in items (1) and (2), above without discrimination as to race, color, religion, or national origin.

TITLE 18, U.S.C., SECTION 247 - CHURCH ARSON PREVENTION ACT OF 1996

Prohibits (1) intentional defacement, damage, or destruction of any religious real property, because of the religious, racial, or ethnic characteristics of that property, or (2) intentional obstruction by force or threat of force, or attempts to obstruct any person in the enjoyment of that person's free exercise of religious beliefs. If the intent of the crime is motivated for reasons of religious animosity, it must be proven that the religious real property has a sufficient connection with interstate or foreign commerce. However, if the intent of the crime is racially motivated, there is no requirement to satisfy the interstate or foreign commerce clause.

TITLE 18, U.S.C., SECTION 248 - FREEDOM OF ACCESS TO CLINIC ENTRANCES (FACE) ACT

This statute prohibits (1) the use of force or threat of force or physical obstruction, to intentionally injure, intimidate or interfere with or attempt to injure, intimidate or interfere with any person or any class of persons from obtaining or providing reproductive health services; (2) the use of force or threat of force or physical obstruction to intentionally injure, intimidate, or interfere with or attempt to injure, intimidate, or interfere with any person lawfully exercising or seeking to exercise the First Amendment right of religious freedom at a place of religious worship; or (3) intentionally damages or destroys the property of a facility, or attempts to do so, because such facility provides reproductive health services or intentionally damages or destroys the property of a place of religious worship. This statute does not apply to speech or expressive conduct protected by the First Amendment. Non obstructive demonstrations are legal.

TITLE 18, U.S.C., SECTION 844(H) - FEDERAL EXPLOSIVES CONTROL STATUTE

Whoever (1) uses fire or an explosive to commit any felony which may be prosecuted in a court of the United States, or (2) carries an explosive during the commission of any felony which may be prosecuted in a court of the United States, including a felony which provides for an enhanced punishment if committed by the use of a deadly or dangerous weapon or device shall, in addition to the punishment provided for such felony, be sentenced to imprisonment for five years but not more than 15 years. In the case of a second or subsequent conviction under this subsection, such persons shall be sentenced to imprisonment for ten years but not more than 25 years.

TITLE 42, U.S.C., SECTION 3631 - CRIMINAL INTERFERENCE WITH RIGHT TO FAIR HOUSING

This statute also makes it unlawful by the use of force or threatened use of force, to injure, intimidate, or interfere with any person who is assisting an individual or class of persons in the exercise of their housing rights.

This statute makes it unlawful for any individual(s), by the use of force or threatened use of force, to injure, intimidate, or interfere with (or attempt to injure, intimidate, or interfere with), any person's housing rights because of that person's race, color, religion, sex, handicap, familial status or national origin. Among those housing rights enumerated in the statute are:

The sale, purchase, or renting of a dwelling;
the occupation of a dwelling;
the financing of a dwelling;
contracting or negotiating for any of the rights enumerated above.
applying for or participating in any service, organization, or facility relating to the sale or rental of dwellings.

TITLE 42, U.S.C., SECTION 14141 - PATTERN AND PRACTICE

This civil statute was a provision within the Crime Control Act of 1994 and makes it unlawful for any governmental authority, or agent thereof, or any person acting on behalf of a governmental authority, to engage in a pattern or practice of conduct by law enforcement officers or by officials or employees of any governmental agency with responsibility for the administration of juvenile justice or the incarceration of juveniles that deprives persons of rights, privileges, or immunities secured or protected by the Constitution or laws of the United States.

Whenever the Attorney General has reasonable cause to believe that a violation has occurred, the Attorney General, for or in the name of the United States, may in a civil action obtain appropriate equitable and declaratory relief to eliminate the pattern or practice.

Types of misconduct covered include, among other things:

1. Excessive Force
2. Discriminatory Harassment
3. False Arrest
4. Coercive Sexual Conduct
5. Unlawful Stops, Searches, or Arrests

Liability of cities and police departments

While an individual officer may be held liable for the excessive use of force, a city or police department may generally be held liable only when it is established that the city or department either failed to properly hire, train, or supervise the officer. A breach of the duty to supervise by a city is cognizable law only when, during the course of employment, the employer becomes aware, or should have become aware, of problems with an employee that indicates his or her unfitness, and the employer fails to take further actions such as investigation, discharge, or reassignment.

Regarding a claim of negligent training, the Eleventh Circuit, in *Lewis v. City of St. Petersburg*,* set out the two-step showing that is required for such a claim to succeed. Thus, the plaintiff must demonstrate:

- A failure to exercise a duty of care causing an injury, and, if that is shown
- Establish that the training program did not involve a discretionary function

* *Lewis v. City of St. Petersburg*, 260 F3rd 1260 (11th Cir. 2004).

For example, in the Baltimore case discussed later in this chapter, the plaintiff contended that the city had failed to train the plaintiff in the following three areas of law enforcement: (1) How to use a flashlight as a defensive weapon, (2) the level of force appropriate to use, and (3) how to deal with intoxicated individuals.

Summary judgment

In most cases where the victim sues the officer, the police force, or the municipality, the defendant (officer, police department, or city) will file a motion for summary judgment. Rule 56(a) of the Federal Rules of Civil Procedure states that a party may move for summary judgment, identifying each claim or defense—or the part of each claim or defense—on which summary judgment is sought. The court shall grant summary judgment if the movant shows that there is no genuine dispute as to any material fact and the movant is entitled to judgment as a matter of law. The court should state on the record the reasons for granting or denying the motion.

Generally, in a motion for summary judgment, the defendant (officer) is claiming that even if all the facts in the plaintiff's cause of action are true, the plaintiff is not entitled to a judgment. For example, if a plaintiff files a civil action against a police officer claiming the excessive use of force, but fails to allege any injuries as the result of this excessive force, a federal district court would probably grant the officer summary judgment because a requirement to recover for the excessive use of force is that the plaintiff (victim) was injured. In another example, if an injured victim files suit for excessive force and includes the city as one of the defendants but fails to allege that the city was neglectful in the hiring, training, or supervision of the officer, the city could probably get the case dismissed as to the city, because these three requirements were not alleged.

Immunity

Absolute immunity

There are, basically, two types of immunity: absolute and qualified. A person has absolute protection for civil law suits in the areas where he or she has absolute immunity. For example, a trial judge has absolute immunity when he or she is exercising the judicial duties of a judge. Absolute immunity is extended to legislators in their legislative functions, executive officers engaged in adjudicative functions, and the president of the United States. The rationale for the grant of absolute immunity is that certain officials, such as trial judges, need the extra protection. Former U.S. Supreme Court justice Louis Powell noted:

> Our decisions have recognized immunity defenses of two kinds. For officials whose special functions or constitutional status requires complete protection from suit, we have recognized the defense of "absolute immunity." The absolute immunity of legislators, in their legislative functions, and of judges, in their judicial functions, now is well settled. Our decisions also have extended absolute immunity to certain officials of the Executive Branch. These include prosecutors and similar officials, executive officers engaged in adjudicative functions, and the President of the United States. For executive officials in general, however, our cases make plain that qualified immunity represents the norm. We have acknowledged that high officials require greater protection than those with less complex discretionary responsibilities.*

Qualified immunity

Qualified immunity is immunity that shields public officials, including police officers, from being sued in

civil court for actions that fall short of violating a clearly established statutory or constitutional right. As noted in *Pearson v. Callahan*, qualified-immunity balances two important issues—the need to hold public officials accountable when they are irresponsible in the exercise of their official powers and the need to shield those officials from harassment, distraction, and liability when they perform their duties in a reasonable manner.† Accordingly, the law is clearly established that a police officer is entitled to qualified immunity if there is no constitutional or statutory violation.

At one time, qualified or "good-faith" immunity included both an objective and a subjective aspect. The U.S. Supreme Court noted that the subjective aspect involved determining whether the government actor in question took his "action with the malicious intention to cause a deprivation of constitutional rights or other injury."‡ This subjective determination would typically require discovery and testimony to establish whether malicious intention was present. Having to go through the costly process of discovery and trial, however, conflicted with the goal of qualified immunity to allow for the dismissal of insubstantial lawsuits without trial.

Because of this dilemma, the Supreme Court altered the test to determine whether qualified immunity was appropriate. The new test, as stated earlier, is that "government officials performing discretionary functions generally are shielded from liability for civil damages insofar as their conduct does not violate clearly established statutory or constitutional rights of which a reasonable person would have known." By applying the reasonable person standard, the Supreme Court established, for the first time, a purely objective standard to determine whether granting a government official qualified immunity was appropriate.[1]

Saucier v. Katz

Katz, president of In Defense of Animals, filed a civil rights suit against Saucier, a military policeman. Katz alleged that Saucier violated his Fourth Amendment rights by using excessive force in arresting him.§ At the time, Katz was protesting during a speech by Vice President Gore's speech in San Francisco. The Supreme Court noted that claims of excessive force in the context of arrests or investigatory stops should be analyzed under the Fourth Amendment's "objective reasonableness standard," not under substantive due process principle.

The court noted that one concern of the immunity inquiry is to acknowledge that reasonable mistakes

---

* *Harlow v. Fitzgerald*, 457 U.S. 800, 807 (1982).

† *Pearson v. Callahan*, 555 U.S. 223 (2009).
‡ *Wood v. Strickland*, 420 U.S. 308, 322 (1975).
§ *Saucier v. Katz et al.*, 533 U.S. 194 (2001).

can be made as to the legal constraints on particular police conduct. It is sometimes difficult for an officer to determine how the relevant legal doctrine, here excessive force, will apply to the factual situation the officer confronts. An officer might correctly perceive all of the relevant facts but have a mistaken understanding as to whether a particular amount of force is legal in those circumstances. If the officer's mistake as to what the law requires is reasonable, however, the officer is entitled to the immunity defense.

The Supreme Court ruled that the first inquiry into a request for qualified immunity must be whether a constitutional right would have been violated on the facts alleged; only if the answer to the first inquiry is affirmative does the question of whether the right was clearly established at the time of the alleged violation have to be answered. The Supreme Court also disagreed with the Ninth Circuit's rationale that only a jury could decide whether the force used in this instance was excessive, making its two-step approach workable even in excessive force claims.

The Supreme Court held that judges of the district courts and the courts of appeals should be permitted "to exercise their sound discretion in deciding which of the two prongs of the qualified-immunity analysis should be addressed first in light of the circumstances in the particular case at hand." Not surprisingly, in the case before them, the court found the issue of qualified immunity easier to determine based on whether any violation (if one occurred at all) was of a clearly established right. Here, the court found that at the time of the officers' actions, it was not clearly established that those actions were unlawful.

Wynn v. City of Lakeland

In any action against a city, police department, or law enforcement officer, the aggrieved citizen needs to overcome the qualified immunity that these parties may have. For example, in *Wynn v. City of Lakeland*, the defendants (city, police department, and individual officers) moved for summary judgment claiming that the officers had qualified immunity in performing their official duties. The court stated: "Viewing the evidence in the light most favorable to arrestee, police officer used excessive force when he struck arrestee in the face with a flashlight, breaking three bones in his face, and thus, officer was not entitled to qualified immunity on arrestee's §1983 claim against him, alleging use of excessive force in violation of Fourth Amendment."*

In the Wynn case, the court noted that qualified immunity offers complete protection for government officials sued in their individual capacities if their conduct does not clearly violate established statutory or constitutional rights of which a reasonable person would have known. To receive qualified-immunity protection, the government official must first establish that he was acting within his discretionary authority at the time of the alleged violation. Once that is shown, the plaintiff (victim) bears the burden of proving (1) that the official violated a constitutional right and (2) that the right was clearly established at the time the official acted.

In the Wynn case, the officer's claim of qualified immunity was based on his version of the confrontation, in which he struck the plaintiff in the face with his flashlight because the officer reasonably believed the plaintiff (arrestee) reached for the officer's Taser. If this were not a qualified-immunity case, the (arrestee's) contrary showing would seemingly create a genuine dispute of fact. However, "in qualified immunity cases, a 'material issue of fact' never exists." In other words, the officer cannot base his claim of qualified immunity, as he attempts to do, on his version of how the events unfolded. The plaintiff's "best case" indicates a different scenario.

A witness testified that, while he did not see the plaintiff's hands, the plaintiff was only stumbling and falling forward in the direction of the officer. Importantly, another witness testified that the plaintiff had his arms at his sides and stumbled forward at the moment of the strike. Consequently, the plaintiff's evidence shows that the plaintiff, whose arms were at his side, was not reaching for the Taser located on the officer's person.

Moreover, at that point, the plaintiff was not under arrest, and an officer had indicated that the plaintiff was free to leave. Under these circumstances, a jury could reasonably find that Officer Taylor used excessive force in striking the plaintiff in the head with a flashlight.

In *Baltimore v. City of Albany, Georgia*, the Eleventh Circuit Court of Appeals rejected a claim of qualified immunity by a police officer who struck an arrestee in the head with a flashlight. Significantly, that claim was complicated by the fact that the strike occurred in a chaotic situation in the face of a hostile crowd.† In that case, the police–citizen encounter occurred on the evening of June 24, 2000. Arrid Baltimore ("Baltimore") and his brother, Saran Baltimore, met at Saran's home around 7:00 p.m. to watch the Mike Tyson–Lou Savarese boxing match. When the fight was over, they left in separate cars to attend an "after-party" at a local club, Charlie and Diane's Lounge. On the way to the club, Baltimore stopped at a convenience store and bought a quart bottle of grapefruit juice. He arrived at the club shortly after his brother got there, and parked down the street. It was close to 11:00 p.m.

* *Wynn v. City of Lakeland*, 727 Fed Supp. 2nd. 1309 (MD, Fla. 2010).

† *Baltimore v. City of Albany*, Ga. 183 Fed. Approx. 891 (2006).

As Baltimore walked toward the club, he saw a crowd, which included several of his acquaintances, standing in the front yard of a house adjacent to the club. He heard someone suddenly yell that the police were coming. Cpl. Joseph Rizer and his riding partner, Officer Ire Hornsby, who were on patrol, saw the crowd, which appeared to be unruly, shouting and cursing, and stopped to investigate. Before exiting their patrol car, they called for backup due to the size of the crowd. As Cpl. Rizer approached the gathering, he saw Baltimore carrying the bottle of grapefruit juice and thought he might be violating the City of Albany's open container law. Rizer drew next to Baltimore to explain the open container law, and as he did, the crowd grew closer and began to turn hostile. So, Rizer decided to remove Baltimore to his patrol car. By this time, the backup, Cpl. Richard Vanstone and Officer Andrew Long, had arrived and parked next to Rizer's patrol car. Baltimore told Rizer that the bottle he was carrying did not contain alcohol, but Rizer was not convinced. Holding Baltimore's left wrist, he reached for his handcuffs; Baltimore resisted and a struggle ensued.

Rizer had Baltimore in a choke hold, and when it appeared that Baltimore would break free, Cpl. Vanstone struck him on the left shoulder with his flashlight. Meanwhile, several men in the crowd, including Saran Baltimore and Eric Green, got involved and went at the officers. During the ensuing melee, Officer Long approached Baltimore from the rear and struck him on the back of the head with his flashlight. The blow brought Baltimore to his knees, and he was handcuffed.

Baltimore (arrestee) suffered a serious wound when he was hit with the flashlight. The district court concluded that Cpl. Rizer acted properly in stopping Baltimore to determine whether he was violating Albany's open container ordinance, and that Baltimore's conviction for disorderly conduct foreclosed Baltimore's §1983 claims for false arrest and malicious prosecution. The case boiled down then to whether striking Baltimore on the head with a flashlight constituted excessive force, and whether the officers were entitled to qualified immunity regarding that act. The court concluded that the striking violated the Constitution, but that the officers—with the exception of Rizer, Singleton, and Long—were entitled to qualified immunity and summary judgment. The appellate court held that Rizer and Singleton were entitled to qualified immunity, but that Officer Long, who had hit Baltimore in the head with a flashlight, was not.

In determining whether an officer is entitled to qualified immunity, one court employed a two-step test: first, the court decides whether the officer violated a plaintiff's constitutional right; if the answer to that inquiry is "yes," then the court proceeds to determine whether the constitutional right was "clearly established

in light of the specific context of the case" at the time of the events in question.*

Messerschmidt v. Millende

In *Messerschmidt v. Millende*,[†] one Shelly Kelly was afraid that she would be attacked by her boyfriend Jerry Bowen when she moved out of his apartment. She requested police assistance. Two officers arrived, but were called away to an emergency. When the officers left, Bowen showed up with a sawed-off shotgun. Kelly ran away and, as she was leaving in her car, Bowen fired five shots into the car. Kelly was unhurt. She met with Detective Messerschmidt to discuss the incident. She mentioned that Bowen was a member of the Mona Park Crips Gang.

After meeting with Kelly, Messerschmidt conducted a detailed investigation of Bowen. The officer noticed that Bowen had been arrested numerous times. The officer prepared affidavits to search Bowen's stepmother's home, where it was believed that Bowen was living, for all weapons that would indicate gang membership. The home was searched, and only the stepmother's shotgun and a box of ammunition was uncovered.

The stepmother filled a civil rights action against the detective, claiming that the warrant was too broad. The trial court agreed that the warrant was too broad. The detective defended on the grounds of qualified immunity.

The Supreme Court held that qualified immunity "protects government officials from liability for civil damages insofar as their conduct does not violate clearly established statutory or constitutional rights of which a reasonable person would have known". Where the alleged Fourth Amendment violation involves a search or seizure pursuant to a warrant, the fact that a neutral magistrate has issued a warrant is the clearest indication that the officers acted in an objectively reasonable manner, or in "objective good faith." Nonetheless, that fact does not end the inquiry into objective reasonableness. The court has recognized an exception, allowing suit when it is obvious that no reasonably competent officer would have concluded that a warrant should be issued. The shield of immunity otherwise conferred by the warrant will be lost where, for example, the warrant was based on an affidavit so lacking in indicia of probable cause as to render official belief in its existence entirely unreasonable. The threshold for establishing this exception is high. In the ordinary case, an officer cannot be expected to question the magistrate's probable-cause determination because it is the magistrate's responsibility to determine whether the officer's allegations establish probable cause and, if so, to issue a

* *Mattos v. Agarano*, 661 F. 3rd. 433 (9th Cir. 2011).
† Messerschmidt v. Millende, 132 S.Ct. 1235 (2012).

warrant comporting in form with the requirements of the Fourth Amendment.

This case does not fall within that narrow exception. It would not be entirely unreasonable for an officer to believe that there was probable cause to search for all firearms and firearm-related materials. Under the circumstances set forth in the warrant, an officer could reasonably conclude that there was a "fair probability" that the sawed-off shotgun was not the only firearm Bowen owned, and that Bowen's sawed-off shotgun was illegal. Given Bowen's possession of one illegal gun, his gang membership, willingness to use the gun to kill someone, and concern about the police, it would not be unreasonable for an officer to conclude that Bowen owned other illegal guns. An officer also could reasonably believe that seizure of firearms was necessary to prevent further assaults on Kelly.

California law allows a magistrate to issue a search warrant for items in the possession of any person with the intent to use them as a means of committing a public offense, and the warrant application submitted by the officers specifically referenced this provision as a basis for the search.

Regarding the warrant's authorization to search for gang-related materials, a reasonable officer could view Bowen's attack as motivated not by the souring of his romantic relationship with Kelly but by a desire to prevent her from disclosing details of his gang activity to the police. It would therefore not be unreasonable—based on the facts set out in the affidavit—for an officer to believe that evidence of Bowen's gang affiliation would prove helpful in prosecuting him for the attack on Kelly, in supporting additional, related charges against Bowen for the assault, or in impeaching Bowen or rebutting his defenses. Moreover, even if this were merely a domestic dispute, a reasonable officer could still conclude that gang paraphernalia found at the residence could demonstrate Bowen's control over the premises or his connection to other evidence found there.

The fact that the officers sought and obtained approval of the warrant application from a superior and a deputy district attorney before submitting it to the magistrate provides further support for the conclusion that an officer could reasonably have believed that the scope of the warrant was supported by probable cause. A contrary conclusion would mean not only that Messerschmidt was plainly incompetent in concluding that the warrant was supported by probable cause, but that the supervisor, the deputy district attorney, and the magistrate were as well.

Rationale for immunity

In *Harlow v. Fitzgerald*, the U.S. Supreme Court discussed the need for government officials and employees to have

some form of immunity.* The Supreme Court noted that there are government officials whose special functions or constitutional status requires complete protection from suits for damages—including certain officials of the executive branch, such as prosecutors and similar officials. However, executive officials in general are usually only entitled to qualified or good-faith immunity. The recognition of a qualified-immunity defense reflects an attempt to balance competing values: not only the importance of a damages remedy to protect the rights of citizens, but also the need to protect officials who are required to exercise discretion, and the related public interest in encouraging the vigorous exercise of official authority.

The court held that to establish a defense of good-faith immunity, a government official must prove both objective and subjective elements. The official must not have actually known and also should not have been able to know that his actions were illegal. Accordingly, many claims will be resolved on summary judgment, and officials will have the freedom to use their discretion in carrying out their tasks.

The resolution of immunity questions inherently requires a balance between the evils inevitable in any available alternative. In situations of abuse of office, an action for damages may offer the only realistic avenue for vindication of constitutional guarantees. The court noted that, in the *Bivens* case, it was damages or nothing. It is this recognition that has required the denial of absolute immunity to most public officers. At the same time, however, it cannot be seriously disputed that claims frequently run against the innocent, as well as the guilty—at a cost not only to the defendant officials, but to society as a whole. These social costs include the expenses of litigation, the diversion of official energy from pressing public issues, and the deterrence of able citizens from acceptance of public office. Finally, there is the danger that fear of being sued will dampen the ardor of all but the most resolute or the most irresponsible public officials in the unflinching discharge of their duties.

Affirmative defense

Qualified or "good-faith" immunity is an affirmative defense that must be pleaded by a defendant official or officer.† Decisions of the Supreme Court have established that the "good-faith" defense has both an "objective" and a "subjective" aspect. The objective element involves a presumptive knowledge of and respect for "basic, unquestioned constitutional rights."‡ The subjective component refers to permissible intentions.

---

* *Harlow v. Fitzgerald*, 457 U.S. 800 (1982).
† *Gomez v. Toledo*, 446 U.S. 635 (1980).
‡ *Wood v. Strickland*, 420 U.S. 308, 322 (1975).

Characteristically, the court has defined these elements by identifying the circumstances in which qualified immunity would not be available. Referring both to the objective and subjective elements, the court held that qualified immunity would be defeated if an official knew or reasonably should have known that the action he took within his sphere of official responsibility would violate the constitutional rights of the plaintiff, or if he took the action with the malicious intention to cause a deprivation of constitutional rights or other injury.

Victim's conduct

In many cases, the officer had probable cause to stop a victim and after a legal stop abused his or her authority by using excessive force. In *Smith v. City of Hemet*, the appellate court held that an arrestee's conviction on his guilty plea to resisting, delaying or obstructing a peace officer did not preclude him suing the officer for excessive use of force under a §1983 action.*

Excessive force used after a defendant has been arrested may properly be the subject of a §1983 action, notwithstanding the defendant's conviction on a charge of resisting an arrest that was itself lawfully conducted. All claims that law enforcement officers have used excessive force, deadly or otherwise, in the course of an arrest must be analyzed under the Fourth Amendment and its "reasonableness" standard.

In analyzing excessive force claims arising before or during arrest under the Fourth Amendment's reasonableness standard, the question is not simply whether the force was necessary to accomplish a legitimate police objective; it is whether the force used was reasonable in light of all the relevant circumstances.

In the Smith case, Smith's wife placed an emergency phone call to the Hemet Police Department reporting that her husband "was hitting her and/or was physical with her." Mrs. Smith informed emergency personnel that her husband did not have a gun, there were no weapons in the house, and he was clad in his pajamas.

Officer Reinbolt was the first officer to arrive at the house to investigate the incident. He observed Smith standing on his front porch and "noticed Smith's hands in his pockets." The officer announced himself and instructed Smith to remove his hands from his pockets. Smith refused, responding with expletives and directing the officer to come to him. The officer then informed Smith that he would approach, but only after Smith removed his hands from his pockets and showed that he had no weapons. Smith again refused to remove his hands from his pockets and instead entered his home.

After the officer advised dispatch of what had transpired, Smith reemerged onto the porch with his hands

still in his pockets. The officer again instructed Smith to show his hands. Smith complied with this instruction, but then refused to follow an order to "put his hands on his head and walk towards the officer's voice." Instead, Smith again asked officer to approach and enter the home with him.

A second officer arrived in response to Officer Reinbolt's radioed request for assistance. Observing Smith's refusal to cooperate with Officer Reinbolt, the second officer contacted dispatch to request additional assistance, including a canine unit. Officer Quinn, a canine handler with the department, arrived shortly thereafter with "Quando," a police canine. Officer Medina also responded to one of the assistance calls.

Officer Quinn instructed Smith to turn around and place his hands on his head. Smith again refused to obey the order, despite being informed that Quando could be sent to subdue him and might bite. Without further warning, Officer Quinn sprayed Smith in the face with pepper spray. Smith responded with expletives and attempted to reenter his residence, but the door had been locked by Mrs. Smith. Several more officers then moved onto the porch, grabbed Smith from behind, slammed him against the door, and threw him down on the porch; Officer Quinn ordered the canine to attack him. Quando bit Smith on his right shoulder and neck area. At some point, either before or after the order to attack, the dog sank his teeth into Smith's arm and clung to it.

With at least four officers surrounding him and Quando's teeth sunk into his shoulder and neck, Smith agreed to comply with the officers' orders and submit to arrest. Although Smith submitted, he admits that he was "curled up" in a fetal position in an attempt to shield himself from the dog and that one of his hands was "tucked in somewhere," still out of the officers' view.

As one of the officers attempted to secure both arms, Quando was instructed by Officer Quinn to bite Smith a second time; this time the dog bit Smith on his left side and shoulder blade. On Officer Quinn's order, Quando ultimately retreated, and the officers dragged Smith off the porch, face down. Once off the porch, Smith continued to shield one of his arms from the dog's attack. Officer Quinn then ordered Quando to bite Smith a third time. This time, the dog bit into Smith's buttock. While all this was transpiring, Smith was pepper-sprayed at least four times, at least two of which sprayings occurred after the police dog had seized him and broken his skin, and at least one after the officers had pinned him to the ground.

Eventually, the officers secured the handcuffs on both of Smith's arms. Officer Reinbolt then washed Smith's eyes out with water from a nearby hose, but did not cleanse the wounds he received as a result of the

---

* In *Smith v. City of Hemet*, 394 F.3d 689 (9th Cir. 2005).

dog bites. Paramedics arrived shortly thereafter and attended to Smith's injuries.

Smith pled guilty in California Superior Court to a violation of California Penal Code §148(a)(1).2. Section 148(a)(1) provides: "Every person who willfully resists, delays, or obstructs any … peace officer … in the discharge or attempt to discharge any duty of his or her office or employment, … shall be guilty of a misdemeanor." Smith was sentenced to 36 months' probation.

Smith filed a complaint under 42 U.S.C. §1983 in the district court, alleging that the officers used excessive force when they sprayed him with pepper spray and sicced the police canine on him. The defendants moved for summary judgment on several grounds, including that the challenged use of force—the pepper spray and police dog—was appropriate and reasonable under the circumstances. The district court granted summary judgment on the basis that Smith's conviction for resisting arrest barred Smith's §1983 action. Judgment for the defendants was entered, and Smith filed an appeal.

The appellate court held Smith would be allowed to bring a §1983 action, however, if the use of excessive force occurred subsequent to the conduct on which his conviction was based. Specifically, Smith would be entitled to proceed if his conviction were based on unlawful behavior that took place while he stood alone and untouched on his porch—that is, if his unlawful conduct occurred while the officers were attempting to investigate his wife's complaint. In such case, a judgment in Smith's favor would not necessarily conflict with his conviction, because his acts of resistance, delay, or obstruction would have occurred while the officers were engaged in the lawful performance of their investigative duties, not while they were engaged in effecting an arrest by the use of excessive force.

The appellate court noted that defendants' argument wrongly focused on Smith's conduct rather than that of the officers. There were two different phases of the officers' conduct here—first, the investigative phase; then, when Smith repeatedly refused to cooperate, the arrest for violating §148(a)(1) and for the underlying offense that otherwise might or might not have led to an arrest.

The officers' allegedly unlawful conduct, which transpired after they decided to use physical force to subdue Smith, occurred during the second phase of their law enforcement activities, during the course of their effort to take Smith into custody. Prior to that time, during the investigative phase, they had issued only verbal commands, all of which were concededly well within the bounds of their general police powers. Smith's obstruction of that investigation came to an end when the officers decided to arrest him. Thereafter, in the course of the arrest, they allegedly engaged in the use of excessive force that rendered the arrest unlawful.

It did not, however, render their preceding investigation unlawful, nor would it invalidate a conviction for obstructing that investigation.

The appellate court explained that a §1983 action was not barred. Smith's success in that action would not necessarily impugn his conviction. Accordingly, the defendants were not entitled to summary judgment on the basis.

Smith alleged that after the officers came onto the porch they used both excessive force, generally, and deadly force, specifically, against him in contravention of the Fourth Amendment. Defendants, in contrast, urged that the force used was at all times reasonable and that the court should therefore affirm the district court's summary judgment order on this alternative ground.

Although the appellate court noted that a Fourth Amendment claim of excessive force is analyzed under the framework outlined by the Supreme Court in *Graham v. Connor*,* all claims that law enforcement officers have used excessive force—deadly or otherwise—in the course of an arrest must be analyzed under the Fourth Amendment and its "reasonableness" standard.

It is clear that, under *Graham*, excessive force claims arising before or during arrest are to be analyzed exclusively under the Fourth Amendment's reasonableness standard. That analysis requires balancing the "nature and quality of the intrusion" on a person's liberty with the "countervailing governmental interests at stake" to determine whether the use of force was objectively reasonable under the circumstances. The Supreme Court has said that the reasonableness inquiry in an excessive force case is an objective one: The question is whether the officers' actions are objectively reasonable in light of the facts and circumstances confronting them. The question is not simply whether the force was necessary to accomplish a legitimate police objective; it is whether the force used was reasonable in light of all the relevant circumstances.

More-specific-provision rule

The "more-specific-provision" rule of *Graham v. Connor* requires that if a constitutional claim is covered by a specific constitutional provision, the claim must be analyzed under the standard appropriate to that specific provision, not under substantive due process.† In the case of *County of Sacramento v. Lewis*,‡ a county sheriff's deputy (Smith) responded to a call along with another officer and observed a motorcycle approaching at high

---

* *Graham v. Connor*, 490 U.S. 386 (1989).
† 490 U.S. 386, 395.
‡ 523 U.S. 833 (1998).

speed with a passenger. The second officer turned on his rotating lights and pulled his patrol car closer to first officer's vehicle. The motorcycle rider, Willard, maneuvered between the two patrol cars and sped off. The officers immediately switched on the emergency lights and began a high-speed chase. The chase ended after the cycle tipped over. One officer's vehicle skidded into the passenger and killed him.

The passenger's parents brought the action under 42 U.S.C. §1983, alleging a deprivation of Lewis's Fourteenth Amendment substantive due process right to life. The district court granted summary judgment for Smith, but the Ninth Circuit reversed, holding, *inter alia*, that the appropriate degree of fault for substantive due process liability for high-speed police pursuits is deliberate indifference to, or reckless disregard for, a person's right to life and personal security.

Justice Souter, writing for the court's majority, stated that issue in this case is whether a police officer violates the Fourteenth Amendment's guarantee of substantive due process by causing death through deliberate or reckless indifference to life in a high-speed automobile chase aimed at apprehending a suspected offender. The court said no, and held that, in such circumstances, only a purpose to cause harm unrelated to the legitimate object of arrest will satisfy the element of arbitrary conduct shocking to the conscience, necessary for a due process violation.

The court noted that the chase ended after the motorcycle tipped over as Willard tried a sharp left turn. By the time the officer slammed on his brakes, Willard was out of the way, but passenger Lewis was not. The patrol car skidded into him at 40 miles an hour, propelling him some 70 feet down the road and inflicting massive injuries. Lewis was pronounced dead at the scene.

The court noted that Officer Smith was faced with a course of lawless behavior for which the police were not to blame. They had done nothing to cause Willard's high-speed driving in the first place, nothing to excuse his flouting of the commonly understood law enforcement authority to control traffic, and nothing (beyond a refusal to call off the chase) to encourage him to race through traffic at breakneck speed, forcing other drivers out of their travel lanes. Willard's outrageous behavior was practically instantaneous, and so was Smith's instinctive response. While prudence would have repressed the reaction, the officer's instinct was to do his job as a law enforcement officer, not to induce Willard's lawlessness, or to terrorize, cause harm, or kill. Prudence, that is, was subject to countervailing enforcement considerations, and while Smith exaggerated their demands, there is no reason to believe that they were tainted by an improper or malicious motive on his part.

The court noted that the Fourth Amendment covers only "searches and seizures," neither of which took place here. No one suggests that there was a search, and the cases foreclose finding a seizure. The court noted that a police pursuit in attempting to seize a person does not amount to a "seizure" within the meaning of the Fourth Amendment. The court explained that a Fourth Amendment seizure does not occur whenever there is a governmentally caused termination of an individual's freedom of movement (the innocent passerby), nor even whenever there is a governmentally caused and governmentally desired termination of an individual's freedom of movement (the fleeing felon), but only when there is a governmental termination of freedom of movement through means intentionally applied. The court illustrated the point by saying that no Fourth Amendment seizure would take place where a pursuing police car sought to stop the suspect only by the show of authority represented by flashing lights and continuing pursuit, but accidentally stopped the suspect by crashing into him.

Graham's more-specific-provision rule is therefore no bar to respondents' suit. The court noted that parents of a motorcyclist who was struck and killed by a police car during a high-speed pursuit could sue under substantive due process because no Fourth Amendment seizure took place.

Summary

- In the majority of cases where the police, city, and so on are sued for violation of a civil rights in federal court, the suit is filed pursuant to Civil Rights Act, 42 U.S. Code §1983.
- The Supreme Court noted that its cases make clear that the Fourth Amendment operates as a limitation on the exercise of federal power, regardless of whether the state in whose jurisdiction that power is exercised would prohibit or penalize the identical act if engaged in by a private citizen.
- The court pointed out that interests protected by state laws regulating trespass and the invasion of privacy, and those protected by the Fourth Amendment's guarantee against unreasonable searches and seizures, may be inconsistent or even hostile.
- Historically, damages have been regarded as the ordinary remedy for an invasion of personal interests in liberty.
- Frequently, state officers may be sued under §1983 in federal court for violations of state tort laws. Generally, the actions are based on allegations of negligence.
- Police officers and other governmental officials have been given power over citizens by local, state, and federal government agencies. This is necessary to enforce laws and ensure justice.

- The powers include the authority to detain, arrest, search persons and property, and to seize property or persons. To prevent abuse of this authority, it is a federal crime for anyone acting under "color of law" to abuse that authority.
- On the federal level, it is the FBI that is the lead authority to investigate possible color-of-law abuses. In a normal year, about 42% of the FBI's total civil rights caseload involves the issue of abuse of authority under color of law.
- To file a color-of-law complaint, one should contact one's local FBI office by telephone, in writing, or in person.
- One may also contact the U.S. Attorney's office in one's district or send a written complaint to Assistant Attorney General, Civil Rights Division.
- FBI investigations vary in length. Once their investigation is complete, the FBI should forward the findings to the U.S. Attorney's office within the local jurisdiction and to the U.S. Department of Justice in Washington, D.C., which will decide whether or not to proceed toward prosecution and handle any prosecutions that follow.
- While an individual officer may be held liable for the excessive use of force, a city or police department may generally be held liable only when it is established that the city or department either failed to properly hire, train, or supervise the officer.
- A breach of the duty to supervise by a city is cognizable law only when, during the course of employment, the employer becomes aware or should have become aware of problems with an employee that indicates his or her unfitness, and the employer fails to take further action such as investigation, discharge, or reassignment.
- In most cases where the victim sues the officer, the police force, or the municipality, the defendant (officer, police department, or city) will file a motion for summary judgment. Rule 56(a) of the Federal Rules of Civil Procedure states that a party may move for summary judgment, identifying each claim or defense—or the part of each claim or defense—on which summary judgment is sought.
- There are, basically, two types of immunity: absolute and qualified. A person has absolute protection for civil law suits in the areas where he or she has absolute immunity.
- Qualified immunity is immunity that shields public officials, including police officers, from being sued in civil court for actions that fall short of violating a clearly established statutory or constitutional right.
- Qualified or "good-faith" immunity is an affirmative defense that must be pleaded by a defendant official or officer.

- Decisions of the Supreme Court have established that the "good-faith" defense has both an "objective" and a "subjective" aspect. The objective element involves a presumptive knowledge of and respect for "basic, unquestioned constitutional rights."
- Excessive force used after a defendant has been arrested may properly be the subject of a §1983 action, notwithstanding the defendant's conviction on a charge of resisting an arrest that was itself lawfully conducted.

Practicum

In March 2001, a Georgia county deputy clocked respondent's vehicle traveling at 73 miles per hour on a road with a 55 miles per hour speed limit. The deputy activated his blue flashing lights, indicating that respondent should pull over. Instead, respondent sped away, initiating a chase down what is in most portions a two-lane road at speeds exceeding 85 miles per hour. The deputy radioed his dispatch to report that he was pursuing a fleeing vehicle, and broadcast its license plate number. Petitioner, Deputy Timothy Scott, heard the radio communication and joined the pursuit along with other officers. In the midst of the chase, respondent pulled into the parking lot of a shopping center and was nearly boxed in by the various police vehicles. Respondent evaded the trap by making a sharp turn, colliding with Scott's police car, exiting the parking lot, and speeding off once again down a two-lane highway.

Following respondent's shopping center maneuvering, which resulted in slight damage to Scott's police car, Scott took over as the lead pursuit vehicle. Six minutes and nearly 10 miles after the chase had begun, Scott decided to attempt to terminate the episode by employing a "Precision Intervention Technique ('PIT') maneuver, which causes the fleeing vehicle to spin to a stop." Having radioed his supervisor for permission, Scott was told to "go ahead and take him out." Instead, Scott applied his push bumper to the rear of respondent's vehicle. As a result, respondent lost control of his vehicle, which left the roadway, ran down an embankment, overturned, and crashed. Respondent was badly injured and was rendered a quadriplegic.

Respondent filed suit against Deputy Scott and others under Rev. Stat. §1979, 42 U.S.C. §1983, alleging a violation of his federal constitutional rights, namely, use of excessive force resulting in an unreasonable seizure under the Fourth Amendment. In response, Scott filed a motion for summary judgment based on an assertion of qualified immunity. The district court denied the motion, finding that "there are material issues of fact on which the issue of qualified immunity turns which present sufficient disagreement to require submission to a jury." On interlocutory appeal, the U.S. Court of Appeals for the Eleventh Circuit affirmed the district court's decision to allow respondent's Fourth Amendment claim against Scott to proceed to trial. Taking respondent's view of the facts as given, the Court of Appeals concluded that Scott's actions could constitute "deadly force" under *Tennessee v. Garner*, 471 U.S. 1, 105 S.Ct. 1694, 85 L.Ed.2d 1 (1985), and that the use of such force in this context would violate respondent's constitutional right to be free from excessive force during a seizure. Accordingly, a reasonable jury could find that Scott violated [respondent's] Fourth Amendment rights. The Court of Appeals further concluded that the law, as it existed at the time of the incident, was sufficiently clear to give reasonable law enforcement officers fair notice that ramming a vehicle under these circumstances was unlawful. The Court of Appeals thus concluded that Scott was not entitled to qualified immunity. The Supreme Court reversed.

As a Supreme Court justice, would you grant the officer immunity?

See *Scott v. Harris* 127 S.Ct. 1769 (2007).

Discussion questions

1. Explain the meaning of the term "under color of law."
2. What are the reasons for qualified immunity?
3. Under what circumstances may a city or police department be held liable for an officer's misconduct?
4. Why is the *Bivens v. Six Unknown Named Agents* case important?
5. How would you file a complaint against a local officer who used excessive force?

Reference

1. Richard G. Schott (September, 2012) Qualified immunity: How it protects law enforcement officers, *FBI Law Enforcement Bulletin.* 79(9).

Citizen review boards and external oversight

Learning objectives

After studying this chapter, the reader should understand the following concepts and issues:

- Purpose of external review boards
- Powers and authority of external review boards
- How review boards differ in the United States, Canada, and the United Kingdom

Introduction

According to the written testimony of Rashad Robinson, Executive Director, Color of Change before the President's Task Force on 21st Century Policing, civilian oversight of police should be expanded. In part of his testimony he stated:

> Civilian oversight: we urge the expansion of strong, empowered state and local level civilian control over law enforcement nationwide. There has been much research done into the criteria of effective civilian oversight boards, but general guidelines include strong political and public support, police cooperation, a proactive approach to identify underlying systemic problems with police and the comprehensive legal power to resolve said issues, as well as control over more than police misconduct, but police hiring and firing, policing priorities, and participatory budgeting as well. We suggest that funding in part for the expansion of community controlled and community based policing come from the termination of all federal anti-drug grants.*

Functions of civilian review boards

Probably one of the most important functions of civilian or citizen review boards is to oversee the processing of citizens' complaints about police misconduct. As noted by Human Rights Watch (HRW), citizen review

agencies should publish reports at least annually, presenting detailed statistics and information relating to complaints, trends, sustained rates for each type of complaint, disciplinary actions stemming from sustained allegations, policy recommendations (as well as the departmental responses to those recommendations), and community outreach efforts. The statistics should include breakdowns on the race and gender of the complainants and officers in question. The reports should also include examples of the types of abuse about which the agency has received complaints during the reporting period.[1] The HRW also contends that review boards should be empowered and financed to conduct investigations on their own initiative.

National associations on civilian oversight of police

The National Association for Civilian Oversight of Law Enforcement (NACOLE) is a nonprofit organization that brings together individuals or agencies working to establish or improve oversight of police officers in the United States.[2] It is the largest and most dominant association dealing with civilian oversight of the police. NACOLE's mission statement states that its mission is to "enhance fair and professional law enforcement responsive to community needs." NACOLE operates under the following goals:

- To provide for the establishment, development, education, and technical assistance of/for the civilian oversight of law enforcement.
- To develop a national forum to provide an informational and educational clearinghouse and a publication resource of educational information for the public and organizations in the field of civilian oversight of law enforcement.
- To encourage the highest ethical standards in organizations which oversee law enforcement.
- To educate the public by developing mechanisms to enhance police and community relations, educate law enforcement agencies, and encourage law enforcement to respond with sensitivity to citizens' issues and complaints.
- To encourage full racial and ethnic representation and participation in this organization and the agencies overseen by its members.

---

* This section was taken from the testimony of Rashad Robinson, before the President's Task Force on 21st Century Policing, January 30, 2015.

Regular members of NACOLE are mayors, county or municipal managers, or others who hold executive positions on a board, council, commission, or committee with authority to direct, control, or oversee the activities or performance of the chief law enforcement officer of a political subdivision. Sworn law enforcement officers are not allowed to be regular members.

NACOLE has two other classes of membership: associate members and student members. Associate members are defined as any persons interested in the oversight of law enforcement. Associate members are able to participate in all association activities, including serving on committees. Student members are defined as individuals currently enrolled, either full or part-time, in a college or university program in the area of criminology, criminal justice, law, sociology, political science, public administration, journalism, or a related field, and who are interested in the oversight of law enforcement. Associate members and student members are ineligible to vote or serve as officers or members of the board of directors.

In January 2015, NACOLE president Brian Buchner noted that, "Civilian oversight has evolved into something far broader than the review of disciplinary decisions or individual investigations of police misconduct. Given the national attention on policing and the strained or broken relationships between police and communities, this is the perfect time to be asking important questions about existing police accountability structures and considering research on effective solutions."[3] Buchner also noted that topics being explored by NACOLE included: studying the impact of critical incidents from Rodney King to Ferguson, attaining the right balance between national policing standards and local values, incorporating community input into the police reform process, using benchmarks to promote constitutional policing, and developing standards for the use of body cameras in policing.

In addition to NACOLE, there are numerous local agencies that deal with police oversight. In most U.S. cities, there is a local oversight agency. NACOLE attempts to organize the local agencies into one strong national voice.

United Kingdom review boards

According to its website, "Her Majesty's Inspectorate of Constabulary (HMIC) independently assesses police forces and policing across activity from neighborhood teams to serious crime and the fight against terrorism—in the public interest."[4]

HMIC is independent of government and the police:
- HM inspectors of constabulary are appointed by the crown—they are not employees of the police service or the government.
- HM chief inspector of constabulary reports to Parliament on the efficiency and effectiveness of police forces in England and Wales.

- HM inspectors have powers to seek information from police forces and to access their premises.

HMIC decides on the depth, frequency, and areas to inspect based on their judgments about what is in the public interest. In making these judgments, HMIC considers the risks to the public, the risks to the integrity of policing, service quality, public concerns, the operating environment, the burden of inspection, and the potential benefits to society from the improvements that might arise from inspection.

The United Kingdom also has the Independent Police Complaints Commission (IPCC). It oversees the police complaints system in England and Wales and sets the standards by which the police should handle complaints. It is independent, making its decisions entirely independently of the police and government. It is not part of the police.[5] The IPCC has its own website that reports on issues involving police misconduct. It may be accessed at: www.ipcc.gov.uk

Police forces deal with the majority of complaints against police officers and police staff. The IPCC considers appeals from people who are dissatisfied with the way a police force has dealt with their complaint. Since November 2012, the responsibility for determining appeals is shared with local police forces. In addition, police forces must refer the most serious cases—whether or not someone has made a complaint—to the IPCC. The IPCC may decide to investigate such cases independently, manage or supervise the police force's investigation, or return it for local investigation.

Other agencies in the United Kingdom that are involved in civilian oversight of the police include the Home Office, Office of the Oversight Commissioner (Northern Ireland) and the Police Ombudsman (Northern Ireland).

Canadian review boards

There are over 20 different oversight agencies in Canada that provide civilian oversight of police departments. For example, the Civilian Review and Complaints Commission for the Royal Canadian Mounted Police (CRCC) provides civilian oversight of the Mounted Police. The Office of the Police Complaint Commissioner, British Columbia provides impartial civilian oversight of complaints involving municipal police in British Columbia, Canada.

Civilian investigative bodies and prosecutorial power

Darius Charney from the Center for Constitutional Rights testified before the President's Task Force on 21st

Century Policing regarding independent investigative bodies of civilian complaints. Mr. Charney stated that, while many jurisdictions around the country currently have governmental agencies independent of the local police department to investigate civilian complaints of police officer misconduct, none of these agencies have the power to actually discipline those officers who the agencies' investigations have found have committed misconduct. In virtually all jurisdictions, the power to impose disciplinary penalties on offending officers rests solely with the commissioner or chief of the police department, as does the decision whether or not to even prosecute the officers through existing administrative disciplinary hearing processes. In the few jurisdictions where the independent investigative bodies have been granted the power to administratively prosecute disciplinary charges against officers against whom they have sustained civilian complaints, that power is restricted to certain categories of misconduct cases and, in New York City, can even in certain cases be removed from the investigative body altogether by the police commissioner.

According to Charney, this lack of independent disciplinary authority has, in turn, resulted in repeated failures by police departments to hold officers who have violated civilians' rights to account in any meaningful way. For example, in New York City, a report by the inspector general of the New York Police Department (NYPD) found that in all substantiated civilian complaints against NYPD officers for improper chokeholds between 2009 and 2013 that were referred to NYPD for formal disciplinary charges against the offending officers, the NYPD either refused to administratively prosecute charges or rejected the recommended disciplinary penalty offered by the independent complaint investigative body, the Civilian Complaint Review Board (CCRB). In addition, in the Floyd stop and frisk litigation, the United States District Court for the Southern District of New York found that the NYPD's disciplinary prosecution arm, the Department Advocate's Office (DAO), repeatedly failed to pursue disciplinary charges against officers against whom the CCRB had sustained misconduct allegations, rejecting CCRB investigators' factual findings and instead conducting its own *de novo* review of the complaint allegations, in which it routinely disregarded the civilian complainant's account of the incident in question, which the CCRB investigator had found to be credible.

These failures have, in turn, seriously undermined the legitimacy of existing civilian complaint and police officer disciplinary processes. While state and municipal labor and civil service laws often make it extremely difficult to transfer final disciplinary authority out of the hands of the chief or commissioner of a local police department, CCRB believes that giving administrative disciplinary prosecutorial power to the independent body that investigates civilian misconduct complaints is a legally and politically viable reform. Accordingly, we recommend that the Department of Justice, through its Community Oriented Policing Services (COPS) or other funding streams, provide funding and technical assistance to state and local jurisdictions to develop disciplinary prosecutorial offices within existing independent civilian complaint investigative agencies.

Investigative powers of civilian oversight groups

Many communities are going to civilian boards or groups to ease the tensions between police and the community. With the strained relations between police and the community, the spotlight in many cases is focused on independent civilian oversight boards or groups. One of the problems, however, is that most civilian oversight boards have no or only limited ability to investigate claims of police misconduct. *Scripps News* claims that, of the more than 200 civilian oversight organizations in the United States, less than one-third have their own investigators, and that the majority of oversight boards rely on police department internal affairs officers to determine if an officer committed misconduct.[6]

According to the *Scripps News* article, oversight groups that work with an independent investigator and have more than advisory power are hard to find. While some boards have the authority to reject the internal affairs investigation and recommendations and return them back for further investigation, they must still take the word of internal affairs that it has been reinvestigated. In addition, many oversight boards' findings are merely advisory, even when the board determines that the officer crossed the line and that there is a need for discipline.

The *Scripps News* article points out that there are frequent disagreements between boards and police departments. The article noted that board members in Baltimore, where there is also an independent investigator, have openly questioned the board's effectiveness and have noted that the board's findings are often ignored by the police department leaders. Many members of the board have resigned out of frustration before their terms ended.

In many of the nation's largest police departments, only a fraction of misconduct allegations is ultimately confirmed. For example, between 2010 and 2015 in San Francisco, there were more than 1100 complaints of improper force used by the police, but only 16 cases were sustained. In Indianapolis during the same period, there were 268 allegations of the improper use of force, but only eight were sustained. Baltimore averaged only five findings of excessive force each year during that period.

The U.S. Department of Justice concluded that Cleveland police officers engaged in a pattern or practice of unreasonable use of force. Yet, the findings of excessive force sustained by the Cleveland police department were exceedingly rare.

There are some success stories regarding independent oversight boards. For example, in Washington, DC, the Officer of Police Complaints observed that an increasing number of black teenagers were being ticketed for riding unlicensed bicycles. The office recommended that this little known ordinance be repealed, and it was.

In New York City, the police department's inspector general reported that the nation's largest police department had failed to document the use of force by police officers. After the report was made public, Commissioner William Bratton rolled out a new policy to take care of this.

Summary

- Rashad Robinson, Executive Director, Color of Change before the President's Task Force on 21st Century Policing, civilian oversight of police should be expanded.
- The use of civilian oversight boards is a proactive approach to identify underlying systemic problems with police and the comprehensive legal power to resolve said issues, as well as control over more than police misconduct.
- Probably on the most important functions of civilian or citizen review boards is to oversee the processing of citizens' complaints about police misconduct.
- As noted by HRW, citizen review agencies should publish reports, at least annually, presenting detailed statistics and information relating to complaints, trends, sustained rates for each type of complaint, disciplinary actions stemming from sustained allegations, policy recommendations (as well as the departmental responses to those recommendations), and community outreach efforts.
- HRW also contends that review boards should be empowered and financed to conduct investigations on their own initiative.
- NACOLE is a nonprofit organization that brings together individuals or agencies working to establish or improve oversight of police officers in the United States.
- NACOLE operates to provide for the establishment, development, education, and technical assistance of/for the civilian oversight of law enforcement.

- Regular members of NACOLE are mayors, county or municipal managers, or others who hold executive positions on a board, council, commission, or committee with authority to direct, control, or oversee the activities or performance of the chief law enforcement officer of a political subdivision.
- In the United Kingdom, HMIC independently assesses police forces and policing in the public interest across activity from neighborhood teams to serious crime and the fight against terrorism.
- HMIC decides on the depth, frequency, and areas to inspect based on their judgments about what is in the public interest. In making these judgments, HMIC considers the risks to the public, the risks to the integrity of policing, service quality, public concerns, the operating environment, the burden of inspection, and the potential benefits to society from the improvements that might arise from inspection.
- The United Kingdom also has the IPCC, which oversees the police complaints system in England and Wales and sets the standards by which the police should handle complaints. It is independent, making its decisions entirely independently of the police and government. It is not part of the police.
- There are over 20 different oversight agencies in Canada that provide civilian oversight of police departments. For example, the Civilian Review and Complaints Commission for the Royal Canadian Mounted Police (CRCC) provides civilian oversight of the Mounted Police.
- Many communities are moving to civilian boards or groups to ease the tensions between police and the community. With strained relations between police and communities, the spotlight in many cases is focused on independent civilian oversight boards or groups. One of the problems, however, is that most civilian oversight boards have no or only limited ability to investigate claims of police misconduct.
- In many of the nation's largest police departments, only a fraction of misconduct allegations is ultimately confirmed.

Discussion questions

1. What powers and functions should be given to civilian oversight boards?
2. How do the civilian oversight boards in the United States differ from those in the United Kingdom?
3. Who should serve on the oversight boards?
4. What reports should the oversight boards publish to the public each year?

References

1. Allyson Collins (1998) *Shielded from Justice: Police Brutality and Accountability in the United States*. New York: Human Rights Watch.
2. NACOLE website at https://nacole.org/membership. Accessed on October 22, 2015.
3. Press release by Brian Buchner on January 6, 2015, at buchner@nacole.org. Accessed on October 22, 2015.
4. HMIC website at http://www.justiceinspectorates.gov.uk/hmic/about-us/. Accessed on October 22, 2015.
5. IPCC website at http://www.ipcc.gov.uk/page/about-us#sthash.wp06oGa1.dpuf. Accessed on October 22, 2015.
6. Ross Jones (November 16, 2015). Many civilian review groups have limited power to resolve allegations of police misconduct, *Scripps News* website at http://www.thedenverchannel.com/news/many-civilian-review-groups-lack-the-power-to-resolve-allegations-of-police-misconduct. Accessed on November 17, 2015.

chapter ten

Investigating and complaining of officer misconduct

Learning objectives

After studying this chapter, the reader should understand the following concepts and issues:

- The best method to file a complaint against a law enforcement officer
- The complaint process
- How a complaint is investigated
- Peace officers' bills of rights
- Use of polygraph tests
- Reporting requirements
- Obtaining discovery of police documents

Complaint process

Many citizens are reluctant to file a complaint against a peace officer for fear of retaliation. Most nations and states within the United States have statutes to prevent retaliation or to protect the complaining citizen. While the statutes are not uniform, there are some similarities. In this section, we will examine the Florida and California statutes and regulations in this area.

The term "complaining citizen" is used as a shorthand way of describing a person who has filed a complaint of misconduct against a police officer or department. It also includes those individuals who are not citizens.

Filing a misconduct complaint

The state of California and many other states have a standard form for filing a complaint against a peace officer or law enforcement agency. California's statutes and regulations provide that a governmental authority, agent, or person acting on behalf of a governmental authority is prohibited from engaging in a pattern or practice of conduct by law enforcement officers that deprive any person of rights, privileges, or immunities secured or protected by state or federal law. The attorney general may bring a civil action for equitable or declaratory relief to eliminate the unlawful pattern or practice.

A typical state statute on the procedure for handling complaints against peace officers is California Penal Code §832.5. That section requires each department or agency which employs peace officers to establish a procedure for investigating citizens' complaints against such officers. Each department or agency is required to make available to the public a written description of the procedure it uses. Complaints, reports, or findings must be retained for a period of at least five years.

The *California Civil Rights Handbook*, Chapter 9, on peace officer misconduct, states that:

> It is the policy of the California Department of Justice that local government will be primarily responsible for citizen complaints against law enforcement agencies and their employees, and that appropriate local resources (e.g., sheriff or police department, district attorney, citizens' review commission and/or grand jury) be utilized for resolution of such complaints prior to a request for intervention by the Attorney General. All complaints filed with the California Department of Justice will be processed and reviewed by the Attorney General's Public Inquiry Unit to determine whether all local remedies have been exhausted. Complaints meeting this criterion are then forwarded to and reviewed by the Attorney General's Criminal Law Division and Civil Rights Enforcement Section. If the complaint alleges that the local district attorney wrongfully declined to criminally prosecute the officer-involved, the Criminal Law Division may review the matter to determine whether the district attorney abused his or her discretion in declining to bring criminal charges and take whatever other action that the Attorney General may deem appropriate. Complaints that raise alleged patterns or practices of the violation of civil rights by a local law enforcement agency may be reviewed by the Civil Rights Enforcement Section for whatever action that the Attorney General may deem appropriate.

Florida statute §112.532(1) provides that when a complaint is made against an officer, the officer has the right to be represented by a chosen representative. However, §112.533 provides that the representative is not authorized to review the complaint and statements against the officer until after the commencement of an investigative interview. Florida provides that the complaint against an officer and all information obtained during the agency's investigation are confidential. But, the officer involved and his or her representative do have the right to review the material.

Filing an effective complaint

There are certain tips that a citizen should adhere to in order to file an effective complaint. Those include:

- Control your emotions when making the complaint. As noted in the famous *Dragnet* TV series, "just the facts, ma'am."
- Do not engage in "name calling."
- Complain in writing. An oral complaint is rarely effective.
- Complain to the proper authority. A quick internet search will probably reveal the name of the proper authority.
- File in a timely manner—do not wait too long before filing the complaint.
- If possible, include corroborating witnesses whose reports are not in conflict with yours.
- Consider sending a copy of your complaint to a state representative or other local politician. Generally, when there is outside pressure, the agency acts in a more efficient manner.
- If there is a standard form such as used in California and many other jurisdictions—use it.

Racial profiling

Numerous complaints are received each year accusing peace officers of racial profiling. A typical state statute designed to prevent racial profiling is California Penal Code §13519.4, which prohibits "racial profiling" by law enforcement officers. The section defines "racial profiling" as the practice of detaining a suspect for no reason other than the color of that person's skin or apparent nationality or ethnicity. The section concludes with the statements that racial profiling violates the due process and equal protection clauses and the prohibition against unlawful searches and seizures embodied in the state and federal constitutions. Every law enforcement officer is required to participate in training on racial and cultural diversity, which includes, but is not limited to, gender and sexual orientation issues.

Mediation

Many law enforcement agencies have mediation procedures. Mediation is a voluntary process for resolving complaints, and it may involve meeting with other community members, police officers, police administrators, and/or an independent monitor. In most jurisdictions,

one has the right to refuse mediation if it is offered. Also, one does not have the right to demand mediation. Whether or not mediation will help achieve one's goals definitely depends on the facts of one's case, and the professionalism of the agency with which one is dealing. If mediation is offered, it is worth tracking down a lawyer or other local insider with knowledge of the mediation process and its likely effect on the results of one's complaint.

Unidentified officer

In most jurisdictions, police agencies must make a good-faith effort to identify the officer on the citizen's behalf. Unless one is going to sue the agency (and thus will have discovery or subpoena power), one will not have much chance to identify the officer oneself. So, if the agency cannot or will not identify the officer, one's best chance is to challenge whether the agency really lived up to its obligations and made a good-faith effort; one should ask them to document what steps they took to identify the officer(s) in question.

Alberta, Canada's Peace Officer Act

A typical process for handling complaints is reflected in Alberta, Canada's Peace Officer Act.

The act requires that the notification of public complaints and reporting to the Peace Officer Program must be accompanied by an incident report form. The form and any accompanying documentation may be faxed, mailed, or e-mailed to the Peace Officer Program.

Under the act, any person may make a complaint in writing regarding a peace officer to the peace officer's authorized employer. The employer must investigate and dispose of the complaint in accordance with the procedures set out in the act and the regulations. The employer must notify the complainant and the peace officer every 45 days as to the status of the complaint until the disposition of the complaint. An incident report form must also be submitted to the Peace Officer Program at poprogram@gov.ab.ca every 45 days until the disposition of the complaint.

A notification of the complaint must also be provided to the Peace Officer Program using the incident report form. Attached to the form should be a copy of the complaint, notification to the involved peace officer, a copy of the letter of acknowledgment to the complainant and any other relevant documentation, and it is to be submitted to the public complaints coordinator at poprogram@gov.ab.ca.

Anonymous complaints: Anonymous complaints, in writing, do not allow for the authorized employer to discharge required legal responsibilities under the act and regulations relating to the complaint notification;

therefore, they are not considered a complaint under §14 of the Peace Officer Act.

However, if the nature of any complaint (anonymous, written, or verbal) is serious, the employer or registrar shall review the matter. In the event that some element of substance to the allegation is uncovered, the employer must report it to the manager of the Peace Officer Program as per §16 of the Peace Officer Act.

Criminal misconduct: Any allegations of criminal misconduct must be turned over to the police service of the jurisdiction and the complainant notified forthwith. Should the police service make a determination that a criminal event has occurred, then the standard complaint process must be followed and the authorized employer is required to keep the file open and provide the required 45 day notifications to the peace officer, complainant, and the Peace Officer Program until such time as the police have concluded their investigation. Should the police service determine that no criminal allegations had occurred, the authorized employer may wish to continue to conduct a code of conduct investigation or conclude the file.

Informal resolution of complaints: Prior to conducting a formal investigation, the authorized employer may attempt to resolve the matter informally with the consent of the complainant and the peace officer(s) involved.

Unfounded authorized-employer-initiated investigations: Unless an internally identified issue fits within the scope of a mandatory reportable event or incident as specified by §19 of the Peace Officer Act, employer-initiated investigations that result in the issue being unfounded do not need to be reported (either initially upon detection or upon conclusion). Records should be kept internally as part of an effective record management system, and be available for audit purposes, to ensure that an employer can demonstrate appropriate dispositions and investigations if challenged.

Appeals of the outcome of a complaint:

Complaint against a peace officer: If the officer is not satisfied with the decision of the authorized employer, he or she may appeal to the director of law enforcement within 30 days using the process outline in the document "How to Resolve a Complaint Concerning the Conduct of a Peace Officer in Alberta."

Complaint against a sheriff: If a sheriff is not satisfied with the decision of the Professional Standards Unit, he or she may appeal the decision to the sheriff appeals delegate within 30 days, using the process outlined in the document "How to Resolve a Complaint Concerning the Conduct of a Sheriff in Alberta."

Reporting requirements for the Peace Officer Program: An employer must provide a report to the director as soon as he or she becomes aware of the following.

Incidents must be reported by the employer on an incident report form. Incidents required to be reported include every incident in which a peace officer, while carrying out his or her duties, may have

- Used excessive force
- Used a weapon or equipment prescribed by the regulations in circumstances referred to in the regulations
- Been involved in an incident involving a weapon used by another person
- Been involved in an incident involving serious injury to or the death of any person, or
- Been involved in any other circumstances referred to in the regulations

Also, any matter of a serious or sensitive nature related to the actions of a peace officer is required to be reported. This may also include:

- Violations of the employer's code of conduct
- Loss of identification
- Suspension or termination of a peace officer
- Use of baton
- Use of conducted energy weapon/tear gas
- Use of firearm discharged at a person/not as part of peace officer duties
- Use of force
- Use of other weapon as detailed on policy
- Use of O/C spray
- Newspaper article indicating involvement in high-speed chase
- Staff member complaining about conduct
- Staff member complaining about intimidation

Complaint dispositions

Many citizens fail to file a complaint against the police because they feel that the complaint will be ignored. In this section, we will look at the results of a report on complaint dispositions sponsored by the Bureau of Justice Statistics, U.S. Department of Justice.[1]

Of the total force complaints received in one calendar year, 94% had a final disposition at the time of data collection. The percentage with a disposition varied only slightly by type of agency.

Among force complaints having a final disposition:

- Thirty-four percent of the complaints were not sustained, meaning that there was insufficient evidence to prove the allegation.
- Twenty-five percent of the complaints were unfounded, meaning that the complaint was not based on facts or the reported incident did not occur.
- Twenty-three percent of the complaints resulted in officers being exonerated, meaning that the

incident occurred, but the officer's action was deemed lawful and proper.

- Eight percent of the complaints were sustained, meaning that there was sufficient evidence to justify disciplinary action against the officer(s).
- Nine percent of the complaints had some other disposition (e.g., the complaint was withdrawn).

The most common disposition for force complaints received by municipal police departments was "not sustained" (37%). One-quarter of force complaints in these agencies were unfounded, and in about one-fifth (21%), officers were exonerated. Eight percent of force complaints were sustained.

Among county police departments, force complaints most frequently resulted in officers being exonerated (35%). One-quarter were not sustained, 17% were unfounded, and 6% were sustained. A larger proportion of complaints in these agencies resulted in some other disposition (17%) as compared to other types of agencies.

About 6 in 10 complaints received by sheriffs' offices resulted in officers being exonerated (32%) or the complaint being unfounded (30%). One-fifth of complaints were not sustained.

Compared to other types of agencies, sheriffs' offices had the highest proportion of complaints that were sustained (12%).

The percentage of force complaints having a disposition varied slightly by agency size, ranging from 97% among agencies having fewer than 250 officers to 93% among those with 1000 or more officers. Forty-two percent of force complaints received by departments with 1000 or more officers were not sustained, which was roughly twice the rate of all other departments. Departments with 1000 or more officers also had the lowest "sustained" rate (6%), roughly half that of all other departments.

Investigating police misconduct

New York mayor's authority to investigate police corruption

The mayor of the city of New York established a special commission headed by the Honorable Milton Mollen, former deputy mayor for public safety and former presiding justice of the Appellate Division Second Department. The purposes of the commission was to investigate allegations of police corruption by holding hearings and examining witnesses, and review the police department's existing procedures to make recommendations for reforms that would better safeguard the integrity of the department. The authority of the mayor to establish an investigatory special commission was

the issue before the court on this petition. This issue arose in the context of a petition by the Police Captains' Endowment Association, the association for all police officers with the rank of captain, deputy inspector, inspector, and deputy chief, which sought an order holding that a special commission appointed by the mayor for the investigation of allegations of corruption, popularly known as the Mollen Commission, was in excess of the mayor's jurisdiction. The city cross moved, seeking dismissal of the petition on the grounds that the mayor was acting within his authority as chief executive officer in establishing the Mollen Commission. The court held that the mayor, in establishing the Mollen Commission, was acting within his authority, and that the Mollen Commission was legally constituted; that the chairman of the commission, Hon. Milton Mollen, had the authority, as a special deputy commissioner of investigation, to subpoena witnesses, as well as having general investigatory powers.

On July 24, 1992, Mayor Dinkins issued Executive Order 42. This executive order established a commission headed by Hon. Milton Mollen to investigate allegations of corruption, the effectiveness of the police department procedures to prevent and detect corruption, and to recommend improvements and reforms in the existing procedures. The Mollen Commission was empowered to hold hearings, receive evidence, and examine witnesses to enable it to perform these tasks. Pursuant to the executive order to comply with New York City Charter §§802, 805, the commissioner of the Department of Investigation designated Mr. Mollen as special deputy commissioner with subpoena power.

The government of the city of New York is modeled on the tripartite distribution of powers among the three branches of government: executive, legislative, and judicial. The purpose of the separation of powers doctrine is to better secure liberty by division of authority. The city council has legislative authority and the mayor may not encroach upon it. Likewise, the mayor is chief executive with the primary responsibility of managing and administering programs. In this case, the establishment of a special commission within the mayor's office for the purpose of investigations, inquiries, holding hearings, and making recommendations was within the mayor's authority.

A special commission to investigate general conditions and make recommendations for reforming procedures does not encroach on the Civilian Complaint Review Board, since, under §440 of the New York City Charter, this body investigates specific complaints against individual members of the police department and recommends disciplinary action. In *Kiernan*, the court upheld the Knapp Commission as within the mayor's authority and determined that, as part of his duty to keep himself informed of the activities of city agencies and to enforce the law, the mayor could establish a commission to investigate conditions in the police department. In holding that the mayor had the independent power to establish the Knapp Commission to investigate systemic problems in the police force, Justice Harry Frank quoted from the dispositive appellate authority as follows (64 Misc.2d, at 621, 315 N.Y.S.2d 74):

> The Mayor is under a duty to communicate to the Council annually a general statement as to the finances, affairs and activities of the City and its agencies, to recommend to the City Council legislation which he deems necessary or desirable. To keep himself informed as to the activities of city agencies, to take measures for the efficient conduct of their business and to cause all provisions of law to be enforced. He may command any investigation which will supply him with the information required.

The petitioners' assertions regarding the merits of the Mollen Commission are not matters properly before this court, see Jones, supra. The contention that a commission differently funded or with different members, would be a better commission involves matters of judgment more appropriately addressed to the policy making branches. The hearings have not yet been held. When the hearing process is completed and the Commission issues its report, the public will be in a better position to judge the merits of the proposed reforms.

The court also finds the assignment of funds within the Mayor's Office to the Mollen Commission is a proper intra-agency transfer that is permitted under New York City Charter § 107(a). Finally the court holds that the commission and its chairman has subpoena powers, pursuant to the designation of the Commissioner of the Department of Investigation implementing City Charter §§ 802, 805 as well as the general investigatory powers.

For the reasons set forth above, the City's cross motion to dismiss the petition is granted.

Police defamation

In *Dunlay v. Philadelphia Newspapers,** an action for defamation was brought by appellee, a sergeant in the Philadelphia Police Department, against appellant, publisher of the *Philadelphia Inquirer.* It was based on an article in the *Inquirer* concerning police corruption. The jury awarded appellee both compensatory and punitive damages. Appellant's motion for judgment *n.o.v.* or new trial was denied. The appellate court concluded that judgment *n.o.v.* should have been entered because appellee failed to prove that appellant published the article with "actual malice" or "reckless disregard of the truth," as required by *New York Times Co. v. Sullivan,* 376 U.S. 254, 84 S.Ct. 710, 11 L.Ed.2d 686 (1964). The case was reversed.

The appellate court noted that literal "truth" of a publication need not be established, only that the statement is "substantially true." The proof of "truth" must go to the "gist" or "sting" of the defamation. The test is "whether the [alleged] libel as published would have a different effect on the mind of the reader from that which the pleaded truth would have produced."

Fixing tickets

In *People v. Anthony, et al.,*† the evidence presented to the grand jury established that defendants, all of whom were New York City police officers and/or Patrolmen's Benevolent Association (PBA) delegates or trustees, engaged in a scheme involving the fixing of summonses given for illegal parking and for moving violations. The investigation into ticket fixing was an outgrowth of an earlier investigation into the illegal activities of Police Officer Jose Ramos (who was separately indicted), which included, among other activities, the sale of large quantities of marijuana and counterfeit DVDs from two barbershops in the Bronx owned by Ramos, as well as a robbery, a burglary, and insurance fraud. The investigation into Ramos' illegal activities included the use of court-authorized eavesdropping on Ramos' cell phone. During the course of the eavesdropping on Ramos, a number of conversations were intercepted in which Ramos was overheard communicating with fellow police officers in order to fix summonses for moving violations that had been issued to people known to Ramos. Those interceptions formed the basis for the court's order, issued on December 23, 2009, authorizing eavesdropping on Police Officer Virgilio Bencosme's cell phone, the court having found that there was probable cause to believe that Bencosme's phone had been used and would continue to be used in furtherance of the crime of grand larceny in the fourth degree and the conspiracy and the attempt to commit this crime. Following the December 23, 2009 order authorizing eavesdropping on Bencosme's phone, the court authorized wiretaps to investigate ticket fixing on 16 additional mobile

---

* 448 A.2d. 6 (Pa Super. 1982).

† 42 Misc.3d 411 (Sup. Crt. Bronx, 2013).

telephones operated by 13 other Bronx police officers who were either delegates or officers of the Bronx PBA or Sergeants' Benevolent Association (SBA). The eavesdropping, which ended on December 14, 2010, resulted in the interception of over 10,000 telephone conversations and text messages.

Discovery requests

One of the leading cases on seeking documents from a police department's internal affairs unit is *Jaramillo v. City of San Mateo.** In this civil rights case, alleging excessive force and retaliation by City of San Mateo police officers, plaintiff Jaramillo sought to discover documents relating to his arrest, including San Mateo's "Internal Affairs" documents. The primary dispute was whether the "official information" privilege shielded the discovery. San Mateo asserted that Jaramillo should have instead deposed witnesses to discover the relevant information. As explained in the following paragraph, the court found that Jaramillo's need to discover relevant information outweighed the qualified "official information" privilege. The court therefore granted Jaramillo's discovery requests, with some modifications to focus the discovery.

The court noted that, here, the requested information was probative of what happened the day of Jaramillo's arrest, what statements witnesses made, what investigation took place, whether San Mateo ratified the officers' conduct, whether San Mateo retaliated against Jaramillo, and whether officers complied with the applicable training and policies. The requested information was therefore relevant. A finding of relevance does not end the court's inquiry. Federal Rule of Civil Procedure 26(c) provides that a court may limit discovery to protect from annoyance, embarrassment, oppression, or undue burden or expense. Furthermore, the federal common law recognizes a qualified privilege for "official information." To determine whether the official information sought is privileged, courts must carry out a case-by-case analysis that weighs the potential benefits of disclosure against the potential disadvantages. If the latter is greater, the privilege bars discovery.

Law enforcement officers' bills of rights

Are officers' bills of rights a protection for police officers or are they used to shield police officers involved in misconduct? Most U.S. states and nations have established a bill of rights for law enforcement officers. In this section, we will explore some of the more popular bills. While officers should have certain protections, those protections should not be used to shield officer misconduct.

In July 1996, Gilbert Gallegos, former national president of the Fraternal Order of Police, testified before a U.S. House of Representatives Subcommittee on Crime that a national law enforcement officers' bill of rights was needed because the rights of police officers do exist; they are spelled out in the U.S. Constitution; and they have been ruled on as a matter of law in the highest court in the land. Yet, according to Gallegos, there was still evidence, overwhelming evidence, that these rights were being ignored by police management, simply because the correct holding of the court had not been consistently applied. Gallegos testified that police officers were not being treated fairly.

Gallegos stated that no police officer or police department wanted to work with a bad or brutal cop. It should also be noted that the bill protected the rights of officers under internal, noncriminal investigations only. He stated that police officers were held to a much higher standard of personal and professional conduct—as well they should be, considering the enormous responsibility they hold. Sometimes, however, this higher standard and increased visibility subjected police officers to false accusations from criminals and others in society who had no other motivation in making such allegations than to disrupt law enforcement activities. He concluded his testimony with the assurance that the bill would not protect bad cops.[2]

Unfortunately, the assurance that a law enforcement officers' bill of rights would not protect bad cops is not correct. Louisiana has an officers' bill of rights. In one reported case, in Shreveport, an officer was conducting a videotaped interview with a DUI suspect. During the interview, the officer turned off the camera. Later, when the camera was turned back on, it showed the suspect on the floor in a pool of blood. The officer was later fired. He appealed his termination to a civil service board. The board found that the officer's rights under the Louisiana officers' bill of rights were violated and ordered the city to rehire him and give him a year and a half of back pay.[3]

In 2015 in Baltimore, Maryland, city police officers dragged Freddie Gray into a van. He emerged a short while later with a fatal injury to his spine. When the local press complained to the Baltimore mayor about the lack of action in the case by the city, Mayor Rawlings-Blake responded that the city officials were unable to "fully engage" with the officers "because of our Law Enforcement Officers' Bill of Rights." The state bill includes a provision that the officers cannot be forced to make any statement for 10 days after the incident and then may only be questioned for a reasonable length of time, at a reasonable hour, and by only one or two investigators, who must be fellow policemen[4] (Box 10.1).

---

* 2013 WL 5692425 (N.D. Cal. 2013).

BOX 10.1   MARYLAND'S LAW ENFORCEMENT OFFICERS' BILL OF RIGHTS

§ 3-104. Investigation or interrogation of law enforcement officer.

(a) In general: The investigation or interrogation by a law enforcement agency of a law enforcement officer for a reason that may lead to disciplinary action, demotion, or dismissal shall be conducted in accordance with this section.

(b) Interrogating or investigating officer: For purposes of this section, the investigating officer or interrogating officer shall be:

   (1) a sworn law enforcement officer; or

   (2) if requested by the Governor, the Attorney General or Attorney General's designee.

(c) Complaint that alleges brutality:

   (1) A complaint against a law enforcement officer that alleges brutality in the execution of the law enforcement officer's duties may not be investigated unless the complaint is sworn to, before an official authorized to administer oaths, by:

      (i) the aggrieved individual;

      (ii) a member of the aggrieved individual's immediate family;

      (iii) an individual with firsthand knowledge obtained because the individual was present at and observed the alleged incident; or

      (iv) the parent or guardian of the minor child, if the alleged incident involves a minor child.

   (2) Unless a complaint is filed within 90 days after the alleged brutality, an investigation that may lead to disciplinary action under this subtitle for brutality may not be initiated and an action may not be taken.

(d) Disclosures to law enforcement officer under investigation:

   (1) The law enforcement officer under investigation shall be informed of the name, rank, and command of:

      (i) the law enforcement officer in charge of the investigation;

      (ii) the interrogating officer; and

      (iii) each individual present during an interrogation.

   (2) Before an interrogation, the law enforcement officer under investigation shall be informed in writing of the nature of the investigation.

(e) Disclosures to law enforcement officer under arrest.- If the law enforcement officer under interrogation is under arrest, or is likely to be placed under arrest as a result of the interrogation, the law enforcement officer shall be informed completely of all of the law enforcement officer's rights before the interrogation begins.

(f) Time of interrogation.- Unless the seriousness of the investigation is of a degree that an immediate interrogation is required, the interrogation shall be conducted at a reasonable hour, preferably when the law enforcement officer is on duty.

(g) Place of interrogation:

   (1) The interrogation shall take place:

      (i) at the office of the command of the investigating officer or at the office of the local precinct or police unit in which the incident allegedly occurred, as designated by the investigating officer; or

      (ii) at another reasonable and appropriate place.

   (2) The law enforcement officer under investigation may waive the right described in paragraph (1)(i) of this subsection.

(h) Conduct of interrogation:

   (1) All questions directed to the law enforcement officer under interrogation shall be asked by and through one interrogating officer during any one session of interrogation consistent with paragraph (2) of this subsection.

   (2) Each session of interrogation shall:

      (i) be for a reasonable period; and

      (ii) allow for personal necessities and rest periods as reasonably necessary.

(i) Threat of transfer, dismissal, or disciplinary action prohibited.- The law enforcement officer under interrogation may not be threatened with transfer, dismissal, or disciplinary action.

(j) Right to counsel:
  (1) (i) On request, the law enforcement officer under interrogation has the right to be represented by counsel or another responsible representative of the law enforcement officer's choice who shall be present and available for consultation at all times during the interrogation.
      (ii) The law enforcement officer may waive the right described in subparagraph (i) of this paragraph.
  (2) (i) The interrogation shall be suspended for a period not exceeding 10 days until representation is obtained.
      (ii) Within that 10-day period, the chief for good cause shown may extend the period for obtaining representation.
  (3) During the interrogation, the law enforcement officer's counsel or representative may:
      (i) request a recess at any time to consult with the law enforcement officer;
      (ii) object to any question posed; and
      (iii) state on the record outside the presence of the law enforcement officer the reason for the objection.
(k) Record of interrogation:
  (1) A complete record shall be kept of the entire interrogation, including all recess periods, of the law enforcement officer.
  (2) The record may be written, taped, or transcribed.
  (3) On completion of the investigation, and on request of the law enforcement officer under investigation or the law enforcement officer's counsel or representative, a copy of the record of the interrogation shall be made available at least 10 days before a hearing.
(l) Tests and examinations - In general:
  (1) The law enforcement agency may order the law enforcement officer under investigation to submit to blood alcohol tests, blood, breath, or urine tests for controlled dangerous substances, polygraph examinations, or interrogations that specifically relate to the subject matter of the investigation.
  (2) If the law enforcement agency orders the law enforcement officer to submit to a test, examination, or interrogation described in paragraph (1) of this subsection and the law enforcement officer refuses to do so, the law enforcement agency may commence an action that may lead to a punitive measure as a result of the refusal.
  (3) If the law enforcement agency orders the law enforcement officer to submit to a test, examination, or interrogation described in paragraph (1) of this subsection, the results of the test, examination, or interrogation are not admissible or discoverable in a criminal proceeding against the law enforcement officer.
(m) Same - Polygraph examinations:
  (1) If the law enforcement agency orders the law enforcement officer to submit to a polygraph examination, the results of the polygraph examination may not be used as evidence in an administrative hearing unless the law enforcement agency and the law enforcement officer agree to the admission of the results.
  (2) The law enforcement officer's counsel or representative need not be present during the actual administration of a polygraph examination by a certified polygraph examiner if:
      (i) the questions to be asked are reviewed with the law enforcement officer or the counsel or representative before the administration of the examination;
      (ii) the counsel or representative is allowed to observe the administration of the examination; and
      (iii) a copy of the final report of the examination by the certified polygraph examiner is made available to the law enforcement officer or the counsel or representative within a reasonable time, not exceeding 10 days, after completion of the examination.
(n) Information provided on completion of investigation:
  (1) On completion of an investigation and at least 10 days before a hearing, the law enforcement officer under investigation shall be:
      (i) notified of the name of each witness and of each charge and specification against the law enforcement officer; and
      (ii) provided with a copy of the investigatory file and any exculpatory information, if the law enforcement officer and the law enforcement officer's representative agree to:

1. execute a confidentiality agreement with the law enforcement agency not to disclose any material contained in the investigatory file and exculpatory information for any purpose other than to defend the law enforcement officer; and

2. pay a reasonable charge for the cost of reproducing the material.

(2) The law enforcement agency may exclude from the exculpatory information provided to a law enforcement officer under this subsection:

(i)   the identity of confidential sources;

(ii) nonexculpatory information; and

(iii) recommendations as to charges, disposition, or punishment.

(o) Adverse material:

(1) The law enforcement agency may not insert adverse material into a file of the law enforcement officer, except the file of the internal investigation or the intelligence division, unless the law enforcement officer has an opportunity to review, sign, receive a copy of, and comment in writing on the adverse material.

(2) The law enforcement officer may waive the right described in paragraph (1) of this subsection.

Officer's privilege against self-incrimination

As discussed in the following cases, a police officer may not be required to testify if such testimony will cause him or her to incriminate him- or herself. However, the protection against self-incrimination does not extend to the cases where the police officer gives a false statement.

The Supreme Court noted in *Garner v. Broderick*, 392 U.S. 273 (1968), that if a policeman had refused to answer questions specifically, directly, and narrowly relating to the performance of his official duties, without being required to waive his immunity with respect to the use of his answers or the fruits thereof in a criminal prosecution of himself, the privilege against self-incrimination would not be a bar to his dismissal.

Garrity v. New Jersey

In *Garrity v. New Jersey*, 87 S.Ct. 616 (1967), police officers were convicted in state court of conspiracy to obstruct justice. The state attorney general was investigating irregularities in the handling of criminal cases in the state municipal courts. Before being questioned during the investigation, each officer was warned that anything he said might be used against him in any state criminal proceedings, that he had the privilege to refuse to answer if the disclosure would tend to incriminate him, but that if he refused to answer he could lose his position with the police department.

The court noted that the petitioners had the choice between self-incrimination or job forfeiture. The option to lose their means of livelihood or to pay the penalty of self-incrimination is the antithesis of free choice to speak out or to remain silent. In the investigation, the state had relied on an earlier statement made by Justice Holmes in *McAuliffe v. New Bedford*, 155 Mass. 216, that:

The petitioner may have a constitutional right to talk politics, but he has no constitutional right to be a policeman. There are few employments for hire in which the servant does not agree to suspend his constitutional right of free speech as well as of idleness by the implied terms of his contract. The servant cannot complain, as he takes the employment on the terms which are offered him. On the same principle the city may impose any reasonable condition upon holding offices within its control.

The court noted that the privilege against self-incrimination would be reduced to a mockery if its exercise could be could be taken as equivalent to a confession; and that the right against self-incrimination is of constitutional statute and a state may not condition it on the exaction of a price. The court held that the protection of the individual under the Fourteenth Amendment against coerced statements prohibits use in subsequent criminal proceedings of statements obtained under threat of removal from office, and that it extends to all, whether they are policemen or other members of our body politic.

People v. Marchetta

In a 1998 case in a New York State court, *People v. Marchetta*, 177 Misc. 2d. 701 (1998), a port authority police officer was convicted of menacing and disorderly conduct based on a statement that he had given in an investigation. The court stated: "Public employees, who are charged with a public trust, do not have an absolute right to refuse to account for their official actions, and at the same time retain their employment."

Officer Marchetta was told that he "must" cooperate in the investigation and was also distinctly informed that he did not have to give evidence against himself. The court noted that the written statement given by the port authority police officer, in connection with police investigation of the incident, which eventually gave rise to charges of menacing and disorderly conduct against him, was made voluntarily and without the officer being under pressure to either incriminate himself or lose his job, and thus was not obtained in violation of his Fifth Amendment right against self-incrimination; the officer was never informed that he would experience any job-related sanction if he did not submit a statement.

False statement

The *Garrity* immunity has been held not to apply where the police officer makes a false statement during the course of a department's internal investigation. In *Herek v. Village of Menomonee Falls*, 226 Wis. 2d 504 (1999), Officer Scott Herek apparently gave a false statement to the investigating officer.

Herek was employed by the City of Milwaukee Police Department from approximately February 1990 to June 1995. In June 1995, Herek began employment with the Village of Menomonee Falls Police Department. In December 1996, approximately three weeks after the expiration of his probationary period, Herek was assigned the investigation of a theft. The theft occurred at a private residence during a party held by a juvenile while his parents were not at home. During the course of the investigation, Herek interviewed certain juveniles who had attended the party. One parent filed a citizen complaint against Herek based on his conduct during these interviews.

On December 30, 1996, a police sergeant was assigned to investigate the complaint. During his investigation, the sergeant conducted personal interviews and obtained affidavits from the juveniles involved in the investigation and their parents. On February 5, 1997, Herek was interviewed. The purpose of the interview was to allow Herek to respond to the allegations of inappropriate conduct. Herek responded to the department's questions and denied that the alleged inappropriate conduct took place.

At the close of his investigation, the sergeant provided the department with a written report, stating his determination that Herek had violated departmental rules and regulations and recommending that charges be filed.

Herek was charged with the violation of six general orders of the department: (1) "Conduct Unbecoming an Officer" for using vulgarities during interviews with the juveniles; (2) "Conformance to Laws" for disclosing juvenile records to other juveniles during the interviews; (3) "Dissemination of Information" for making disparaging remarks about a fellow officer and disclosing information regarding a separate investigation; (4) "Required Reports" for failing to note a statement by one juvenile implicating another juvenile in the theft; (5) "Truthfulness" for providing false information when questioned regarding the alleged conduct; and (6) "Miranda Warnings" for failing to administer a Miranda warning to a suspect. The department sought suspension without pay or other disciplinary action deemed appropriate by the civil service commission.

Prior to the commencement of the hearing, Herek filed a motion to dismiss the untruthfulness charge based on the department's failure to provide warnings under *Garrity v. New Jersey*, 385 U.S. 493, 87 S.Ct. 616, 17 L.Ed.2d 562 (1967). The commission denied Herek's motion, finding that the law did not mandate the suppression of his statements based on the lack of *Garrity* warnings and that his statements had not been coerced, involuntary, or given as a result of a denial of due process.

On July 22, 1997, after hearing approximately six days of testimony from approximately 22 witnesses, the commission issued a decision and order concluding that there was just cause for discipline and ordering that Herek be removed from office, effective immediately.

The court noted that what is proscribed as unconstitutional is to condition public employment on a waiver of the privilege against self-incrimination. When duress is inherent in the "choice" given, the individual being questioned is deprived of the opportunity to make a free and reasoned decision. Such circumstances have been aptly characterized as ones that force a public employee to select "between the rock and the whirlpool."

The court concluded that it was undisputed that Herek made false statements during the department's interview. He now sought to suppress those statements, which were the basis for the charge of untruthfulness, under the cloak of *Garrity*. However, the court noted that they did not know of any case law which extends *Garrity* immunity to false statements made during the course of a disciplinary investigation. Indeed, the case law is to the contrary. For various reasons, the court deemed it dispositive that Herek gave false statements during the interview. The court dismissed Herek's claim that he should not have been removed from office.

Failure of a polygraph test

When an officer fails a polygraph test, is that sufficient basis to take disciplinary action against the officer? This was question in the case of *Morgan v. Tandy* (2000 WL 682659, U.S. Dist. Ct. S.D. Indiana). Daniel Morgan worked as a juvenile probation officer for Shelby County courts. He was accused of sexual misconduct. Morgan was directed to take a polygraph test. After the judges were told that Morgan had "failed" the test, they fired him.

The court, in its decision, noted that the *Garrity* line of cases establishes three core principles. First, if a public employee answers his employer's questions under an explicit threat that he will lose his job if he invokes his Fifth Amendment privilege against self-incrimination, his answers cannot be used against him in a criminal proceeding. Second, unless a public employee has been given at least use immunity for his answers to questions, he may not be fired for invoking his Fifth Amendment privilege. Third, however, if the public employee has been given at least use immunity, he may be fired if he continues to refuse to answer questions that are specifically, directly, and narrowly related to his performance of official duties.

The court also noted that in *Garrity* itself, police officers were questioned about allegedly fixing traffic tickets. The officers were told they would be discharged if they refused to answer questions about the allegations. Faced with that prospect, the officers answered the questions. The officers' answers were then used against them in criminal proceedings resulting in convictions. The Supreme Court reversed the officers' convictions.

The court's decision noted that, a year after *Garrity*, the Supreme Court extended its reasoning to hold that where a public employee invokes his Fifth Amendment privilege against self-incrimination, the employee may not be fired for that reason. In *Gardner v. Broderick*, 392 U.S. at 273 (1968), a police officer appeared before a grand jury under subpoena to testify about suspected bribery and corruption in the police force. Prior to testifying, the officer was informed of his Fifth Amendment privilege against self-incrimination, but was then asked to sign a "waiver of immunity" form. The officer was told that if he did not sign the waiver, he would be fired pursuant to a state statute. The officer refused to sign the waiver and was fired for his refusal. The Supreme Court held that the employer violated the officer's Fifth Amendment privilege by firing him for refusing to waive his privilege against self-incrimination. The court made clear, however, that as long as the employee was protected from possible use of answers in a criminal proceeding, the employer could insist on answers on pain of dismissal.

The court stated that under the *Garrity* line of cases, Morgan could establish a violation of his Fifth Amendment privilege in one of two general ways. The first would be to show that he was coerced into waiving his Fifth Amendment privilege by the threat of discharge, that he answered questions based on that threat, and that his answers were then used against him in a criminal proceeding. Morgan did not allege that he had been charged with a criminal offense, let alone that he had been convicted on the basis of his answers.

The court stated that if Morgan had been fired because he had decided not to take the polygraph test, or because he had refused to answer certain questions he found out of bounds, or if his answers were being offered against him in a criminal case, he might have a viable claim under the *Garrity* line of cases.

He did not allege that any of those things happened. Morgan did not cite and the court did not find any cases extending *Garrity* and its progeny to the point that an employee who has answered questions—even under coercive circumstances—may prohibit an employer from considering those answers in making decisions about his employment. Because there was no set of facts consistent with his complaint that Morgan could establish to prove Count I of his complaint, it failed to state a claim for relief.

The second way would be for Morgan to show he was fired for exercising his Fifth Amendment privilege, which would require him to show that the defendants questioned Morgan about his job, that Morgan exercised his Fifth Amendment privilege against self-incrimination, and that Morgan was fired for exercising his Fifth Amendment privilege. There was no set of facts consistent with Morgan's complaint that would support this theory. Morgan did not allege he was fired for exercising his Fifth Amendment privilege. Morgan submitted to the polygraph test. He alleged that he was fired based on the results of the test.

The court did find, however, that a reasonable public official would have and should have understood that he could not fire a public employee based on this stigmatizing—even poisonous—charge and then publicize the charge without first giving the employee a fair hearing in which he could try to clear his name. Subjecting an employee to an *ex parte* polygraph test is not equivalent to providing due process of law.

In summation, the court held that, while the results of the test could be used, Morgan had a right to a hearing prior to dismissal.

Interrogation of officers

According to Jeffrey Noble and Geoffrey Alpert, the interrogation of police officers after a use-of-force incident have caused concern among many citizens. The concern is that officers receive different treatment from other citizens after an encounter involving physical force. The normal citizen is interrogated immediately after the incident, but law enforcement policy is to provide officers with a cooling-off period before they may be interrogated.[5]

This law enforcement policy is based on research concluding that the psychological trauma of critical incidents may create perception and memory distortion. This distortion may result in inadvertent contradictions in the reports. Experts have concluded that delaying interviews of officers for a few hours to several days should enhance their memory and produce more accurate statements.

Noble and Alpert note that this policy differs from the practice of immediately questioning civilians. They point out that conventional wisdom is that interviewing or interrogating soon after the events produces more accurate and truthful statements and reduces the opportunity to fabricate a story.

The authors noted that when officers use deadly force, proper law enforcement procedures typically require the initiation of at least two concurrent investigations to determine the appropriateness of the use of force: a criminal investigation, which determines if an officer's use of force constituted a criminal action, and an administrative query, to ensure that the individual followed department policies and procedures.

The authors note that, just as everyone else, police officers have the right to protect their own interests during each of these investigations. However, while officers may assert their own right to refuse to speak with investigators, they may aggressively seek statements from other citizens during the critical time period soon after the incident to get to the truth. Investigators ask for a cooling-off period for officers, but not for any other citizen equally impacted by such a stressful event.

Noble and Alpert propose that, rather than providing a cooling-off period to police while not applying it equally to citizens, agencies should train investigators to conduct interviews in a manner that recognizes the impact of the traumatic event on witnesses' minds. Interviewers should gain information through a "cognitive interviewing process," which avoids common approaches in which interviewers do most of the talking; questions focus too specifically; witnesses are discouraged from providing information unrelated to the specific question; interviewers determine question sequence, sometimes based on a checklist.

The authors recommend that, rather than focus on the narrow issue of when and even how to conduct an interview following a critical incident, agencies may find it more important to have strong, strict, and clear policies and procedures. Treating all parties fairly and equally will likely result in an increase in public trust in the police without any reduction in the fair and impartial fact finding important in these investigations.

Recruiting

The President's Task Force on 21st Century Policing noted in their summary report that police recruitment plays a significant role in improving the quality and performance of individual officers and departments.

Changing police culture begins with recruitment practices:

- Strengthen police recruiting standards and procedures to ensure the highest quality law enforcement officers with the skill sets and personalities that support a change in the culture of policing.
- Require thorough vetting of police recruits, including past employment, criminal record checks, and evaluation of psychological fitness to target the skill set needed for effective community policing and a culture of respect and inclusion.
- Increase entry-level education requirements such as requiring a minimum of a two-year degree.
- Starting pay for entry-level positions is not enough to justify a student loan.

Summary

- Many citizens are reluctant to file a complaint against a peace officer for fear of retaliation.
- Most nations and states within the United States have statutes to prevent retaliation or to protect the complaining citizen.
- The term "complaining citizen" is used as a shorthand way of describing a person who has filed a complaint of misconduct against a police officer or department. It also includes those individuals who are not citizens.
- Most states have a standard form for filing a complaint against a peace officer or law enforcement agency.
- It is the policy of states to investigate all complaints of misconduct against law enforcement officers.
- Control your emotions when making the complaint. As noted in the famous *Dragnet* TV series, "just the facts, ma'am."
- Do not engage in "name calling."
- Complain in writing. An oral complaint is rarely effective.
- Complain to the proper authority. A quick internet search will probably reveal the name of the proper authority.
- Many law enforcement agencies have mediation procedures. Mediation is a voluntary process for resolving complaints, and it may involve meeting with other community members, police officers, police administrators, and/or an independent monitor.
- Any allegations of criminal misconduct must be turned over to the police service of the jurisdiction and the complainant notified forthwith.
- Prior to conducting a formal investigation, the authorized employer may attempt to resolve the

POLICE CORRUPTION, ROLE MALFEASANCE, AND LEWD BEHAVIOR: DOES THE DEGREE INHIBIT POLICE MISBEHAVIOR?

The function of education itself is to produce a character best suited to the organization of society, that is, best able to carry out the injunctions of law. Education molds the inner life of the members of society to conform to their legally imposed outer life.

—**Plato.**[6]
Diana Bruns, PhD, Professor,
University of Texas,
Permian Basin

Dr. Diana Bruns has nearly 20 years of experience in higher education teaching in the areas of research methods; comparative criminal justice systems; race, gender, class and crime; statistics; criminology; sociology, and drugs and behavior at eight different institutions of higher education. Diana has been the chairperson of three different criminal justice programs over the past 15 years and has published in the areas of criminal justice, social work, higher education, sociology, business and management. Her research interests include issues in policing (training and education) and community policing, assessment and leadership in higher education, family violence, and evaluation research and program development.

She has published over 30 articles in areas of criminal justice, sociology, social work, business, management and higher education and is the Liaison and Representative for the International Police Executive Symposium (consultative status) for quarterly annual meetings at the United Nations meetings in New York City, Geneva, and Vienna including the Commission on the Status of Women in NYC, New York. Most recently, Dr. Bruns chaired and organized the 25th Annual Meeting of the International Police Executive Symposium entitled, *Crime Prevention and Community Resilience: Police Role with Victims, Youth, Ethnic Minorities and Other Partners*, in Sophia, Bulgaria, July 27–August 1, 2014 (27 countries and 43 presenters).

Abstract: The relationship between a college education and police performance has found mixed results in the literature. However, in general, a college degree is associated with higher levels of tolerance, civility, responsibility, dependability, and maturity. Policy implications for recommending college degrees are discussed as a means of reducing police misconduct, corruption, and deviance.

INTRODUCTION

Police misconduct and corruption are worldwide issues. Globally, there is a negative correlation between police corruption and citizen trust in the police. In general terms, police corruption refers to police personnel who utilize their positions and authority for personal rather than public benefit. More broadly, corruption refers to any violation of rules even when there is no personal gain, as in perjury, physical abuse of prisoners, sexual misconduct, robbery, and racial profiling.[7] From 1964 to 1974, the President's Commission on Law Enforcement and Administration of Justice, the National Advisory Commission on Criminal Justice Standards and Goals, and the American Bar Association Project on Standards for Criminal Justice advised that *all police officers obtain a four-year degree*. However, over 40 years later, most police departments have ignored such recommendations. Police misconduct leads to an ineffective police department, which may further result in the breakdown in intergovernmental cooperation, civil lawsuits, a less trusting community, and damaged external relations and cooperation.

The intended goals of higher education include:

- Broadening one's perspective
- Becoming more reliable from an organizational perspective
- Utilizing better judgment
- Promoting greater flexibility in decision-making and positive interaction outcomes
- Being more likely to take initiative

- Becoming more creative in solving problems
- Becoming more humanistic[8]
- Promoting critical thinking, conceptual development, and moral reasoning[9]

According to Kuh, Kinzie, Buckley, Bridges and Hayek:[10]

> Student success is linked with a plethora of desired student and personal development outcomes that confer benefits on individuals and society. These include becoming proficient in writing, speaking, critical thinking, scientific literacy, and more highly developed levels of personal functioning represented by self-awareness, confidence, self-worth, social competence, and sense of purpose.

The purported intentions of higher education in general are to develop individuals into citizens—a growth in appreciation for human differences, allegiance to democratic values, a sophisticated sense of identity.[11,12] More eloquently stated:

> The product of the activity of the teaching collective consists not only on the total amount of the graduate's general and professional knowledge, abilities, skills, and competencies, but also his physical and mental health, his culture, active social involvement, and civic patriotic qualities.[13]

For many years, the literature has demonstrated the following findings: College-educated officers are more ethical than their noneducated counterparts.[14,15] Officers with a college degree hold higher service standards and are more humanistic in their behavior.[16,17] Effective strategies for decreasing police misconduct include requiring college education for police officers, promoting ethics, and implementing community policing programs.[18] Patterson argues that higher education and policing collaboratively improve police professionalism, accountability, and legitimacy on an international level.[19] This study explores the possibility that a simple solution to this worldwide problem of corruption be rectified by requiring police officers to obtain higher education.

BACKGROUND OF STUDY

This study used a phenomenological qualitative approach using content analysis of incidents of police corruption found in news headlines from a variety of news outlets in 2012 in the United States. While all members of society are considered to be innocent until proven guilty, examples of news article titles included:

- Sherriff riding around high on methamphetamine with a gun.
- Sexual predator with a badge.
- Police officer on the other side of the law.
- Officer turns back on oath to protect and serve, instead used badge and authority against a citizen and our system of justice.
- Dirty cops—no one is above the law.
- Cops using drugs, stealing property—even from the dead, committing other acts of corruption, extorting sex from female suspects, soliciting sex for overlooking crimes.
- Endangering the public they take an oath to protect.

GENERAL STATEMENT OF RESEARCH PROBLEM OR PURPOSE

The purpose of this analysis is to determine whether the extent of a college education may impact officer behavior while on the job, and if this standard should be raised across the board within all departments.
Research Questions:

1. Does the lack of a college education increase the risk of police misconduct?
2. Can raising the requirements for police departments to include candidates having a college education decrease misconduct on the force?
3. Does the lack of higher education and proper training influence factors such as abuse of power, excessive force, and misconduct?

LITERATURE REVIEW

The number of police departments in the United States requiring college degrees is surprisingly low (1%). Approximately 82% of police departments only require a high school diploma/general educational development (GED) certificate. Nine percent of U.S. police departments require a two-year degree.[20] As of 2014, 36% of police officers had obtained a four-year degree.[21] Nearly 90% of the police chiefs in large police departments in the United States hold at least a four-year college degree.[22]

Hickman and Reaves reviewed training academy curricula, finding that 83% of training academies use interpersonal skills or mediation training;[23] 98% use ethics training, and 95% have diversity training. Regarding higher education in general, this is what we do know: Officers who obtain a bachelor's degree prior to being hired are less likely to hold supportive attitudes regarding abuse of authority, police corruption, role malfeasance, and lewd behavior.[24] Earlier research suggests that the attitudes of officers who acquired a degree at any point in their career became slightly more positive and stronger regarding policing issues, enhanced responses to citizen behaviors, respect for the impact of community-oriented policing, and police officer information.[25] Does a degree inhibit police misbehavior?

The literature is vast with a myriad of similar findings. Officers with less than two years of college are four times more likely than officers with two or more years of college to face discipline by the commission for moral character or violations.[26] College-educated officers perceive their education to be beneficial to their work.[27] Officers with no college education (high school only) account for a disproportionate number of discipline cases.[28] Regarding behavioral issues, officers with a college education have fewer disciplinary problems than officers with a high school diploma/GED.[29,30] Officers with a high school diploma/GED are three times more likely to face commission discipline than those with an associate's or bachelor's degree.[31]

Additional support for an argument for an educated global police force includes the view that a college degree creates an environment where one can analyze alternative resolutions to moral and ethical dilemmas in policing.[32,33] As cognitive development increases, so does functioning in ethical decision-making.[34]

METHODOLOGY

The study, which is qualitative in nature, is a review of archival data/documents comprised of 122 cases of police misconduct and/or corruption (out of hundreds) randomly selected from hundreds of nationwide cases of police misconduct/corruption in 2012. The study began with 150 sample headlines, but some were disqualified due to incomplete information regarding the level of education of the subject of the headline. As a result, 122 headlines were reviewed in the study. Content came from news headlines located in 28 different states, where department sizes ranged from 15,000 to 34,500 officers. Public records were reviewed for the emergence of officers who committed acts of misconduct and whether or not they held a four-year college degree.

FINDINGS AND INTERPRETATION

Demographic information and level of education

The average age of the person(s) referred to in the news headlines was 38 years ($M = 38.54$; $SD = 10.24$) with ages ranging from 22 to 63 years. Males represented 88.5% ($n = 108$) of the sample, with females representing 11.5% ($n = 11$). Nearly 70% of subjects were Caucasian, with 18% African American and 13% Hispanic. Of the 122 cases, 92% of officers had a high school diploma or a GED. The remaining 10 officers in the study had some college degree or a bachelor's degree. Based on the large variation in sample size, tests for group differences were not attempted (Tables 10.1 and 10.2).

ACTS OF MISCONDUCT AND CORRUPTION

While all types of misconduct and corruption can be found in Tables 10.3 and 10.4, the most frequently found forms of misconduct included the possession of stolen weapons (11.5%), misuse of police authority (9.8%), obstruction of federal investigations (8.2%), felony drug trafficking (8.2%), and extortion (8.2%).

Table 10.1 Description of the sample

Age		M = 38.54,	SD = 10.24	Range (22–63)
Gender	Male	n = 108	88.5%	
	Female	n = 14	11.5%	
Race/ethnicity	Caucasian			68.9%
	African American			18.0%
	Hispanic			13.1%

Table 10.2 Frequencies and percentages of educational attainment

Education level	f	Percentage
High school/GED	112	91.8%
Some college	4	3.3%
Bachelor's degree	6	4.9%

Note: N = 122.

Table 10.3 Frequencies and percentages of act of misconduct/corruption

	f	Percentage
Possession of stolen guns	14	11.5%
Misuse of police authority	12	9.8%
Obstruction of federal investigation	10	8.2%
Felony drug trafficking	10	8.2%
Extortion	10	8.2%
Stealing property while serving warrants	8	6.6%
Drug conspiracy	8	6.6%
Solicitation of prostitutes	6	4.9%
Falsifying drug charges	6	4.9%
Violating civil rights	6	4.9%
Public corruption	4	3.3%
Domestic violence	4	3.3%

Table 10.4 Other acts of misconduct/corruption

Sexual abuse of minors

Accepting bribes over $5000.00

Caught having sex in squad car with minor

Stealing government funds

Custodial sexual misconduct

Viewing child pornography in squad car

Robbery of drug dealers set up to look like raid

Bank robbery

DUI in squad car

Public indecency on duty

Stealing money at traffic stop

Disorderly conduct

Coercing women into sex as bribe

Plotting to kidnap and cook women—cannibalism (n = 1)

CONCLUSION

Even with the advancement toward a professional policing organization in the last 20 years, there is little agreement on how a college education fits in with recruitment, hiring, training, and promotions. Higher education has been seen by many as a pathway to better performance and increased professionalism, while also helping to decrease police misconduct. The standard high school (GED) requirement for most departments was instituted when most of the general population either had one as well or did not even finish high school. In today's highly competitive labor market, over 25% of the general population possess at least a baccalaureate degree.[35] However, the policing field has not followed the same percentage increase. This has actually put the policing field at an extreme disadvantage when it comes to recruitment. Furthermore, it has (in the eyes of some) created a negative perception of the professional organization.

With the paradigm shift in society, technology, and organizational design, the policing field needs higher educated officers to be able to understand the new global environment. As stated earlier, higher education and increased performance (anticorruption) is mixed; however, the skills necessary for the new complex world of policing are enhanced through a college education. It is recommended that the design and implementation of training programs increases the integrity of both recruits and officers.[36] Great thought must be put into the nature and type of education officers receive before they become police officers.[37] Another issue to be addressed regarding the corruption problem is that many corrupt officers had issues prior to hire and should not have been employed in the first place. Promoting cognitive development (moral, conceptual, ego) among recruits has implications for society in terms of potential deterrence of corruption.[38]

Worldwide anticorruption programs must be merged with identified efforts to professionalize police forces.[39] Recruitment, selection, and training are the foundations of a professional policing organization. They are the building blocks for any corruption-free department. An external oversight committee with the ability to investigate, hold individuals responsible for their actions, and dispense consequences would remove internal cultural complications (related to internal policing culture—the "thin blue line"). Just as in professional sports, when the team does not win, it is time to bring in new leadership. A corruption-free environment requires leadership from the top. There must be a vocal leadership leading from the front insisting on change and leading by example. It is essential that senior leadership be held responsible for what occurs under their supervision. From an organizational standpoint, targeting corruption (unfreezing the organization) can help to change the behaviors (making changes) and improve outcome measurement (refreezing the organization).

A final recommendation rests upon expanding into a global community policing structure. The public can be one of a department's best sources of information regarding corrupt behavior. This would allow for a more informed public and a better external relationship between the two entities/parties. The idea is to develop a win-win outcome for both sides. The policing field will be perceived as more professional (and a vested interest will be established, thereby changing the attitudes of officers toward the occupation). The public will believe that the police are there to offer assistance instead of focusing on the "us versus them" perception.

This study is not without limitations, as it is exploratory in nature and the findings cannot be generalized to police officers across the country, because this study did not involve a random sample of all news services across the United States. Furthermore, it is virtually impossible to find all cases of misconduct/corruption across U.S. police departments as well as the level of education and training of the officers involved.

An ending note to reflect on:

- If we require higher education, does the quality of education matter? We must take this into consideration with both online and traditional classroom settings. This may be variable in determining the impact of higher education.[40]

matter informally with the consent of the complainant and the peace officer(s) involved.

- About 6 in 10 complaints received by sheriffs' offices resulted in officers being exonerated (32%) or the complaint being unfounded (30%). One-fifth of complaints were not sustained.

- One of the leading cases on seeking documents from a police department's internal affairs unit is *Jaramillo v. City of San Mateo*. In this civil rights case, alleging excessive force and retaliation by City of San Mateo police officers, plaintiff Jaramillo sought to discover documents relating to his arrest, including San Mateo's "Internal Affairs" documents.

- Most U.S. states and nations have established a bill of rights for law enforcement officers.
- A police officer may not be required to testify if such testimony will cause him or her to incriminate him- or herself. However, the protection against self-incrimination does not extend to the cases where the police officer gives a false statement.

Discussion questions

1. Why should a person keep rational when filing a complaint against a law enforcement officer?
2. Why should complaints be made in writing?
3. What is the purpose of peace officers' bills of rights?
4. Should law enforcement officers be allowed be required to testify on matters that would incriminate themselves? Justify your answer.

References

1. Mathew Hickman (June, 2006) BJS special report: Citizen complaints about police use of force. Washington, DC: U.S. Department of Justice.
2. As reported on Fraternal Order of Police website at http://www.fop.net/legislative/issues/leobr/index.shtml. Accessed on October 1, 2015.
3. As reported on the CATO Institute website at http://www.policemisconduct.net/one-bill-of-rights-for-you-two-bills-of-rights-for-them/. Accessed on October 1, 2015.
4. As reported on the *Huffington Post* website in an article entitled "Take a look at the Law Enforcement Officers' Bill of Rights" posted at http://www.huffingtonpost.com/2015/04/27/law-enforcement-bill-of-rights_n_7153106.html. Accessed on October 1, 2015.
5. Jeffery Noble and Geoffrey Alpert (September, 2013) Criminal interrogations of police officers after use-of-force incidents, *FBI Law Enforcement Bulletin*. 82(9).
6. Gould, J. (1955) *The Development of Plato's Ethics*. Cambridge University Press. Cambridge, UK.
7. Bayley, D. and Perito, R. (2011) Police corruption: What past scandals teach about current challenges. Special report for the United States Institute of Peace. Washington, DC.
8. Carlan, P. and Byxbe, F. (2000) The promise of humanistic policing: Is higher education living up to society expectations? *American Journal of Criminal Justice*, 24(2), 235–246.
9. Morgan, B., Morgan, F., Foster, V., and Kolbert, J. (2000) Promoting the conceptual development of law enforcement trainees: A deliberate psychological educational approach. *Journal of Moral Education*, 29(2), 203–218.
10. Kuh, G., Kinzie, J., Buckley, J., Bridges, B., and Hayek, F.A. (2006) What matters to student success: A review of the literature. Commissioned report for the National Symposium on Postsecondary Student Success: Spearheading a Dialog on Student Success. National Postsecondary Education Cooperative, p. 5.
11. Magdola, B. (2004) Self-authorship as the common goal of the 21st century education. In *Learning Partnerships: Theory and Models of Practice to Educate for Self-Authorship*. Sterling, VA: Stylus.
12. Kuh, G., Kinzie, J., Buckley, J., Bridges, B., and Hayek, F.A. (2006) What matters to student success: A review of the literature. Commissioned report for the National Symposium on Postsecondary Student Success: Spearheading a Dialog on Student Success. National Postsecondary Education Cooperative.
13. Popova, S. and Rozov, N. (2012) Improving upbringing activity in an institution of higher learning. *Russian Education and Society*, 54(11), 65–79.
14. Tyre, M. and Braunstein, S. (1992) Higher education and ethical policing. *FBI Law Enforcement Bulletin*, 61, 6–10.
15. Shernock, S. (1992) The effects of college education for police entry level and promotion: A case study. *Journal of Criminal Justice Education*, 3, 71–92.
16. Miller, J. and Fry, L. (1976) Reexamining about education and assumptions about education in law enforcement. *Journal of Police Science and Administration*, 4, 187–196.
17. Regoli, R. (1976) The effects of a college education on police cynicism. *Journal of Police Science and Administration*, 4, 340–345.
18. Hunter, R. (1999) Officer opinions on police misconduct. *Journal of Contemporary Criminal Justice*, 15, 155–170.
19. Paterson, C. (2011) Adding value? A review of the international literature on the role of higher education in police training and education. *Police Practice and Research*, 12(4), 286–297.
20. Reaves, B. (December, 2010) *Local Police Departments, 2007*. U.S. Department of Justice: Office of Justice Programs.
21. United States Bureau of the Census, Current Population Survey. (2014) http://www.census.gov.
22. Benson, B. (2004) View from the top: The frustrations of police chiefs, and how to solve them. *The Police Chief*, 71(8).
23. Hickman, M., and Reaves, B. (2006) *Local Police Departments, 2003*. (NCJ210118). Washington, DC: U.S. Department of Justice, Bureau of Justice Statistics.
24. Telep, C. (2011) The impact of higher education on police officer attitudes toward abuse of authority. *Journal of Criminal Justice Education*, 22(3), 392–419.
25. Weisburd, D., Greenspan, R., Hamilton, E., Bryant, K., and Williams, H. (2001) *The Abuse of Police Authority: A National Study of Police Officers' Attitudes*. Washington, DC: Police Foundation.
26. Delattre, E. (2002) *Character and Cops: Ethics in Policing*. Washington, DC: AEI Press.
27. Rydberg, J., Nalla, M., and Mesko, G. (2012). The perceived value of a college education in police work in Slovenia. *Journal of Criminal Justice and Security*, 12(14), 408–423.
28. Cunningham, S. (2003) Discipline and educational levels of law enforcement officers, an exploratory report. Paper presented at the 110th Annual IACP Conference, Philadelphia, PA.
29. Aamodt, M. (2004). *Research in Law Enforcement Selection*. Boca Raton, FL: Brown Walker Press.

30. Fullerton, E. (2002) Higher education as a prerequisite to employment as a law enforcement officer. Dissertation, University of Pittsburgh.

31. Delattre, E. (2002) *Character and Cops: Ethics in Policing.* Washington, DC. AEI Press.

32. Morgan, B., Morgan, F., Foster, V., and Kolbert, J. (2000) Promoting the conceptual development of law enforcement trainees: A deliberate psychological educational approach. *Journal of Moral Education*, 29(2), 203–218.

33. Lynch, G. (1976) The contributions of higher education to ethical behavior in law enforcement. *Journal of Criminal Justice*, 4, 285–290.

34. Rest, J., and Narvaez, D. (1994) *Moral Development in the Professions: Psychology and Applied Ethics.* Hillsdale, NJ: Lawrence Erlbaum Associates.

35. United States Bureau of the Census. (2010) http://www.census.gov.

36. Bayley, D. and Perito, R. (2011) Police corruption: What past scandals teach about current challenges. Special report for the United States Institute of Peace. Washington, DC.

37. Rydberg, J., Nalla, M., and Mesko, G. (2012) The perceived value of a college education in police work in Slovenia. *Journal of Criminal Justice and Security*, 12(14), 408–423.

38. Morgan, B., Morgan, F., Foster, V., and Kolbert, J. (2000) Promoting the conceptual development of law enforcement trainees: A deliberate psychological educational approach. *Journal of Moral Education*, 29(2), pp. 203–218.

39. Orces, D. (2008) Corruption victimization by the police. Latin America Public Opinion Project, Americas Barometer Insights, 3. www.AmericasBarometer.org. Accessed on July 17, 2012.

40. Roberg, R. and Bonn, S. (2004) Higher education and policing: Where are we now? *Police Strategies and Management*, 27(4), 469–486.

Index